THE EDEXCEL POETRY ANTHOLOGY: THE COMPLETE STUDENT GUIDE

DAVID WHEELER

Red Axe Books

ISBN: 978-1911477266

Find us at:

www.dogstailbooks.co.uk

CONTENTS

RELATIONSHIPS

Introduction

I hope you find this revision guide useful. It consists of an individual analysis of each poem in The Edexcel Anthology – Relationships. The analysis of each poem follows the same pattern: there is a section on the poet and the context in which the poem was written and some facts about each author; unfamiliar words are explained; and then each poem has a commentary which focuses on both what the poem is about and the style, form and structure that the poet uses. A final section on each poem summarizes the poem's overall impact and effect. There are no colours, few illustrations, but you will get a clear sense of what each poem is about and each poem's overall effect.

Who or what is this book for?

Perhaps you missed that crucial lesson on one particular poem that you find hard to understand? Good lessons are better than this book, because through different activities and through careful questioning and probing your teacher will help you to arrive at an understanding, an appreciation of the poem that you work out for yourself – and that process is invaluable – it's a process of thinking and exploring as a group, in a pair perhaps and as an individual, and, no matter how good the notes that your class-mates made, those notes are no substitute for having been there and gone through the process of the lesson. So, maybe, through absence, you feel a little out of touch with some of the poems: this book will help you.

Alternatively, you may want to read about ideas which you have not encountered in class. Alternatively, you may have the sort of teacher who allows you to respond in your own way to the poems; that is a completely valid and worthwhile approach, of course, but it does not suit every student: some students like to have clear guidelines about the meaning of what they read and to have various interpretations suggested to them so that they are at least aware of the overall gist of the poem. It still leaves you free to make up your own mind and have your own ideas, but it does provide a starting point – this book will give you that starting point.

You may be trying to revise the poems in the final days and weeks before the exam and want a quick refresher on poems that you first studied in class a long time ago; maybe it was a Friday afternoon and you weren't paying complete attention; maybe you were late for the lesson and never quite 'got' what the poem is about; maybe you were distracted by something more interesting happening outside and spent the lesson gazing out of the window. This book will help you get to grips with those poems.

It is very unlikely, but you may be reading these poems on your own for the very first time – this book will help you too, because I have assumed that you know nothing about the poem or about poetry, and the commentary on each poem is written so that you can start from scratch. Of course, some of you might find this a tiny bit condescending – and I apologize for that. I should also apologize if there are ideas in this book which are different from ones you have encountered before in class. There are as many different ways to read a poem as there are readers, and each reader might have a slightly different view of a particular poem – as we shall see. For example, most readers (pupils, teachers, professional critics) would agree that 'London' by William Blake is critical of the society he lived in; most would agree that 'London' is a bitter attack on the London that he lived in, but quite what the final verse means is open to a variety of interpretations!

So... if you want a book that tells you what each poem means; comments on features of style and structure; suggests the tone or the overall impact of each poem; gives you the necessary background knowledge to understand each poem – then this is it. At the end you will find a glossary of poetic terms, but after this introduction, there is a commentary on each poem – each commentary is self-contained and can be read on its own. Throughout the book I have used the words that I would use if I were teaching a lesson on these poems – if I use words you don't know or haven't heard, then look them up. Part of education, part of writing well about Literature is the way you yourself write, so to expand your vocabulary is a good thing. Terms which have specific literary meanings are all in the glossary at the back of the book.

Help Yourself!

I hope you find this book helpful in some ways, perhaps many ways. It deliberately does not include very detailed information about the authors for two reasons. Firstly, it would be a waste of space. Secondly, the internet is a rich source of information about writers and their work – an internet search on any of your studied poets or poems will throw up all sorts of interesting resources, including student chat boards, online revision chat-rooms as well as more obvious sources of information like Wikipedia or web sites associated with a particular author. Where there is detailed biographical information here, it is because it is vital to an understanding of the poem.

But do be warned – all the information you can possibly find about a particular poet may help to clarify something you already sensed about the poem, but it is no substitute for engagement with the poem itself. And in the examination the examiner does not want to read a potted biography of the poet whose poem you have chosen to write about. Besides - generalizing from what we know about a writer or his/her era is a dangerous thing: for example, it is important to be aware of William Blake's political beliefs and to be aware that he wrote 'London' during the years of the French Revolution – some might say that without such an awareness the poem cannot be fully appreciated and understood – BUT that will not help you explain the impact of individual words and lines and images at all, nor will it help you write well in the examination. Very often I have started my commentary on a poem with necessary information to help you understand it, but you don't need to reproduce all that information in the exam - it is there to help you fully understand significant details about the poem; to try to reproduce the process of discovery that a good lesson will guide you through. But it probably has little place in the examination.

You may be the sort of student who is doing English Language or English Literature because it is compulsory at your school. But it may also be that as you progress through the course you come to feel that English is a subject that you like and are good at; you may even be intrigued or fascinated by some of the poems in the anthology. If that happens, then do not rely on this book. Look on the internet for resources that will further your interest. For example, if one poet makes a special impact on you – read some of their other work; you will find a lot of it available on-line. Many of the poets in the Literary Heritage sections are now out of copyright – their work is freely available on-line. Many of the contemporary poets have their own websites which can be a fascinating source of extra information and contain links to other poems or biographical information. So there are many ways in which you can help yourself: it's a good habit to get into, especially if you start thinking about the possibility of doing English at A level.

But please remember this is no substitute for a close engagement with the poems themselves. And just as importantly – this book is no substitute for a good lesson which allows you to think about the poem's language and ideas, and then slowly come to an understanding of it. After understanding it (and that is an emotional as much as a logical understanding of it), you may come to appreciate it. What does that mean? Well, as you go through the course and read more and more poems then you may find that you prefer some to others. The next step is to identify why you prefer some poems to others: in this there are no right answers, but there are answers which are clearer and better expressed than others. And preference must be based on reasons to do with the way the poem is written or its overall emotional impact: it's your job to put what you think and feel into words – I cannot help you do that. I can merely point out some of the important features and meanings of the poems. As you grow in confidence and perhaps read other writing on these poems or listening to your teacher or your classmates, then you will start to formulate your own opinions – stealing an idea from one person, a thought from somewhere else and combining all these different things into your own view of the poem. And that is appreciation. As soon as you say you prefer one poem to another you are engaging in a critical reaction to what you have read – in exactly the same way that people prefer one film to another or one song or performer to another.

Romanticism

In this cluster of poems the first three are designated Romantic poems and it is important that you have an understanding of what Romanticism was. It has very little to do with the word 'romantic' as we apply it today to an event like Valentine's Day.

Romanticism is the name given to the artistic, political and cultural movement that emerged in England and Germany in the 1790s and in the rest of Europe in the 1820s and beyond. It was a movement that saw great changes in literature, painting, sculpture, architecture and music, and found its catalyst in the new philosophical ideas of Jean Jacques Rousseau and Thomas Paine, and in response to the American, French and industrial revolutions. Its chief emphasis was on freedom of individual self-expression, sincerity, spontaneity and originality, but it also looked to the distant past of the Middle Ages for some of its inspiration. In Romantic thought the nature of the poet changed: no longer was a poet someone who could manipulate words well and with skill; the poet was a special individual with a unique vision to communicate and with special insights to communicate through his poetry.

The key characteristics of Romantic poetry in English are:

- a reverence for and veneration of the natural world.
- a belief that the poet was a special person who had important truths to communicate and whose experiences were more intense than those of ordinary people.
- an emphasis on individualism and intense emotion.

- an increased interest in ordinary people – the rural poor and the urban working classes.

- a political radicalism, best summed up by the watchwords of the French Revolution – liberty, fraternity, equality.

- an overwhelming emphasis on the sensibility and imagination of the poet.

- an interest in medieval and ancient history.

- a veneration of Shakespeare.

- a desire to be original and to reject the orthodoxies of the immediate past.

Of course, not all the poets that we label 'Romantic' displayed all these characteristics all through their careers.

Contemporary Poetry & the Literary Heritage

You will probably have noticed that the poems within each section or cluster of your anthology are designated as Literary Heritage poems. Why? Contemporary poetry consists of poems written in the very recent past by living poets and they are here because as you study English or English Literature, it is felt to be important that you realize that poetry is not dead and poetry is not only written by dead white Englishmen: it is alive and it is being written now all over the English-speaking world by men and by women from a wide variety of backgrounds. So the contemporary poems are there to remind you that poetry is alive and well and thriving. Indeed, as I have already mentioned, many of the contemporary poets have their own websites or perform poetry readings which you may be lucky enough to attend during your course. You can also see some performances of these poems on the internet.

The poems in the first half of the anthology are generally by dead white Englishmen, although there are some poems by women. That sounds dismissive (dead white Englishmen), but it's not meant to be. They are in the anthology to remind you that writers have been writing poetry in English for hundreds of years and that what happens over those centuries is that an agreement emerges about which poems are some of the greatest or most significant ever written in the English Language. How does such agreement emerge? Well, mainly through people continuing to read the poems, responding to them and enjoying them; another concrete way is for the poems to appear in anthologies – which ensures them an even wider audience. The point you need to grasp is that writing in English poetry has been going on for hundreds of years and what has been written in the past influences what is written now. Many contemporary poets will have read the poems that you will read in the Literary Heritage sections. So when you read, for example, 'Love's Philosophy' by Percy Shelley for the first time, you will be joining the millions of English-speaking people all over the world who have read and enjoyed that sonnet. Organizations like the BBC have also run public votes where members of the public can vote for their favourite poem – another way that we know which poems are popular. Such poems then become part of the canon' such as those by Robert Browning and his wife, Elizabeth Barrett Browning That is not to say, however, that there is only agreement about the value of poems from the distant past: some like those by Charles Causley and Seamus Heaney are from the closing decades of the 20th century; they are included because already there is widespread agreement that these poets are important and influential and that their poems are rewarding to read and study and enjoy.

So part of our heritage, part of the culture of speaking English, whether you speak English in Delhi or London or Manchester or Lahore or Trinidad or Liverpool or Auckland or Toronto or Cape Town or Chicago, is centuries of English poetry and a continuing poetic culture which is rich and vibrant, and includes voices from all over the English-speaking world.

The Secret of Poetry

The secret of poetry, of course, is that there is no secret. Nonetheless, I have come across lots of students who find poetry challenging or off-putting or who don't like it for some reason. I find this attitude bizarre for all sorts of reasons. But some students are very wary of poetry or turned off by it. If you are – rest assured: you shouldn't be!

Poetry is all around us: in proverbial sayings, in popular music, in the nursery rhymes we listen to or sing as children, in playground skipping chants, even in the chanting heard at football matches. All these things use the basic elements of poetry: rhythm and rhyming and very often the techniques of poetry – alliteration, repetition, word play. Advertisements and newspaper headlines also use these techniques to make what they say memorable. Ordinary everyday speech is full of poetry: if you say that something is 'as cheap as chips' you are using alliteration and a simile; if you think someone is 'two sandwiches short of a picnic', if someone is 'a pain in the arse', then you are using metaphors – the only difference is that when poets use similes and metaphors they try to use ones that are fresh and original – and memorable, in the same away that a nursery rhyme or your favourite song lyrics are memorable. Even brand names or shop names use some of the techniques of poetry: if you have a Kwik Fit exhaust supplier in your town you should note the word-play (the mis-spelling of Kwik) and the assonance – the repetition of the 'i' sound. There must be several hundred ladies' hairdressers in the UK called 'Curl Up and Dye' – which is comic word-play. You may go to 'Fat Face' because you like what they sell, but I hope that when you go next time, you'll spare a thought for the alliteration and assonance in the shop's name.

Poets also play with words. So when students tell me they don't like poetry, I don't believe them – I feel they have simply not approached it in the right way. Or perhaps not seen the link between the poetry of everyday life and the poetry they have to study and analyze for GCSE.

Poetry has been around a very long time: the earliest surviving literature in Europe consists of poetry. As far as we can tell poetry existed even before writing, and so poems were passed down by word of mouth for centuries before anyone bothered to write them down. If something is going to be passed down and remembered in this way, then it has to be memorable. And, as we shall see, poets use various techniques and tricks and patterns to make what they write easy to remember or striking in some way - just as you may remember the words to your favourite song or to a nursery rhyme that was recited to you as a small child. Let us take one example. The opening sentence of Charles Dickens' novel *A Tale of Two Cities* is

It was the best of times; it was the worst of times.

It is not poetry, but it is very memorable, because Dickens uses simple repetition, parallelism and paradox to create a very memorable sentence. Parallelism because the two halves of the sentence are the same – except for one word; and paradox because the two words – best and worst – seem to contradict each other. Now look at this recent slogan from an advert for Jaguar cars:

Don't dream it. Drive it.

This uses the same techniques as Dickens: parallelism and paradox (or juxtaposition) and it also uses alliteration. It is all about manipulating words to give them greater impact – to make them memorable.

As I am sure I will repeat elsewhere, it is always vital to read a poem aloud: your teacher might do it very well, you might be lucky enough to hear one of the living poets in the anthology read their poems aloud or you can access many recordings via the internet. I think reading a poem aloud is a good way to revise it: it has been claimed that when we read something aloud we are reading twenty times slower than when we read with our eyes – and that slowness is vital, because it allows the sound of the poem, the turn of each phrase and the rhythm of each poem to stand out. As we shall see, the way a poem sounds is absolutely crucial to its impact – for one thing, it helps you pick out techniques such as alliteration and assonance.

One of the things we will discover is that poetry is partly about pattern – patterns of sounds, of words, of rhythm; patterns of lay-out too, so that a poem and the way it is set out on the page - often separated into separate stanzas (don't call them verses) – is vital. If you quickly glance at a page from the anthology, you would probably assume that what is on the page is a poem – because we have certain expectations of the way that poems look. So what? You have probably been aware for a long time that poets often organize what they write into stanzas. For me this is an absolutely crucial part of poetry because as human beings we are in love with patterns, we are addicted to patterns – and that is one of the many reasons we love poetry or find it so appealing. Patterns dominate our lives. We may have patterns on our clothes, our furnishings, our curtains, our carpets. But patterns rule our lives more completely than that: seen from above even a housing estate has patterns – the street lights at regular intervals, the garages and gardens in the same relationship to the houses; a spider's web on a frosty morning; the unique patterns of snowflakes; a honeycomb; your school uniform perhaps; the rhythm of your day, of the timetable you follow at school, of your week, of the seasons and of the year. And where patterns do not exist we like to invent them: the periodic table of elements (which you may be familiar with from Chemistry) does not exist as a table out there in nature – it's the human need to organize and give things a pattern which is responsible for the way it looks. Or look at a map of the world, criss-crossed by lines of longitude and latitude – and invented by the human mind as an aid for navigation.

What on earth has this to do with poetry? Well, poetry, especially from the past, likes to follow patterns and this structure that poets choose is something we instinctively like; it is also important when poets set up a pattern, only to break it to make whatever they are saying even more memorable because it breaks the pattern. We will see this happen in some of the poems in the anthology.

Let us look at it another way. Take the sonnet: if you choose to write a sonnet, you are committing yourself to trying to say what you want to say in 140 syllables, arranged in equal lines of 10 syllables each and fitted to a complex rhyming scheme. It is very hard to do, so why bother?

Partly because it is a challenge – to force you to condense what you want to say into 140 syllables concentrates the mind and, more importantly, makes for language that can be very condensed and full of meaning. And, of course, the sonnet has been around for centuries so to choose to write one now means you are following (and hoping to bring something new and surprising) to a long-established form.

So what is poetry? *The Oxford Concise Dictionary of Literary Terms* defines it as:

Language sung, chanted, spoken, or written according to some pattern of recurrence that emphasizes the relationships between words on the basis of sound as well as sense: this pattern is almost always a rhythm or metre, which may be supplemented by rhyme or alliteration or both. All cultures have their poetry, using it for various purposes from sacred ritual to obscene insult, but it is generally employed in those utterances and writings that call for heightened intensity of emotion, dignity of expression, or subtlety of meditation. Poetry is valued for combining pleasures of sound with freshness of ideas....

Remember some of these phrases as you read this book or as you read the poems in the Anthology – which poems have intensity of emotion? Are there some which have a freshness of ideas? Or do some make you think about things more deeply (subtlety of meditation)? Perhaps there are poems which make you do all three? What can I possibly add to the Oxford Book of Literary Terms? Think of your favourite song – whatever type of music you listen to. The song's lyrics will share many of the characteristics of poetry, but the words will be enhanced by the music and the delivery of the vocalist. Is it a song that makes you happy or sad? Angry or mellow? Whatever it makes you feel, a song takes you on an emotional journey – and that is what poems do too, except they lack musical accompaniment. So think of a poem as being like a song – designed to make you feel a particular emotion and think particular thoughts; like some songs, the emotions, the thoughts, may be quiet complex and hard to explain but the similarity is there. And that is another reason why it is important to hear the poems read aloud – they are designed to be listened to, not simply read. Short poems like the ones in the Anthology are often called lyric poems – and that is because hundreds of years ago they would have been accompanied by music. Before 1066 Anglo-Saxon bards telling even long narrative poems used to accompany themselves on a lyre – a primitive type of guitar and up to Elizabethan times lyric poems were set to music and performed.

Making Connections

As you can see from what is written above, a lot of the work in English on the Anthology is about making connections – the exam question will explicitly ask you to do this. As you study the Anthology or read this book you should try to make connections for yourself. Free your mind and make unusual connections. You might feel that some poems take you on a similar emotional journey; some poems might use metaphor or personification in similar ways; some poems were written at the same time as others and are connected by their context.

If you can connect poems because of their written style or something like structure or technique, then that will impress the examiner more than if you simply connect them by subject matter. The poems are already connected by simply being in the Anthology, so to start an answer, for example, by stating that two poems are about 'Conflict' is a waste of words. You should try to do some thinking for yourself as you read this book and reflect on the poems in the anthology– because it is a good habit to get into and helps prepare you mentally for the exam.

Do you have a favourite word? If you do, you might like to think about why you like it so much. It may well have something to do with the meaning, but it might also have something to do with the sound. Of course, some words are clearly onomatopoeic like *smash*, *bang* and *crack*. But other words have sound qualities too which alter the way we react to them – and they are not obviously onomatopoeic. For example, the word *blister* sounds quite harsh because the letter *b* and the combination of *st* sound a little unpleasant; and, of course, we know what a *blister* is and it is not a pleasant thing. On the other hand, words like *fearful* or *gentle* or *lightly* have a lighter, more delicate sound because of the letters from which they are made. Words like *glitter* and *glisten* cannot be onomatopoeic: onomatopoeia is all about imitating the sound that something makes and *glitter* and *glisten* refer to visual phenomena, but the the *gl* at the start and the *st* and *tt* in the middle of the words make them sound entirely appropriate, just right, don't they?

Think of it another way: just reflect on the number of swear words or derogatory terms in English which start with *b* or *p*: *bloody, bugger, bastard, plonker, pratt, prick, prawn* – the list goes on and on. The hard *c* sound in a word like *cackle* is also unpleasant to the ear. So what? Well, as you read poems try to be aware of this, because poets often choose light, gentle sounds to create a gentle atmosphere: listen to the sounds. Of course, the meaning of the word is the dominant element that we respond to, but listen to it as well.

You don't need to know anything about the history of the English language to get a good grade at GCSE. However, where our language comes from makes English unique. English was not spoken in the British Isles until about 450 CE when tribes from what is now Holland invaded as the Roman Empire gradually collapsed. The language these tribes spoke is now known as Old English – if you were to see some it would look very foreign to your eyes, but it is where our basic vocabulary comes from. A survey once picked out the hundred words that are most used in written English: ninety-nine of them had their roots in Old English; the other one was derived from French. The French the Normans spoke had developed from Latin and so when we look at English vocabulary – all the words that are in the dictionary – we can make a simple distinction between words that come from Old English and words that come from Latin – either directly from Latin or from Latin through French. [I am ignoring for the moment all the hundreds of thousands of words English has adopted from all the other languages in the world.]

So what? I hear you think. Well, just as the sounds of words have different qualities, so do the words derived from Old English and from

Latin. Words that are Old English in origin are short, blunt and down-to-earth; words derived from Latin or from Latin through French are generally longer and sound more formal. Take a simple example: house, residence, domicile. *House* comes from Old English; *residence* from Latin through French and *domicile* direct from Latin. Of course, if you invited your friends round to your residence, they would probably think you were sounding rather fancy – but that is the whole point. We associate words of Latinate origin with formality and elegance and sometimes poets might use words conscious of the power and associations that they have. Where a poet has used largely Latinate vocabulary it creates a special effect and there are poems in the Anthology where I have pointed this feature out. Equally, the down to earth simplicity of words of English origin can be robust and strong.

Alliteration is a technique that is easy to recognize and is used by many poets and writers to foreground their work. It can exist, of course, in any language. However, it seems to have appealed to writers in English for many centuries. Before 1066 when the Normans invaded and introduced French customs and culture, poetry was widely written in a language we now call Old English, or Anglo Saxon. Old English poetry did not rhyme. How was it patterned then? Each line had roughly the same number of syllables, but what was more important was that each line had three or four words that alliterated. Alliterative poetry continued to be written in English until the 14th century and if you look at these phrases drawn from everyday English speech I think you can see that it has a power even today: busy as a bee, cool as a cucumber, good as gold, right as rain, cheap as chips, dead as a doornail, kith and kin, hearth and home, spick and span, hale and hearty. Alliteration can also be found in invented names. Shops: Coffee Corner, Sushi Station, Caribou Coffee, Circuit City. Fictional characters: Peter Pan, Severus Snape, Donald Duck, Mickey Mouse, Nicholas Nickleby, Humbert Humbert, King Kong, Peppa Pig. The titles of films and novels: *Pride and Prejudice, Sense and Sensibility, Debbie Does Dallas, House on Haunted Hill, Gilmour Girls, V for Vendetta, A Christmas Carol, As Good as it Gets, The Witches of Whitby,*

The Wolf of Wall Street. Alliteration is an easy way to make words and phrases memorable.

So what? Well, as you read the poems and see alliteration being used, I think it is helpful to bear in mind that alliteration is not some specialized poetic technique, but is part of the fabric of everyday English too and it is used in everyday English for the same reasons that it is used by poets – to make the words more memorable.

An Approach to Poetry

This next bit may only be relevant if you are studying the poems for the first time and it is an approach that I use in the classroom. It works well and helps students get their bearing when they first encounter a poem. These are the Five Ws. They are not my idea, but I use them in the classroom all the time. They are simply five questions which are a starting point, a way of getting into the poem and a method of approaching an understanding of it. With some poems some of the answers to the questions are more important than others; with some poems these questions and our answers to them will not get us very far at all – but it is where we will start. I will follow this model with each commentary. They are also a good way to approach the unseen poem. The five questions to ask of each poem you read are:

- Who?

- When?

- Where?

- What?

- Why?

WHO? Who is in the poem? Whose voice the poem uses? This is the first and most basic question. In many poems the poet speaks as themselves, but sometimes they are ventriloquists – they pretend to be someone else. So first of all we must identify the voice of the poem. We must ask ourselves to whom the poem is addressed. It isn't always right to say – the reader; some poems are addressed to a particular individual. And, of course, there may well be other people mentioned in the poem itself. Some poetry is quite cryptic, so who 'you' and 'they' are in a poem make a crucial difference to the way we interpret it. Why are poems 'cryptic'? Well, one reason is that they use language in a very compressed way – compressed perhaps because of the length of each line or the decision to use rhyme.

WHEN? When was the poem written and when is it set? This is where context is important. We know our context: we are reading the poem now, but when the poem was written and when the poem is set (not always the same, by any means) is crucial to the way we interpret it. The gender or background of the poet might be important, the society they were living in, the circumstances which led them to write the poem – all these things can be crucial to how we interpret the poem.

WHERE? Where is the poem set? Where do the events described in the poem take place? With some poems this question is irrelevant; with others it is absolutely vital – it all depends on the poem. In the Anthology you will find some poems which depend on some understanding of where they are set for them to work; you will find other poems where the location is not specified or is irrelevant or generalized – again it depends on the poem.

WHAT? This means what happens in a poem. Some poems describe a place; some describe a particular moment in time; some tell a story; some have a story buried beneath their surface; some make statements – some may do several or all of these things at once. They are all potentially different, but what happens is something very basic and should be grasped before you can move on to really appreciate a poem. Very often I have kept this section really short, because it is only when you start to look closely at language that you fully understand what is going on.

WHY? This is the hardest question of all and the one with a variety of possible answers, depending on your exact view of the poem in question. I like to think of it asking ourselves 'Why did the poet write this poem?' Or what is the overall message or emotional impact of this poem? To answer it with every poem, we need to look at all the other questions, the way the poet uses language and its effect on us, and try to put into words the tone of the voice of the poem and the poem's overall impact. Students in the classroom often seem puzzled by my asking them to discuss the poem's tone. But it boils down to this - if you were reading the poem out loud, what tone of voice would you use? What is the mood or atmosphere of the poem? Does the poet, or whoever the poet is pretending to be, have a particular attitude to what he or she is writing about? Answering these questions helps us discuss the tone of the poem. But you may not agree with everybody else about this and this is good: through disagreement and discussion, our understanding of what we read is sharpened. In the commentaries on each poem in this Anthology this question 'Why?' is answered at the very end of each commentary, because it is only after looking closely at the poet's use of language, form and structure that we can begin to answer it. If you feel you know the poem well enough, you might just use the section 'Why?' for each poem as a quick reminder of what its main message is. For all the poems the 'Why?' section consists of a series of bullet points which attempt to give you the words to express what the poem's main point is.

A Word of Warning

This book and the commentaries on individual poems that follow are full of words to do with literature – the technical devices such as metaphor, simile, oxymoron. These are the vocabulary to do with the craft of writing and it is important that you understand them and can use them with confidence. It is the same as using the word *osmosis* in Biology or *isosceles* in Maths. However, in the examination, it is absolutely pointless to pick out a technique unless you can write something vaguely intelligent about its effect – the effect is vital! The examiner will know when a poet is using alliteration and does not need you to point it out;

the sort of writing about poetry that consists of picking out technical devices and saying nothing about their effect or linking them in some meaningful way to the subject matter is worthless. I will suggest, in each commentary, what the effect might be, but we can generalize and say that all techniques with words are about making the poem memorable in some away – and this 'making something memorable' is also about foregrounding language. Language that is foregrounded means that it is different from normal everyday language and that it draws attention to itself by being different – it would be like if we all went round every day and tried to use a metaphor and alliteration in everything that we said or if we tried speaking in rhyme all day – people would notice!

Warming Up

Before we look at any of the poems from the anthology, I want to briefly examine some poems (which focus on relationships) to give you a taste of the approach that will be followed throughout the rest of the book. So we will start by looking at some completely different poems. I am going to subject all the poems to a full analysis, but I will demonstrate with the poems some crucial ways of reading poetry and give you some general guidance which will stand you in good stead when we deal with the poems in the anthology itself. This is not meant to confuse you, but to help. I cannot stress enough that these poems are not ones that you will be assessed on. They are my choice – and I would use the same method in the classroom – introducing a class very slowly to poetry and 'warming up' for the anthology by practising the sorts of reading skills which will help with any poem. Besides, you may find the method valuable in your preparation for answering on the unseen poem in the exam.

Here is the first poem we will consider – one of the most famous love poems in the English Language – Sonnet 116 by William Shakespeare:

SONNET 116

Let me not to the marriage of true minds
Admit impediments. Love is not love
Which alters when it alteration finds,
Or bends with the remover to remove:
O no; it is an ever-fixed mark,
That looks on tempests, and is never shaken;
It is the star to every wandering bark,
Whose worth's unknown, although his height be taken.
Love's not Time's fool, though rosy lips and cheeks
Within his bending sickle's compass come;
Love alters not with his brief hours and weeks,
But bears it out even to the edge of doom.
   If this be error and upon me proved,
   I never writ, nor no man ever loved.

Context

Shakespeare is the most famous writer England has ever produced and his plays are known throughout the world. 'Sonnet 116' by William Shakespeare is part of a sonnet sequence of 154 sonnets – also known as a sonnet cycle. Readers have commented that in the sonnets as a whole, Shakespeare covers every aspect of arguably the most important and strongest human emotion – love - as well as our most powerful instinct – sexual desire and the whole range of what happens in what we now call human relationships. Unlike Shakespeare's plays (most of which were unpublished during his lifetime), the sonnets were published in 1609. What does this tell us? We are not entirely sure: it is generally felt that it shows that poetry was held in higher regard than writing plays, so perhaps Shakespeare published the sonnets to achieve fame and wealth; there is also the fact that in Shakespeare's era there were no copyright laws – so once a play was published, there was nothing to stop any theatre putting a play on without giving the writer any performance fees.

Of the 154 sonnets some are very famous and appear in many anthologies. These very famous ones are well-known by the general public too: in the past, BBC Radio 4 has sometimes run public surveys to discover the nation's favourite poem or the nation's favourite love poem and Shakespeare's sonnets are frequently voted into the top ten. If you like 'Sonnet 116', then you might like to read some of his others. They are readily available on-line and are known by their number and the first line:

Sonnet 18 – Shall I compare thee to a summer's day?

Sonnet 29 – When in disgrace with Fortune and men's eyes

Sonnet 55 – Not marble or the gilded monuments

Sonnet 57 – Being your slave what should I do?

Sonnet 71 – No longer mourn for me when I am dead

Sonnet 91 – Some glory in their birth, some in their skill

Sonnet 129 – The expense of spirit in a waste of shame

Sonnet 130 – My mistress' eyes are nothing like the sun

Because so little is known about Shakespeare's private life, there has been endless speculation about who the sonnets are addressed to – but none of this speculation helps us get any closer to the individual sonnets and their meaning and impact. Personally I find it of no interest whatsoever, because for me the words are what make the sonnets memorable and worth reading now – over four hundred years since they were first published.

'Sonnet 116' is often used in modern marriage services (nowadays some churches allow couples considerable freedom in choosing some of the words they use during the service) and I have even seen cards for sale which reproduce the words of the sonnet – these cards are intended to be sent to people who are getting married. The whole sonnet presents a love that is steadfast and loyal and unchanging in the face of other changes. We will look closely at the language and tone of the sonnet, but also consider a deeper and darker interpretation.

impediments – obstacles.

or...remove – or ends when one person leaves or stops the relationship.

ever-fixèd – permanent, not moving.

bark – ship.

time's fool – the fool of time, subject to time and ageing.

bending sickle – a scythe and its curved shape; the Grim Reaper carries a sickle; sickles and scythes are long-handled tools used for chopping down tall crops or weeds; here it is used metaphorically – Time chops us down because we succumb to age and finally death.

compass – range.

bears it out – endures it.

doom – Doomsday, the end of the world in Christian mythology, the day of Final Judgement when Christ will come to earth again and decide who goes to Heaven and who to Hell. Shakespeare uses this to suggest that love will last forever – until the end of time or the end of the world.

Who? The voice of the poet – but the commentary that follows suggests the implied presence of other people.

When? The sonnets were published in 1609, but most scholars believe that Shakespeare began to write them in the 1590s. Within the poem no particular time is specified.

Where? No particular place is specified, so the location does not seem important.

What? Shakespeare states that true love will never change and then explores this assertion through a series of images in order to prove or demonstrate that love will never change.

Commentary

The opening sentence of the sonnet is justly famous: the recurrence of the letter *m* which both alliterates and is within certain words and the way the first line runs on into the second

Let me not to the marriage of true minds

Admit impediments

creates a gentle, calm, mellifluous tone which is appropriate to the sense: assonance on the letter / allows creates euphony, which is all enhanced by the enjambment. The next sentence too

Love is not love

Which alters when it alteration finds.

is often quoted on its own and offered as a universal truth: true love never changes no matter what happens. This second sentence is memorable not just because of the sentiment but because of the words: the repetition of the word *love* as well as *alter/ alteration* and the soft sounds of the letter / and *w* and *f.* So far the sonnet is quite clearly concerned with marriage and *alters* is a pun on what we find at the eastern end of a church the altar. *Impediment* too is a word, a very important word, in the Church of England marriage service. In the marriage service the priest says to the congregation, before the couple exchange their vows of marriage:

Does anyone know of any just cause or impediment why these two should not be joined together in holy matrimony?

Impediment here means an obstacle. At this point in the service, centuries ago, this was the moment when someone in the congregation could mention an obstacle – such one of the couple being already married or promised to someone else or below the legal age to marry or whatever. The final line of the quatrain continues this pattern of repetition – *remover/remove*.

The second quatrain introduces new images in an effort to define what love is. Line 5 begins with a dramatic exclamation – *O no* – and then introduces a metaphor based on ships and navigation. Love is *ever-fixèd*: it never changes and can endure the fury of tempests without being shaken; love is like a star that guides sailors who would otherwise be lost (*wandering*) and they measure the height of the star (love) even before they understand whether the star will help them navigate. Shakespeare uses assonance – *star* assonates with the rhyme words *bark* and *mark* – and *whose worth's unknown* – repeats the same sound with *o* – which also goes back to the exclamation at the start of the quatrain. This creates a sort of aural harmony even though he is writing about potentially dangerous things – tempests, and ships that are lost.

The third quatrain changes the line of thought again. It starts with a bold statement – *Love's not Time's fool*; Shakespeare means that true love will not alter even though time changes our physical appearance as we age. Time destroys *rosy lips and cheeks*. Note the consonance on *c* in *sickle's compass come*. Line 11 deliberately echoes the opening quatrain with its use of *alters*. The whole quatrain is held together not just by sense and subject matter and rhyme, but also alliteration – *bending, brief, but bears*. The final line says that love will last until Doomsday, the end of time.

The sonnet ends with an assertive couplet. Shakespeare states that if he is wrong – that if love is impermanent or transitory then it follows that he, the poet, never wrote a word and no human being ever really loved.

This poem is usually read as a definition of love or true love: an emotion that survives time and tempests, that will never change, no matter what happens. This is why it is so popular in connection with marriages – it serves, people think, as a vow of love that will last forever. Perhaps its power has a lot to do with its sounds: we have noted the clever use of repetition; the euphony created by the soft consonants in the opening quatrain; and, perhaps, its appeal has something to do with Shakespeare's straightforward imagery of stars and ships, rosy cheeks, death personified with his bending sickle. However, a closer reading will show that there is another possibility, another way to interpret this very famous poem.

Remember that in the first sentence Shakespeare had said he was not going to admit impediments – he is going to say nothing at this point of the marriage service. This suggests that Shakespeare is writing about the marriage of someone else and asserting that he still loves that person and his love will never change, despite the fact that they are marrying someone else and not him. It is ironic, isn't it, that the sonnet is so often used in marriage services: this is a poem about the end of a relationship – a relationship that is ending because one of the people involved in the relationship is getting married. Consequently, the speaker's feelings are of sadness and a sense of betrayal, but they are controlled by the strict form of the sonnet which helps to restrain the terrible sadness the speaker feels.

In the light of this reading of the poem, the poem's imagery still fits with what I wrote earlier in the summary, but some of the images take on a darker, sadder tone and atmosphere. The simile involving the *wandering bark* works as a simile, but it might also suggest Shakespeare's emotional state now that his former lover has rejected him to marry someone else – he is like a ship drifting. Love that bears it out until the edge of doom, means a love that will never die and will keep going until Doomsday, but that word *doom* perhaps suggests the terrible sadness that Shakespeare feels at the end of the relationship: in a sense it is almost like the end of the world for him. *Bears it out* suggests a determination to keep going despite the heartbreak he feels – and he does, in a sense, keep going, because the sonnet reaches its conclusion.

Why?

This world-famous poem

- offers a definition of love which many readers have found comforting and inspiring.

- asserts that true love lasts forever and will endure absence and time and even death.

- uses simple repetition and wonderfully crafted combinations of sound to create euphony.

BUT it might also be read as

- a poem full of heartbreak and sadness at the loss of a loved one who marries someone else.

Here is the second poem that we will look at as an unseen:

The Sick Rose

O rose, thou art sick!
  The invisible worm,
That flies in the night,
  In the howling storm,

Has found out thy bed   5
  Of crimson joy,
And his dark secret love
  Does thy life destroy

thou – you

thy - your

Who? The voice of the poet, the invisible worm, a rose.

When? In the night during a storm.

Where? Hard to say... in the bed of the rose.

What? Just using what we know from the poem, we can say that an invisible worm discovers the dark secret love of the rose and destroys it during a storm.

It is obvious that this method will not get us very far with this type of poem or, at least, will not get us beyond a superficial interpretation of what it means. Before you read any further, please read my comments below about William Blake's poem 'London', on page 40 because Blake is also the author of 'The Sick Rose'.

What can we say with any certainty about this poem? Its mood is sinister. It is night-time and there is a howling storm. An invisible worm has found out where the rose has its bed and is coming to take its life. *Found out* suggests that the bed needs to be hidden. Paradoxically, although the worm is going to destroy the life of the rose, the worm has a *dark secret love* for the rose: this is now especially disturbing – a love which is dark and secret and which is destructive of life. Not only is it night and, therefore, dark, but the love of the worm is also dark and secret and destructive. We expect love to be a positive emotion which brings good things to our lives.

When faced with this poem many readers want to interpret the poem symbolically – otherwise it becomes a poem about horticulture. The poem is full of words that we associate with love - *rose, bed, joy, love*. In addition, in our culture sending someone roses, especially red roses, is a token of love. But this is a love which has gone wrong and is destructive. Many readers also find the shape of the worm rather phallic – suggestive of the penis. Think of all the types of love which might be considered 'wrong' or destructive. This is the list I came up with, but I am sure you can think of many others:

- Love for someone who does not love you back.

- Love for someone who is already married or in a relationship.

- Love which cannot be expressed.

- Love that transmits disease through unprotected sex.

- Love between two people from different religions.

- Love which is against the law.

- Love which is unwanted by the person you love.

- Love between two people of different class backgrounds.

- Love between two people of the same gender.

- Love or sexual expressions of love which are condemned by the church or by religious doctrine or law.

- Love which is possessive and selfish.

The point of this list is really to show that Blake's power of compression suggests a love that has gone wrong and leaves us to interpret it. To say that 'The Sick Rose' is about any one of the situations listed above would be totally wrong; to say that it suggests them all and encompasses them all, suggests the power of Blake's writing.

Furthermore, if you have read 'London' and its section later in this book and if you remember that the rose is the national symbol of England, then this poem becomes even more than a poem about love gone wrong – it becomes (perhaps) a poem about the state of England and a warning that it will soon be destroyed. You don't have to identify exactly what or who the worm is – the poem does that for you: the worm is destructive and capable of killing – it is a symbol of ALL the things Blake hated in his society. Blake's point is that the rose is sick and is about to be destroyed by sinister, invisible powers.

Finally, if you need any proof of Blake's power to compress meaning, just look at how many words I have used in an attempt to give meaning to his words: Blake uses (including the title) only thirty-seven! This is part of the poem's power and art – that it uses powerful words and imagery from which we can extract a multitude of meanings.

Why? This astonishingly compressed and darkly evocative poem is

- a protest about the England that Blake lived in.

- a protest about the way the church and society saw certain types of love as wrong.

- a warning that love – or what we call love- can be destructive if it is not fulfilled.

- a plea for tolerance and inclusion for those who conventional morality condemns.

The third poem we will examine is 'Porphyria's Lover' by Robert Browning, whose poem 'My Last Duchess' is in the anthology: when you have read them both you will be able to see interesting connections between the two poems.

'Porphyria's Lover' – Robert Browning

The rain set early in to-night,
    The sullen wind was soon awake,
It tore the elm-tops down for spite,
    And did its worst to vex the lake:
    I listened with heart fit to break.
When glided in Porphyria; straight
    She shut the cold out and the storm,
And kneeled and made the cheerless grate
    Blaze up, and all the cottage warm;
    Which done, she rose, and from her form
Withdrew the dripping cloak and shawl,
    And laid her soiled gloves by, untied

Her hat and let the damp hair fall,
    And, last, she sat down by my side
    And called me. When no voice replied,
She put my arm about her waist,
    And made her smooth white shoulder bare,
And all her yellow hair displaced,
    And, stooping, made my cheek lie there,
    And spread, o'er all, her yellow hair,
Murmuring how she loved me — she
    Too weak, for all her heart's endeavour,
To set its struggling passion free
    From pride, and vainer ties dissever,
    And give herself to me for ever.
But passion sometimes would prevail,
    Nor could to-night's gay feast restrain
A sudden thought of one so pale
    For love of her, and all in vain:
    So, she was come through wind and rain.
Be sure I looked up at her eyes
    Happy and proud; at last I knew
Porphyria worshipped me; surprise
    Made my heart swell, and still it grew
    While I debated what to do.
That moment she was mine, mine, fair,
    Perfectly pure and good: I found
A thing to do, and all her hair
    In one long yellow string I wound
    Three times her little throat around,
And strangled her. No pain felt she;

I am quite sure she felt no pain.
As a shut bud that holds a bee,
 I warily oped her lids: again
 Laughed the blue eyes without a stain.
And I untightened next the tress
 About her neck; her cheek once more
Blushed bright beneath my burning kiss:
 I propped her head up as before,
 Only, this time my shoulder bore
Her head, which droops upon it still:
 The smiling rosy little head,
So glad it has its utmost will,
 That all it scorned at once is fled,
 And I, its love, am gained instead!
Porphyria's love: she guessed not how
 Her darling one wish would be heard.
And thus we sit together now,
 And all night long we have not stirred,
 And yet God has not said a word!

Context

Robert Browning was born in 1812 and became one of the most famous English poets of the Victorian era. He was married to Elizabeth Barrett Browning who was a semi-invalid with an over-protective father. The couple were married in secret and then went to live in Italy. Browning's best work is often set in the past and he was a master of the dramatic monologue, in which the imagined speaker of the poem reveals their innermost thoughts and feelings, often going on to uncover uncomfortable truths about themselves.

porphyria – a rare disorder of the blood that may cause mental, nervous or skin problems.

vex – annoy, anger.

soiled – dirty, unclean.

dissever – to separate, to part in two.

oped – opened.

tress – a long lock of hair.

Who? The poem is a dramatic monologue spoken by the male lover of Porphyria.

When? One dark stormy might. Browning uses the weather as a pathetic fallacy for the turbulent human emotions in the cottage.

Where? In an isolated cottage.

What? The speaker, without a word of explanation or regret, tells of Porphyria's visit to him and his subsequent murder of her. The speaker spends the night alone with the body of his dead lover.

Commentary

'Porphyria's Lover' by Robert Browning dramatizes the conflicts between social pressures and romantic love; the tension between female submissiveness and the male urge to possess, to control and to act; the tension between momentary pleasure and the human need to preserve and keep that transitory pleasure; and the tension between strong religious faith and religious doubt.

In 'Porphyria's Lover' Browning presents a speaker who is insane. The poem was originally published in 1836 in the London journal *Monthly Repository* (Hawlin, 44) and was paired with another poem with an identical rhyme scheme, metre, line length and overall length (Ryals,

166). The paired poems were printed under the title 'Madhouse Cells' and the other poem, 'Johannes Agricola in Meditation', shares a similar preoccupation to 'Porphyria's Lover' – what Ryals calls the desire or will for 'total possession of another person' (166).

The poem is a dramatic monologue – a type of poem that Browning would continue to write throughout his career, but in this early example the monologue seems to be addressed to the reader; later dramatic monologues, such as 'My Last Duchess' and 'Fra Lippo Lippi' where Browning developed the form by including within the poem other characters to whom the monologue is addressed (Ryals, 87). In 'Porphyria's Lover' the speaker is isolated in many ways as we will see. The speaker is recounting the events of the previous evening, so the poem is written after the main event of the poem (which Browning, as the poet, cleverly delays until line 42.). The speaker – the lover of Porphyria – has a tender tone as he recounts the events of the previous evening: indeed, Hawlin comments that his 'whole perspective is… gentle or feminized' (46). However, the speaker is also mad, and the crucial event of the poem in line 42, throws his previous solicitude and apparent love and care for Porphyria into a dark and deadly ironic light.

Browning's monologues are frequently voiced by eccentrics, lunatics, or people under emotional stress. Their ramblings illustrate character by describing the interactions of an odd personality with a particularly telling set of circumstances. In both 'Porphyria's Lover' and 'My Last Duchess', Browning uses this mode of exposition to describe a man who responds to the love of a beautiful woman by killing her. Each monologue offers the speakers' reasons for the desired woman from subject to object: in 'My Last Duchess', the Duke may have jealously murdered his wife, but keeps a portrait of her behind a curtain so no-one can look upon her smile without his permission; in 'Porphyria's Lover', the persona wishes to stop time at a single perfect moment and so kills his lover and sits all night embracing her carefully arranged body. It should be noted that in 'My Last Duchess' the woman's murder is at best implied, while in 'Porphyria's Lover' it is described quite explicitly by the speaker. The unchanging rhythmic pattern may also suggest the persona's insanity.

The 'Porphyria' persona's romantic egotism leads him into all manner of monstrously selfish assumptions compatible with his own longings. He seems convinced that Porphyria wanted to be murdered, and claims 'No pain felt she' while being strangled, adding, as if to convince himself, 'I am quite sure she felt no pain.' He may even believe she enjoyed the pain, because he, her lover, inflicted it. When she's dead, he says she's found her 'utmost will,' and when he sees her lifeless head drooping on his shoulder, he describes it as a 'smiling rosy little head', possibly using the word 'rosy' to symbolise the red roses of love, or to demonstrate his delusion that the girl, and their relationship, are still alive. More likely, however, is the thought that blood returning to her face, after the strangulation, makes her cheeks 'rosy.' Her 'rosy little head' may also be a sly reference to the hymen; Porphyria leaves a 'gay feast' and comes in from the outside world wearing 'soiled gloves'; now her blue eyes, open in death, are 'without a stain.' The lover may also be a fetishist, indicated by the fact that he refers to her hair numerous times throughout the poem, and strangles her with it. He also refers to the 'shut bud that holds a bee' which backs up the view of it being a sexual fetish.

It is impossible to know the true nature of his relationship to Porphyria. An incestuous relationship has been suggested; Porphyria might be the speaker's mother or sister. Another possibility is that she is a former lover, now betrothed, or even married, to some other man. Alternatively, they may be divided by social class.

Other sources speculate that the lover might be impotent, disabled, sick, or otherwise inadequate, and, as such, unable to satisfy Porphyria. There is much textual evidence to support this interpretation: he describes himself as 'one so pale / for love of her, and all in vain.' At the beginning of the poem, the persona never moves; he sits passively in a cold, dark room, sadly listening to the storm until Porphyria comes through 'wind and rain', 'shuts the cold out and the storm,' and makes up his dying fire. Finally, she sits beside him, calls his name, places his arm around her waist, and puts his head on her shoulder; interestingly, she has to stoop to do this. She is active; he is passive – suggesting impotence perhaps. At the poem's midpoint, the persona suddenly takes action, strangling Porphyria, propping her body against his, and boasting that afterwards, *her* head lay on *his* shoulder.

In line with the persona's suggested weakness and sickness, other scholars take the word 'porphyria' literally, and suggest that the seductress embodies a disease, and that the persona's killing of her is a sign of his recovery. Porphyria, which usually involved delusional madness and death, was classified several years before the poem's publication; Browning, who had an avid interest in such pathologies, may well have been aware of the new disease, and used it in this way to express his knowledge.

Much has been made of the final line: 'And yet, God has not said a word!' Possibly, the speaker seeks divine approval for the murder. He may believe God has said nothing because He is satisfied with his actions. God may be satisfied because: He recognises that the persona's crime is the only way to keep Porphyria pure; or, because He doesn't think her life and death are important compared to the persona's. The persona may also be waiting in vain for some sign of God's approval. Alternatively, the line may represent his feelings of emptiness in the wake of his violence; Porphyria is gone, quiet descends, and he's alone. The persona may also be **schizophrenic**; he may be listening for a voice in his head, which he mistakes for the voice of God. It has also been postulated that this is Browning's statement of 'God's silence,' in which neither good nor bad acts are immediately recompensed by the deity.

The final line may also register the persona's sense of guilt over his crime. Despite his elaborate justifications for his act, he has, in fact, committed murder, and he expects God to punish him – or, at least, to take notice. The persona is surprised, perhaps a little uneasy, at God's continued silence. An alternative reading of the last line is to identify a slightly gleeful tone in it – confirming once again that the speaker is insane.

There is no doubt of his insanity; exactly why he kills Porphyria is open to debate and interpretation.

The poem is set in an isolated rural cottage: Browning implies this because Porphyria who has walked through a storm to meet her lover is completely wet and immediately takes off her 'dripping cloak and shawl' (line 11) and her 'soiled gloves' (line 12). Browning uses the storm as a pathetic fallacy in at least three ways: firstly, it is an effective contrast with the warmth and love within the cottage once Porphyria lights the fire and makes advances to her lover; secondly, it can be seen as Browning foreshadowing the later, violent events of the poem; and, thirdly, it might even be seen as symbolizing the tortured inner feelings of Porphyria's 'murderously jealous lover' (Hair & Kennedy, 88) – feelings which he keeps under careful control. Knoepflmacher argues that Browning presents very well the 'contrast between a cold outside world and a warm interior' (158) and Porphyria herself can be seen as 'the passionate outsider penetrating that interior who brings warmth to the immobile dreamer within' (158). However, this can be seen as an example of prolepsis, since, despite the speaker's self-delusional assertions, in death Porphyria's body will rapidly lose all its warmth.

The relationship between the two lovers is presented by Browning as a clandestine one, but one which Porphyria wants: she has, after all, braved a storm to visit her lover and the way she 'put my arm about her waist,/And made her smooth white shoulder bare' (lines 16 -17) clearly suggests that the relationship is sexual. It seems that Browning suggests that it has to be clandestine because Porphyria and her lover are from different classes: Martens asserts that the poem is essentially about a man's 'pathological love for a socially-superior woman' (39). Browning suggests this through the speaker's words: he says that Porphyria is 'too weak... from pride' (lines 22 & 24) – presumably a pride issuing from her social superiority and the disgrace she would suffer if her love for this man became known, and he goes on to say that she is 'too weak' (line 22) to allow her 'struggling passion free' (line 23) and 'give herself to me forever' (line 25), because she is socially bound by what the speaker dismisses as 'vainer ties' (line 24) – presumably her sense of responsibility to her family. Browning presents the speaker as being very distraught at this situation: it explains why he does not respond in line 15 when she calls him and he comments that, because he cannot have her forever or is dependent on her secret visits to him, it seems that his love for her is 'all in vain' (line 30). But passion prevails – Browning hints perhaps that they make love and, as they do so, the man notices how Porphyria is looking at him and realizes 'I knew/Porphyria worshipped me' (lines 33 -34). He goes on:' That moment she was mine, mine, fair,/Perfectly pure and good' (line 38). But it is only a moment of intense feeling and, given what Browning has suggested about the nature of their relationship and his dependence on her coming to him when she can and not when she or he both want, he decides to preserve the moment and strangles her with her own hair. The repeated 'mine, mine' in line 37 convey his extreme possessiveness and Knoepflmacher writes that 'by draining Porphyria of her life, he can assume... control' (160). This can easily be seen as symptomatic of the masculine desire to possess and control, the human desire to preserve forever a moment of happiness, and we might even see the speaker as rebelling against a rigid class system which keeps him and his lover apart. However, by killing Porphyria, Browning presents the insane speaker as having wholly abrogated all moral responsibility for his actions and acted in defiance of human law and morality.

Mirroring the speaker's desire for control, the poem's structure is highly controlled. On the page the poem looks highly regular and it is: Browning conveys his speaker's thoughts with a regular unvarying rhyme scheme which consists of units of five lines which rhyme ABABB, CDCDD and so on. This tightly-controlled and very regular rhyme scheme could be said to mirror the speaker's own need for control and his obsession with Porphyria; at the same time, despite the horrific nature of his crime, his speaking voice remains calm and untroubled – just as the poem is very formally and regularly structured. Hawlin (42) describes the rhyme scheme as 'assymetrical' – presumably meaning that we might expect the six line unit to rhyme like this – ABABAB – but the rhyme scheme that Browning has chosen with the fifth and sixth line rhyming with each other, means that in terms of rhyme, the six line unit turns back on itself – an attempt surely to accentuate the self-obsessed, inward-looking nature of the speaker. In other words, the speaker is concerned only with his own feelings, despite his apparent concern for Porphyria – (No pain felt she;/I am quite sure she felt no pain' (lines 42 – 43). As Bailey asserts, the speaker has a 'megalomaniac stance towards his lover' (53), and he is 'self-deceiving' (Hair & Kennedy, 88). This self-deception and the evidence of his insanity continues after Porphyria is dead: the speaker thinks that her eyes 'laughed… without a stain' (line 46) and that 'her cheek once more/Blushed bright beneath my burning kiss' (lines 48 -49).

Browning uses a lot of enjambment – twenty-two times in a poem of sixty lines - so that over a third of the lines run on and are not end-stopped. On the one hand, it could be said that this enjambment helps convey the impression of a real voice that is speaking, but there is perhaps another purpose: in so many lines the words and syntax break through the end of the line and this is a poem about a speaker who breaks accepted morality by committing murder. Furthermore, the lines which build up to and describe Porphyria's murder – lines 32 to 42 – use an excessive amount of enjambment which perhaps help to convey the speaker's frenzy, emphasize his breaking of the rules and quicken the rhythm of the poem to its climax, as well as imitating the speedy act of strangling his lover. Browning's use of heavy, full-stop caesuras is equally significant. He uses only two: one in line 15 after Prophyria 'sat down by my side/And called me.' (lines 14 – 15) – a caesura which is used to emphasize the speaker's lack of response to her; the second in line 42 after 'strangled her' – which again serves, for the reader, to emphasize the enormity of the crime he has committed. The caesura helps to foreground the act of murder. However, Browning presents the speaker as so delusional that he argues that in killing his lover he was doing what she would have wanted: he describes her head as 'so glad it has its utmost will' (line 54) and he claims in his insanity that his killing of her is 'her darling one wish' (line 58). The speaker's final observation – that on the subject of the murder 'God has not said a word!' (line 60) – certainly shows the speaker's contempt and insouciance towards religious diktats forbidding murder.

Browning's 'Porphyria's Lover' is a deeply disturbing poem, enhanced by the strict regularity of the rhyme scheme and the control that Browning exerts over it. What appears to be a passionate story of the secret tryst of two lovers turns into a tale of sudden and violent murder, and a crazed and deluded justification of it. Ryals states that 'there has been some disagreement as to whether the lover kills Porphyria because he loves her or hates her' (271): it could be argued that such a question is irrelevant because, love her or hate her, he seeks to possess her completely and forever. It can be seen that the poem raises other issues – the unfairness of the British class system, the habitual, historical male need to dominate and a growing scepticism about God – but these are overshadowed by the pathological and wholly solipsistic megalomania of the speaker.

Works Cited

Bailey, Suzanne. *Cognitive Style and Perceptual Difference in Browning's Poetry.* London: Routledge, 2010. Print.

Browning, Robert. 'Porphyria's Lover'. *Poetry Foundation.* Web. October 28th, 2013.

Hair, Donald S. & Kennedy, Richard S. *The Dramatic Imagination of Robert Browning: A Literary Life.* Columbia, Mi: University of Missouri Press, 2007. Print.

Hawlin, Stefan. *Robert Browning.* London: Routledge, 2012. Print.

Knoepflmacher, U. C. 'Projection of the Female Other: Romanticism, Browning and the Victorian Dramatic Monologue'. Pp. 147 – 168 in Claridge, Laura & Langland, Elizabeth (eds.). *Out of Bounds: Male Writers and Gendered Criticism.* Boston, Ma: University of Massachusetts Press, 1990. Print.

Martens, Britta. *Browning, Victorian Poetics and the Romantic Legacy: Challenging the Personal Voice.* London: Aldgate Publishing Ltd, 2011. Print.

Ryals, Clyde de L. *Robert Browning: The Poems and Plays of Robert Browning, 1833 – 1846.* Columbus, Oh: Ohio State University Press, 1983. Print.

In 'Porphyria's Lover' Browning:

- uses dramatic monologue to present a solipsistic, psychopathic maniac;

- to suggest an illicit love affair, perhaps caused by social differences;

- uses a rigid rhyme scheme and metre to suggest the speaker's confidence and rigidity of thinking, but also uses caesura brilliantly at key moments;

- presents an insane mind obsessed with full possession of his lover;

- in the poem presents possessive love as a life-denying force.

Finally, we will look at a very famous poem called 'The Voice' by Thomas Hardy:

'The Voice'

Woman much missed, how you call to me, call to me,
Saying that now you are not as you were

When you had changed from the one who was all to me,
But as at first, when our day was fair.

Can it be you that I hear? Let me view you, then,
Standing as when I drew near to the town
Where you would wait for me: yes, as I knew you then,
Even to the original air-blue gown!

Or is it only the breeze, in its listlessness
Travelling across the wet mead to me here,
You being ever dissolved to wan wistlessness,
Heard no more again far or near?

   Thus I; faltering forward,
   Leaves around me falling,
Wind oozing thin through the thorn from norward,
   And the woman calling.

Context

listlessness – the state of being listless, lacking energy.

mead – meadow or field.

wan – pale.

wistlessness – 'to wist' is an old English verb meaning to know. So 'wistlessness' is literally the state of being no longer known.

Who? The poet speaks as himself, addressing his dead wife.

When? After his wife's death. The poem comes from a sequence known as *Poems 1912-13*.

Where? An outdoor setting suggested by the final stanza, the wet mead and the wind and the falling leaves.

What? The poet is haunted by the voice of his dead wife and he reminiscences about how happy they were at the start of their relationship. The final stanza breaks the pattern of the previous three stanzas to suggest Hardy's forlorn sadness, his heart-felt confusion and his lack of direction.

Before we can get to grips with this poem we need to know something about Hardy's personal life. In 1870, while on an architectural mission to restore the parish church of St Juliot in Cornwall (he was a trained architect), Hardy met and fell in love with Emma Lavinia Gifford, whom he married in 1874. In 1885 Thomas and his wife moved into Max Gate, a house Hardy had designed himself and his brother had built. Although they later became estranged and the love between them faded, her subsequent death in 1912 had a traumatic effect on him and after her death, Hardy made a trip to Cornwall to revisit places linked with their courtship; his *Poems 1912–13* reflect upon her death. In 1914, Hardy married his secretary Florence Emily Dugdale, who was 39 years his junior. However, he remained preoccupied with his first wife's death and tried to overcome his remorse by writing poetry. 'The Voice' is one of the most celebrated poems about his dead wife.

In the first stanza Hardy imagines the voice of his dead wife calling him. The first line is metrically very complex. It starts arrestingly with a trochaic foot – 'woman' – which is followed by an alliterative spondee – 'much missed' before ending the line on a falling dactylic metre – 'call to me, call to me' and the repetition of the words suggests that he keeps hearing her voice in his mind. The falling dactylic metre conjures up a mood of forlorn sadness and plangent regret, and Hardy uses the same way to end the first and third lines of the first three stanzas. The rest of the first stanza uses very simple English words to describe a complex emotional situation. Hardy imagines that his dead wife, Emma, is telling him that she has changed back to the person he knew when he first met her – 'as at first, when our day was fair'. In other words, she has changed from when their marriage developed problems – when she has changed from the one who was all to him – and has changed back to her original self.

The second stanza opens with a direct question: 'Can it be you that I hear?' – which is given added force by the caesura which follows it. If he can hear her voice, he wants to see her too – 'Let me view you then.' Hardy summons up an image of Emma when they had just met and she would wait for him on the edge of town. The last three syllables of the stanza are stressed – 'air-blue gown' – which suggests the striking immediacy of Hardy's memory and its force and clarity even though he is thinking of events from decades before.

There is a radical change of tone in the third stanza and the use of pathetic fallacy to present the way Hardy is feeling. He wonders whether it is not Emma's voice that he can hear at all but

…is it only the breeze, in its listlessness
Travelling across the wet mead to me here.

The dactyl which ends line one maintains the tone of febrile frailty and sadness: after all, Hardy knows that Emma is dead 'dissolved to wan wistlessness' and death is final: Emma is 'Heard no more again far or near' and the alliteration on 'w' and the sibilance of 'wan wistlessness' contributes to a subdued sense of sadness.

The final stanza breaks completely the pattern Hardy established in the first three: so great is his regret that he loses control of the shape and pattern of the poem. The first line is interesting:

Thus I; faltering forward

The caesura after 'Thus I' enacts Hardy's own faltering, while the alliteration on the soft 'f' suggests hesitation and frailty and is continued in the 'falling' of the leaves in the next line. There is pathetic fallacy too: it is autumn and the leaves are falling as a precursor to winter. The north wind is blowing too so it will be very cold. The line:

Wind oozing thin through the thorn from norward

is an interesting combination of vowel sounds with short 'i' sounds (wind and thin) contrasting with longer 'o' (*oozing, through, thorn, norward*) which suggests the wind gusting through the thick thorn bush. There is also alliteration on 'th' – a difficult sound to say and which stresses the effort with which the wind blows. The poem ends where it began with 'the woman calling'.

There is something grammatically interesting about the last stanza too: technically it is not a complete sentence because it contains no finite verb – there is no completed action which suggests that there is no escape for Hardy from these feelings and that he will always hear Emma's voice, always regret how their marriage fell apart. All the verbs Hardy uses are non-finite, present participles – 'faltering', 'falling', 'oozing', 'calling' – which suggest a never-ending sequence of events that he cannot control (after all he is 'faltering'). Hardy also ends each line of the last stanza with a trochaic foot and this falling, feminine rhythm also contributes to its sadness.

This poem shows Hardy at the height of his powers as a poet.

Endings

This may seem like an obvious point, one hardly worth drawing attention to, but you have seen from the poems discussed above that the endings of poems are absolutely vital and crucial to their overall effect. In 'The Sick Rose' the final word – *destroy* – carries threat and menace. You will find in many of the poems in the Anthology the ending – the final stanza, the final line, the final sentence, even sometimes the final word – changes what has gone before and forces us to see things differently. So be aware of this as you read and as you revise. When you are writing about poems, the way they end and the emotional conclusion they achieve is a simple way to compare and contrast them. It may not be easy to express what it is exactly that they do achieve, but make sure you write something about the endings, because the endings are often the key to the whole poem. Remember – a poem (like a song) is an emotional journey and the destination, the ending, is part of the overall message, probably its most important part.

'La Belle Dame sans Merci: A Ballad' – John Keats

Author & Context

John Keats (31 October 1795 – 23 February 1821) was an English Romantic poet. He was one of the main figures of the second generation of Romantic poets along with Lord Byron and Percy Bysshe Shelley, despite his work having been in publication for only four years before his death. Although his poems were not generally well-received by critics during his life, his reputation grew after his death, so that by the end of the 19th century, he had become one of the most beloved of all English poets. He had a significant influence on a diverse range of poets and writers.

The poetry of Keats is characterised by sensual imagery, most notably in the series of odes. Today his poems and letters are some of the most popular and most analysed in English literature. Keats suffered from tuberculosis, for which, at the time, there was no cure and as a result, perhaps, many of his poems are tinged with sadness and thoughts of mortality, as well as having a keen eye for the beauties of nature and the pains of unrequited love.

La Belle Dame sans Merci – the beautiful woman without pity.

what can ail thee – what can trouble or afflict you.

loitering -waiting around with no fixed purpose.

sedge – a type of grass whish flourishes in watery places.

woe-begone – consumed with woe and sadness.

meads – meadows and fields.

steed – his horse.

manna – delicious food for body and mind.

grot – a cave.

in thrall – to be held like a slave.

gloam – twilight, dusk.

sojourn – to stay for a period of time.

Who? An unidentified speaker asks a knight-at-arms what is wrong with him: he or she speaks for the first three stanzas. The knight then tells his story.

When? The knight and the people he sees in his dream suggest a medieval setting, centuries before Keats was alive.

Where? An indeterminate outdoor setting: the knight says he is on the cold hill's side and the setting is rural.

What? The knight met La Belle Dame Sans Merci of the title. They seemed to fall in love and she took him to her grot. He fell asleep and dreamt a dream before walking up on the cold hillside, alone and deeply sad.

Commentary

This is one of hundreds of anonymous ballads which were passed down orally before being written down.

Lady Maisrey

She called to her little pageboy,
Who was her brother's son.
She told him quick as he could go,
To bring her lord safe home.

Now the very first mile he would walk
And the second he would run,

And when he came to a broken, broken bridge,
He bent his breast and swum.

And when he came to the new castell,
The lord was set at meat;
If you were to know as much as I,
How little you would eat!

O is my tower falling, falling down,
Or does my bower burn?
Or is my gay lady put to bed
With a daughter or a son?

O no, your tower is not falling down,
Nor does your bower burn;
But we are afraid ere you return,
Your lady will be dead and gone.

Come saddle, saddle my milk-white steed,
Come saddle my pony too,
That I may neither eat nor drink,
Till I come to the old castell.

Now when he came to the old castell,
He heard a big bell toll;
And then he saw eight noble, noble men,
A bearing of a pall.

Lay down, lay down, that gentle, gentle corpse,
As it lay fast asleep,
That I may kiss her red ruby lips,
Which I used to kiss so sweet.

Six times he kissed her red ruby lips,

Nine times he kissed her chin.
Ten times he kissed her snowy, snowy breast,
Where love did enter in.

The lady was buried on that Sunday,
Before the prayer was done;
And the lord he died on the next Sunday,
Before the prayer begun.

I have included this anonymous ballad to give you a sense of the tradition Keats was drawing on when he wrote 'La Belle Dame Sans Merci'. It is also written in the traditional ballad stanza. I chose it also because it involves love and death, and a way of telling the story which is elliptical – in which important parts are left out and the readers are left to their own conclusions. Keats' poem is filled with such features.

"La Belle Dame sans Merci" is a popular form given an artistic sheen by the Romantic poet, Keats. Keats uses a stanza of three iambic tetrameter lines with the fourth line shortened which makes the stanza seem a self-contained unit, giving the ballad a deliberate and slow movement, and is pleasing to the ear although the short last line could also be argued to add an air of doubt, of uncertainty and incompleteness. Keats uses a number of the stylistic characteristics of the ballad, such as simplicity of language, repetition, and absence of details; like some of the old ballads, it deals with the supernatural. Keats's economical manner of telling a story in "La Belle Dame sans Merci" is the direct opposite of his lavish manner in "The Eve of St. Agnes". Part of the fascination exerted by the poem comes from Keats' use of understatement. It is a love story, but not a happy or uncomplicated one. The shortened last line suggests a lack of completeness and, as such, is appropriate to the events of the poem and the overall sense of melancholy and anguish that pervades it. The poem became famous in the Victorian period and several Pre-Raphaelite artists produced work inspired by the poem and reproduced here.

Keats sets his simple story of love and death in a bleak wintry landscape that is appropriate to it: *The sedge has wither'd from the lake/And no birds sing!* The repetition of these two lines, with minor variations, as the concluding lines of the poem emphasizes the fate of the unfortunate knight and neatly encloses the poem in a frame by bringing it back to its beginning. Keats relates the condition of the trees and surroundings with the condition of the knight who is also broken.

In keeping with the ballad tradition, Keats does not identify his questioner, or the knight, or the destructively beautiful lady. What Keats does not include in his poem contributes as much to it in arousing the reader's imagination as what he puts into it. La belle dame sans merci, the beautiful lady without pity, is a femme fatale, a Circe-like figure who attracts lovers only to destroy them by her supernatural powers. She destroys because it is her nature to destroy. Keats could have found patterns for his "faery's child" in folk mythology, classical literature, Renaissance poetry, or the medieval ballad. With a few skilful touches, he creates a woman who is at once beautiful, erotically attractive, fascinating, and deadly.

Some readers see the poem as Keats' personal rebellion against the pains of love. In his letters and in some of his poems, he reveals that he did experience the pains, as well as the pleasures, of love and that he resented the pains, particularly the loss of freedom that came with falling in love. However, the ballad is a very objective form, and it may be best to read "La Belle Dame sans Merci" as pure story and no more. Certainly the poem stands out from the others in the Anthology by having a clear narrative element – although the sadness that love can cause is touched upon in several different poems.

The first three stanzas of the poem are spoken by an unidentified speaker who questions the knight-at-arms. It is winter and the knight is clearly unwell:

I

O what can ail thee, knight-at-arms,
  Alone and palely loitering?
The sedge has wither'd from the lake,
  And no birds sing.

II

O what can ail thee, knight-at-arms!
  So haggard and so woe-begone?
The squirrel's granary is full,
  And the harvest's done.

III

I see a lily on thy brow
  With anguish moist and fever dew,
And on thy cheeks a fading rose
  Fast withereth too.

The lily is a flower associated with death, while on the knight's cheeks there is a *fading rose*, suggesting a fading or lost love. The questions serve the simple task of arousing the reader's interest, while the state of the knight is pitiful: he is *alone and palely loitering, haggard* and *woe-begone* and *anguish* is apparent on his fevered brow.

The knight then tells his story and how he has come to be in this situation. The knight met a lady *in the meads*; she was *full beautiful, a faery's child* (which introduces a supernatural element). It is clear that the knight is attracted to the woman and captivated by her appearance:

Her hair was long, her foot was light,

And her eyes were wild.

The knight shows his love for the woman by making a *garland* for her head and *bracelets* and

She looked at me as she did love,

And made sweet moan.

The word *as* is important in the quotation used above because it means she looked at him as if she did love him, but it does not mean that she necessarily does.. In the next stanza the knight seems to take full possession of the woman by placing her on his *prancing steed* and his obsession and infatuation with the woman is total:

And nothing else saw all day long,

For sidelong would she bend, and sing

A faery's song.

The faery's child, the woman, feeds the knight on *roots of relish sweet,/And honey wild. And manna-dew*

and then

...in language strange she said –

'I love thee true'.

The next stanza represents the climax of their love:

She took me to her Elfin grot,

And there she wept and sighed full sore.

And there I shut her wild wild eyes

With kisses four.

The kisses four feel like a consummation of their love and they certainly calm the wildness in her eyes. The woman lulls him to sleep and then the knight has a disturbing dream: *Ah! Woe betide!:*

I saw pale kings and princes too'

Pale warriors, death-pale were they all

They cried – 'La belle dame sans merci

Hath thee in thrall!'

I saw their starved lips in the gloam,

With horrid warning gapèd wide,

And I awoke to find me here

On the hill's cold side.

Of course, the wintry, lifeless landscape, underlined by the repetition of the *hill's cold side* acts as a pathetic fallacy for the knight's sense of futility and despondency.

The final stanza reminds us of the barrenness of the landscape:

And this is why I sojourn here,
Alone and palely loitering,
Though the sedge is withered from the lake,
And no birds sing.

A key word in the final stanza is *this* in the first line. Is the knight hoping to meet La belle dame sans merci again, once more to come under her spell? Is he so broken by his experiences that he can do nothing but palely loiter, enervated by the glimpse of love that he has seen but from which he is banished? Has his taste of love with the faery's child soured his feelings about love forever? Or has his taste of love left him bereft and lifeless until he tastes it again?

In his other poems Keats writes extensively about love. However, in 'La Belle Dame Merci', by choosing the impersonal ballad form, Keats distances himself personally from the poem and its sentiments. Nonetheless, a clear picture of love emerges through the unusual story of the knight and his encounter with La belle dame sans merci.

This poem is typical of some poems in the Anthology because it deals with the anguish and torment of unrequited love, but it is not typical in many more ways. It is set in a vague medieval past and the ballad form de-personalizes it and distances it from the poet's own feelings – most of the poems in the Anthology are deeply personal.

Why?

In this poem:

- Keats presents the anguish and torment of lost love.

- at the same time in stanzas VI, VII and VIII Keats presents the alluring pleasures of romantic love.

- uses the ballad form to present an intriguing story of a haggard knight at arms who has been broken in some way by love.

- successfully imitates the traditional ballad through his use of the ballad stanza, repetition, hints of the supernatural, illogical turns of events and the anonymity of the speakers.

- uses pathetic fallacy to great effect.

'A Child to his Sick Grandfather' - Joanna Baillie

Author

Joanna Baillie (11 September 1762 – 23 February 1851) was a Scottish poet and dramatist. Baillie was very well-known during her lifetime and, though a woman, intended her plays not for the closet but for the stage. Admired both for her literary powers and her sweetness of disposition, she hosted a literary society in her cottage at Hampstead. Baillie died at the age of 88, her faculties remaining unimpaired to the last. Baillie's lyric poems often take the form of meditations on nature and youth. She was the author of *Poems: Wherein It Is Attempted to Describe Certain Views of Nature and of Rustic Manners* (1790), *Metrical Legends of Exalted Characters* (1821), *Dramatic Poetry* (1836), and *Fugitive Verses* (1840).

Joanna Baillie was regarded as a pre-eminent woman poet in her lifetime, comparable to Sappho, and a forerunner of nineteenth-century British women's poetry. Elizabeth Barrett Browning hailed her as "the first female poet in all senses in England". But this poet was Scottish, wrote in Scots as well as English, and was a major contributor to the Scottish ballad and song revival. As Scullion remarks, "although so long resident in London, she was celebrated as a Scottish woman of letters" (161).

stocked – stocking or socks.

corse – body.

vexed – upset.

dad – here used as an abbreviation of 'grandad'.

wot – know.

lank -

scant – sparse, few in number.

crown – top of the head.

wan – pale.

doff – take off.

aye – always.

bide – wait.

partlet – a hen.

bosom – chest.

Who? The speaker is the grandson; his words are addressed to his grandfather. The poem is written in the present tense.

When? As his grandfather approaches death.

Where? In the family home it would seem.

What? The grandson's monologue is full of love and tenderness for his grandfather and he talks about things they have done together.

Commentary

This poem is written in eight stanzas of six lines each. Each verse is written in rhyming couplets, with the first seven lines in iambic tetrameters (four stresses with a generally iambic rhythm; the last line is slightly shorter – an iambic trimeter (three stresses). This rigid structure and the simple rhyme scheme are appropriate for a speaker who is a child and who sees things in simple terms.

In the first stanza the speaker notices that his grandad is *old and frail* and that his legs have begun *to fail*; indeed, he no longer uses his walking stick because it

Can scarce support your bended corse.

The speaker remembers a time when his grandfather's stick was used by the speaker as a pretend horse but now

While back to wall, you lean so sad,

   I'm vexed to see you, dad.

In the second stanza the speaker reminisces

You used to smile and stroke my head,

And tell me how good children did.

But now his grandfather *seldom [takes him] on his knee*, but the speaker is

   … right glad.

   To sit beside you dad.

The speaker concentrates on his grandfather's physical decline in the third stanza:

How lank and thin your beard hangs down!

Scant are the white hairs on your crown;

How wan and hollow are your cheeks!

The speaker is watching the slow descent towards death of his beloved grandfather, but his love and compassion are made completely clear and are inherently touching:

… yet, for all his strength be fled,

   I love my own old dad.

In stanza four the perspective shifts to the community they are living in: housewives are brewing potions (presumably to make the grandfather better or to reduce his suffering), while gossips come to ask for you, the child tells his grandfather. Furthermore

… good men kneel, and say their prayers;

And everybody looks so sad,

> *When you are ailing, dad.*

Despite the age of the speaker his attitude is not innocent: he knows what may be coming and the first line of the fifth stanza asks

You will not die and leave us then?

The speaker promises that the rest of the household will be quiet as the grandfather sleeps

And when you wake we'll aye be near

> *To fill old dad his cheer.*

The speaker makes various promises in the sixth stanza to lead his grandfather by the hand, to help him during meals and to sit and talk with him. Once again we get the impression of the tenderness of the child's compassion.

The seventh stanza goes into detail about a story that the speaker, the grandson will tell his grandfather about a chicken and a fox – because you love a story, dad?

The final stanza begins with a promise of

> *… a wondrous tale*

Of men all clad in coats of mail

With glittering swords….

But the end of life is near

... you nod, I think?

Your fixed eyes begin to wink;

Down on your bosom sinks your head –

You do not hear me, dad.

And so the grandfather dies, tragically and poignantly, being talked to by his grandson.

This is a good poem, simple and yet very effective, which shows a close bond between the different generations of a family, and the care that the child has for his dying grandfather. Baillie does not need to write any stanzas recounting the child's grief – we know from the poem and the closeness that they have shared in the past that the child will be bereft and disconsolate. Moreover, what can the child say except express his grief and sadness: this does not need to be written; Baillie is crediting her readers with basic empathy.

Why?

In this poem Baillie

- chooses a child's perspective which is typical of Romantic poetry as they valued the innocence of children very highly.
- imitates the child's voice and concerns accurately.
- writes a sad and moving poem, made more sad by the use of a child narrator.

'She Walks in Beauty' – Lord Byron

Author and Context

Lord George Gordon Byron (1788-1824) was as famous in his lifetime for his personality cult as for his poetry. He created the concept of the 'Byronic hero' - a defiant, melancholy young man, brooding on some mysterious, unforgivable event in his past. Byron's influence on European poetry, music, novel, opera, and painting has been immense, although the poet was widely condemned on moral grounds by some of his contemporaries.

George Gordon, Lord Byron, was the son of Captain John Byron, and Catherine Gordon. He was born with a club-foot and became extremely sensitive about his lameness. Byron spent his early childhood years in poor surroundings in Aberdeen, where he was educated until he was ten. After he inherited the title and property of his great-uncle in 1798, he went on to Dulwich, Harrow, and Cambridge, where he piled up debts and aroused alarm with bisexual love affairs. Staying at Newstead in 1802, he probably first met his half-sister, Augusta Leigh with whom he was later suspected of having an incestuous relationship.

In 1807 Byron's first collection of poetry, *Hours of Idleness* appeared. It received bad reviews. The poet answered his critics with the satire *English Bards and Scotch Reviewers* in 1808. Next year he took his seat in the House of Lords, and set out on his grand tour, visiting Spain, Malta, Albania, Greece, and the Aegean. Real poetic success came in 1812 when Byron published the first two cantos of *Childe Harold's Pilgrimage* (1812-1818). He became an adored character of London society; he spoke in the House of Lords effectively on liberal themes, and had a hectic love-affair with Lady Caroline Lamb. Byron's *The Corsair* (1814), sold 10,000 copies on the first day of publication. He married Anne Isabella Milbanke in 1815, and their daughter Ada was born in the same year. The marriage was unhappy, and they obtained legal separation next year.

When the rumours started to rise of his incest and debts were accumulating, Byron left England in 1816, never to return. He settled in Geneva with Percy Bysshe Shelley, Mary Wollstonecraft Shelley, and Claire Clairmont, who became his mistress. There he wrote the two cantos of *Childe Harold* and "The Prisoner of Chillon". At the end of the summer Byron continued his travels, spending two years in Italy. During his years in Italy, Byron wrote *Lament of Tasso*, inspired by his visit to Tasso's cell in Rome, *Mazeppa* and started *Don Juan*, his satiric masterpiece.

After a long creative period, Byron had come to feel that action was more important than poetry. He armed a brig, the Hercules, and sailed to Greece to aid the Greek rebels, who had risen against their Ottoman overlords. However, before he saw any serious military action, Byron contracted a fever from which he died in Missolonghi on 19 April 1824. Memorial services were held all over the land. Byron's body was returned to England but was refused burial by the deans of both Westminster and St Paul's. Finally, Byron's coffin was placed in the family vault at Hucknall Torkard, near Newstead Abbey in Nottinghamshire.

climes – a country or region.

raven – a bird with jet black plumage.

tress – a plait or braid of hair.

o'er - over.

Who? Byron writes as himself. The poem is about Mrs John Wilmot, who was in mourning and was Byron's cousin by marriage.

When? Sometime in 1813 – it is said that Byron wrote the poem the morning after meeting Mrs Wilmot and it was published in *Hebrew Melodies* in 1814.

Where? At night at an evening function.

What? The poet praises the lady's beauty and links it to the purity of her character.

Commentary

"She Walks in Beauty" is a poem written in 1813 by Lord Byron, and is one of his most famous works. It was one of several poems to be set to Jewish tunes from the synagogue by Isaac Nathan, which were published as *Hebrew Melodies* in 1815.

It is said to have been inspired by an event in Byron's life: while at a ball, Byron met Anne Hathaway (Mrs Wilmot), his cousin by marriage through John Wilmot. She was in mourning, wearing a black dress set with spangles, as in the opening lines;

> *She walks in beauty, like the night*
> *Of cloudless climes and starry skies*

He was struck by her unusual beauty, and the next morning the poem was written.

'She Walks in Beauty' is not typical of the love poems of the past, because it is largely descriptive. Indeed, it is a poem in which we get a sense of what the woman looks like and what she is wearing. Furthermore, in many love poems of the past (and some in the Anthology) are very intimate: the poet addresses the female recipient of the poem. But not in this poem: the speaker's audience is anyone who reads the poem. Byron's poem attempts to praise the appearance and moral purity of the woman he is writing about. In many other love poems, we learn little about the woman involved, but that is not true of Byron's poem. In many of the love poems of the past there is an emphasis on the poet's feelings: in Byron's poem his feelings are implied perhaps, but completely subservient to his description of the woman the poem is about. Unusually for a love poem, we get a real sense of what the woman is like. Byron's feelings towards her are not like many love poems of the past where the male writers are obsessed with their feelings or seducing the woman into bed. The poem comes across as objective praise by a disinterested observer. Furthermore, it also subverts the convention that beautiful women have fair hair and are blonde in complexion – although many of Shakespeare's sonnets are addressed to the so-called Dark Lady of the sonnets.

The poem is written in iambic tetrameters with only one variation: the opening trochaic foot of line 4.

Byron begins the poem with a simple simile: Mrs Wilmot is like the night and the alliteration in the second line foregrounds the image still further. Byron then indulges in hyperbole by claiming that

All that's best of dark and bright

Meet in her aspect and her eyes.

She is lit by moonlight and starlight which Byron which Byron calls a *tender light* which is denied to *gaudy day*, gaudy being used pejoratively.

The second stanza stresses the absolute perfection of her appearance:

One shade the more, one ray the less

would have *impaired* the beauty of this woman. Byron claims she has a *nameless grace/Which waves in every raven tress* and he links her external beauty with her inner thoughts and feelings, claiming that in her face one can discern

... thoughts serenely sweet [which] express

How pure, how dear their dwelling place.

The third stanza is full of praise for the recipient of the poem. Byron says that on her *cheeks* and on her *brow* - which are *so soft, so calm, yet eloquent,* are

The smiles that win, the tints that glow,

But tell of days in goodness spent.

In short, according to Byron's poem, she is the perfect woman: perfect in looks and in personality, character and intellect. She has

A mind at peace with all below,

A heart whose love is innocent.

Why is this such a famous poem?

- Byron acts as an objective observer so we are more likely to believe him.
- the regular iambic tetrameters do not distract from the harmony of the woman he describes – in fact, they enhance it and make it easy to memorize.
- the night-time setting is romantic and links with Mrs Wilmot's hair and complexion.
- the language is simple and easy to understand.
- Byron uses alliteration throughout but in an unobtrusive way.
- Byron establishes a clear link between the woman's beauty and her character – something unique in this Anthology.

Further reading: *Hebrew Melodies* ISBN: 978-1511897449

'A Complaint' – William Wordsworth
Author and Context

William Wordsworth was born in 1770 in Cockermouth on the edge of the English Lake District. He had a life-long fascination with nature and it is from the natural world that he took much of his inspiration. He died in 1850, having been made Poet Laureate in 1843. Wordsworth began to write *The Prelude* in 1798 and kept working on it and revising it until his death. It was not published until 1850, three months after his death. He published many poems during his own lifetime, but many readers feel that *The Prelude* is his finest work.

In his early years as a poet he was very friendly with the English poet Samuel Taylor Coleridge. In 1798 they published together a collection of poems called *Lyrical Ballads* with a longer version being published in 1800. Lyrical Ballads was to prove one of the most influential collections of poetry and Wordsworth and Coleridge collaborated closely over it. However, the years passed and disagreements between the two poets became bitter and they were estranged. This poem is Wordsworth's reaction to that failed friendship.

Who? Wordsworth writes about the breakdown of his friendship with Samuel Taylor Coleridge – at least it is widely assumed that the poem is about Wordsworth's relationship with Coleridge. The two poets had been very close during the 1790s and had collaborated together.

fond – affectionate.

When? In the early years of the nineteenth century.

Where? No specific location.

What? Wordsworth writes of the enormous inspiration that Coleridge gave him and his sadness that their friendship has waned.

Commentary

This poem consists of three stanzas which have the same pattern: the first four lines form a quatrain, rhyming ABAB and the stanza ends with a rhyming couplet.

The first line sums up the current situation:

There is a change – and I am poor.

Wordsworth means poor in an intellectual or artistic sense. He goes on to praise Coleridge's influence on him by using the metaphor of a fountain, *Whose only business was to flow* and help and inspire Wordsworth in his writing. Coleridge's inspiration was vital to Wordsworth. He says of the fountain:

And flow it did; not taking heed

Of its own bounty, or my need.

The caesura in the fifth line helps to suggest that the *fountain* has stopped flowing, but Wordsworth clearly appreciated Coleridge's friendship, calling it a *bounty*.

The second stanza starts positively and pays tribute to Coleridge's influence as Wordsworth recalls the two poets' friendship and collaboration. The second stanza starts with two happy exclamations:

What happy moments did I count!

Blest was I then all bliss above!

However, the third line of the stanza starts with the word *Now* and Wordsworth proceeds to describe their current relationship. He begins by paying tribute to Coleridge, still using the metaphor of the fountain. He describes Coleridge's friendship as a

> *... consecrated fount*

Of murmuring, sparkling, living love –

the three adjectives in this line showing the old intensity of their friendship and showing platonic love for Coleridge. But all this has changed:

What have I? shall I dare to tell?

A comfortless and hidden well.

The fountain bursting with energy has been replaced by a well – which brings no comfort and is hidden. Wells contain stagnant water; fountains gush and burst water everywhere – the metaphor is well-chosen.

In the final stanza Wordsworth holds out the hope that his relationship is not over by starting the final stanza:

A well of love – it may be deep –

I trust it is – and never dry.

Perhaps this is Wordsworth seeking some reconciliation with Coleridge. In the next two lines he appears to resign himself to the more distant relationship they now have:

What matter? If the waters sleep

In silence and obscurity.

However, in the final two lines he reveals his real feelings:

Such change, and at the very door

Of my fond heart, hath made me poor.

In terms of tone this poem is very varied: Wordsworth writes with real passion and enthusiasm about the past and Coleridge's deep impact on him; however, overall the tone is disconsolate and full of sadness at an intimacy that once meant so much has been allowed to decline from a fountain to a well. Perhaps Wordsworth intended the poem as a conciliatory gesture to revive their friendship.

Why?

In this poem of abandoned friendship Wordsworth:

- gives a vivid and passionate account of their former intimacy and friendship.
- uses natural imagery vividly to convey emotion.
- admits to uncertainty about how the friendship has declined.
- writes sadly about the loss of the friendship.

'Neutral Tones' – Thomas Hardy

Author and Context

 Thomas Hardy (1840 – 1928) is best known as a novelist. He wrote 15 novels, most of which are set largely in Dorset and the surrounding counties, and which deal with the ordinary lives of ordinary people in stories in which they struggle to find happiness and love – often battling against fate or their own circumstances. His final two novels *Tess of the D'Urbervilles* (1891) and *Jude the Obscure* (1895) both portray sex outside marriage in a sympathetic way and there was such a hysterical public outcry about the novels that Hardy stopped writing fiction and devoted the rest of his life to poetry. Although much of his poetry reflects his interest in nature and ordinary things, this poem is also typical of his work in that it is intensely personal and may reflect the intense unhappiness he felt in his first marriage.

Neutral – this can refer to the landscape, drained of vivid colours, but can also refer to the lovers in the poem – who are presented as being completely indifferent to one another.

Tones – like 'neutral' above this can refer to colour (or the lack of it), but also to the mood of the former lovers.

chidden – this is the past of 'to chide'. To chide means to tell off or to reprimand. Here it is as though God had told off the white sun.

sod – turf, the earth with grass on it.

rove – wander.

bird-a-wing – a bird in flight.

curst - cursed

Who? There is no reason to assume that the speaker is not Hardy himself. His lover is with him in the poem and this is seen in Hardy's use of the third person plural – 'we'.

When? On a cold winter's day. Hardy wrote the poem in 1867 at the age of 27, but it was not published until 1898.

Where? In the countryside beside a pond.

What? Hardy is looking back with bitterness and intense sadness at the end of a relationship.

Commentary

This is a bitter and pessimistic poem about the break-up of a relationship – one which Hardy remembers vividly and which still causes him pain and anguish. As a 'break up' poem, it is hard to think of a better one in the English Language – unless it's Byron's 'When We Two Parted'. Hardy uses pathetic fallacy throughout the poem, so the details of the weather and the landscape match and mirror the emotions of the two lovers.

The first stanza sets the scene. It is a bleak winter's day and the speaker and his former lover are standing by a pond. The landscape seems stripped of all fertility and strength. There are a few grey ash leaves scattered about and the sun, source of heat and light and life, is 'white, as though chidden of God' – chidden for being 'white' and for not offering any heat or real light on this miserable day? The sod is starving just as this relationship is starved now of any real love or affection.

In the second stanza Hardy directly addresses his lover, the first line using parallelism – 'eyes on me/eyes that rove'. Her eyes are like eyes that wander over 'tedious riddles of years ago' – suggesting that the relationship has been going on for years but that it has become 'tedious' – monotonous and uninteresting – a long time ago. They exchange some words (which Hardy does not bother to use in the poem) and he writes that the words they exchange – 'lost the more by our love': the words they speak now are trivial and meaningless and are in contrast to the love they once felt for each other. They are dull and irrelevant now (lost the more) in comparison with the love they once enjoyed (our love).

Hardy begins the third stanza with a scathing and oxymoronic simile by writing:

The smile on your mouth was the deadest thing

Alive enough to have strength to die –

which stresses the winter sterility of nature around them, but also accuses his lover of hypocrisy – why should she be smiling given the state of their relationship? Is it for form's sake or to try and keep up the pretence that they still mean something to each other? But then his lover makes 'a grin of bitterness' which is compared to 'an ominous bird-a-wing'. Some readers of Hardy have made the point that in his poems he uses birds in an ominous and usually pessimistic way – which is only interesting because it contrasts so sharply with the Romantic poets' use of birds in their poems. The Romantics (who preceded Hardy) almost always use birds as symbols of hope, poetic inspiration or the uplifting power of nature. Hardy – it could be argued – is more modern in his sensibility using birds as symbols of something negative and life-denying.

Hardy in the final stanza is writing from an imagined present and writes:

Since then, keen lessons that love deceives,

And wrings with wrong, have shaped to me

Your face, and the God-curst sun, and a tree

And a pond edged with grayish leaves.

'Since then' suggests the incident is long ago. Hardy suggests that he has been in love since then, but without success: he has learnt 'keen lessons' that 'love deceives', and whenever he does his mind thinks back to this unsuccessful meeting by the pond. The alliteration of 'wrings with wrong' sounds unpleasant and the venom (partly in the sound, partly in the meaning) of 'God-curst sun' is very bleak and powerful. In artistic terms Hardy brings the poem full circle to end where he began – the pond, the tree, the gray leaves. The pond is stagnant like the relationship, and is part of the pathetic fallacy used through the poem – the dead leaves, the white sun. The landscape is drained of all colour – just as the relationship is drained of all love.

Byron's 'When We Two Parted' is clearly about one individual woman. Hardy's poem is based on a meeting with one individual woman, but he has learnt 'keen lessons that love deceives' since then, which suggests a series of unsuccessful relationships, with the one in 'Neutral Tones' being the first of many. And in what ways can love deceive? Our first thought might be infidelity, but that is not very subtle. Hardy might mean pretending to yourself that you love someone or falling in love with someone before discovering what they are really like or just falling in love with the wrong person. I'm sure you can think of other possibilities. Hardy is claiming that at the end of any relationship he thinks back to this scene by the pond because of its sterile desolation: perhaps it was also the end of his first serious love affair.

Hardy chooses to use a regular rhyme scheme and the poem is made up of four rhyming quatrains written in iambic tetrameter – eight syllables to the line with four stressed syllables. However, Hardy uses enjambment skilfully and there is some metrical variation: 'God-curst sun' consists of three stressed syllables which adds force and power to the words themselves.

In 'Neutral Tones' Hardy

- writes a devastatingly bleak poem about the end of a relationship.

- uses pathetic fallacy in a masterly way to convey the human emotions in the poem.

- writes with a sense of experience about the bitter feelings that relationships can cause.

- apportions no blame for the breakdown of the relationship.

- uses imagery well to convey the sterility of the landscape and by extension the sterility of the relationship.

'My Last Duchess' – Robert Browning

Context

Robert Browning was born in 1812 and became one of the most famous English poets of the Victorian era. He was married to Elizabeth Barrett Browning who was a semi-invalid with an over-protective father. The couple were married in secret and then went to live in Italy. Browning's best work is often set in the past and he was a master of the dramatic monologue, in which the imagined speaker of the poem reveals their innermost thoughts and feelings, often going on to uncover uncomfortable truths about themselves.

This poem is based on real historical events. Duke Alfonso II of Modena and Ferrara (1559 – 1597) married Lucrezia de Doctors and she died four years after the wedding in mysterious circumstances. This is the starting point for Browning's poem. Victorian Britain was rather obsessed with the Italian Renaissance. Many of Browning's monologues are set in Renaissance Italy. The Renaissance, around the period 1450 – 1650, was a cultural and intellectual movement which happened all across Western Europe and it involved the rediscovery of many of the skills that had been forgotten or ignored since the fall of the Roman Empire, especially in painting, art and sculpture. We can understand why the Renaissance began in Italy and the Italians felt themselves to be the heirs of the ancient Romans. In Italy the ruins and ancient buildings were a constant visual reminder of the arts of Rome. The artistic achievement of the Renaissance was helped by a system of patronage: wealthy dukes, merchants and princes commissioned great artists to create paintings and sculptures, just as in the poem the Duke of Ferrara has commissioned Fra Pandolf to paint the portrait of his first wife and Claus of Innsbruck has sculpted Neptune taming a sea-horse.

But the Renaissance, especially in Italy, had a sinister side to it. Many of the wealthy and powerful patrons of art were just as capable of paying to have an enemy assassinated or poisoned because their power and wealth allowed them to do so. What seems to have fascinated the Victorians was the co-existence in the Italian renaissance of art works of stunning beauty alongside moral and political corruption. As Victorian Britons they hoped to emulate the cultural achievements, but looked down upon (even as they were fascinated by) the moral corruption.

Fra Pandolf – an imaginary painter who supposedly painted the portrait of the Duchess.

a day – for many days.

countenance – face.

durst – dared.

mantle – a cloak.

favour – a thing (a jewelled brooch perhaps or a flower) worn as a token of love or affection.

officious – too forward in offering unwelcome or unwanted services.

nine-hundred-years-old name – this simply means that the title the Duke of Ferrara was first created nine-hundred years before the poem is set.

forsooth – truly.

the Count, your master – this phrase is important because it makes clear that the speaker of the poem is talking to a servant of the Count, who is visiting (it later becomes clear) to discuss the marriage of his daughter to the narrator.

munificence – generosity.

nay – no.

Neptune – the God of the Sea.

Claus of Innsbruck – an imaginary sculptor who has sculpted the statue of Neptune for the Duke.

Who? The Duke of Ferrara talks to the representative of an unnamed count who is there to arrange for his daughter to marry the Duke – she will be his next duchess. The poem is written in the present tense.

When? In the 16th century, in the Duke's palace. This is very important because Browning and his fellow Victorians were fascinated by the Italian Renaissance period.

Where? In Ferrara in northern Italy.

What? The speaker tells the story of his first marriage by reference to a portrait of his first wife which hangs on the wall.

Commentary

'My Last Duchess' by Robert Browning is a very famous and much-anthologized poem. It is a dramatic monologue – that is to say the poet adopts the voice of someone else and speaks throughout as that person. It was first published in 1842 and is one of many dramatic monologues that Browning wrote.

The speaker in the poem is the Duke of Ferrara, an Italian nobleman from the 16th century – we are told this from the note at the beginning. This immediately tells us the location of the poem (Italy) and the social background of the speaker – he is a powerful and wealthy aristocrat.

As the poem develops we come to understand that the Duke (pictured here) is talking to a representative of the family of his fiancée, his future wife, and that they are talking in the Duke of Ferrara's palace. We can be even more precise and say that for most of the poem they are standing in front of a portrait of the Duke's former wife (now dead). The Duke talks about his dead wife and, in doing so, reveals a great deal about his character, the sort of man he is. We also learn the terrible fate of his first wife.

The opening sentence refers the reader to a painting hanging on the wall. The painting is so good that his previous wife is

Looking as if she were alive.

Browning establishes that the painter was skilled and produced a *wonder* – a masterpiece. The painter fussed over the portrait and over the duchess – *his hands worked busily a day.* In line 5 we realize for the first time that the duke is speaking not to the readers as such, but someone else; he invites him to sit and look at the portrait of his dead wife. He says he mentioned Fra Pandolf *by design* – perhaps to imply that he was an exceptionally well-known and highly sought-after painter (but remember that he has been made up by Browning). The fact that the Duke could pay for his services shows how rich he is.

The long sentence that begins on line 5 may be a little hard to follow. Note that in lines 9-10 the duke reveals that the painting is normally concealed by a curtain which only he is allowed to open; this suggests, perhaps, a man who is used to being obeyed, even in petty things like a curtain covering a painting. When people like the person he is talking to – *strangers like you* – see the painting, the duke says, they are always moved to ask him (he's always there because he controls the curtain!) what caused the *depth and passion* in the look on the duchess's face. You might note the phrase *its pictured countenance* – I know he is talking about a painted image, but it may strike you as unusual that he doesn't use the word *her* when talking about his dead wife. This one word suggests that he treated her like an object in life and, now that her portrait is on his wall, she is still an object – only now he can exert complete control over her. We might also note that the visitor hasn't asked about the *earnest glance* in the duchess's face – perhaps only the duke sees it. He seems to like the painting of her very much indeed and we will return to this idea later in this commentary.

The duke continues by saying that his visitor is not the first person to ask him why she looked so passionate in the portrait. The duke states

.... Sir, 'twas not

Her husband's presence only, called that spot

Of joy into the Duchess' cheek.

Her husband's presence – are we to assume that he was there in the room all the time while she had her portrait completed? I think we are – it fits with what we are starting to find out about his character. The duke seems to have been jealous when other men paid any attention to his wife – something she appears to have enjoyed since it brings *a spot of joy* to her face. He seems to have seen Fra Pandolf as some sort of rival and repeats things that the painter said to his wife in lines 16 – 19. You may feel that the duke really suspected that Fra Pandolf was his wife's secret lover or you may feel that the duke thought she was a little too easily impressed by male attention.

The duke then expands on his wife's faults. She was *too soon made glad*; she was *too easily impressed*; she could not discriminate –

...she liked whate'er

She looked on and her looks went everywhere.

She looked on everything with the same undiscriminating affection.

My favour at her breast – some precious brooch pinned on her breast and given her by the duke was given the same importance as the sunset or some cherries brought to her by a servant or riding a white mule along the terrace of the palace. You might feel that riding a white mule is a slightly eccentric thing to do – but she is the wife of a wealthy and very powerful man and she can do what she likes, whatever takes her fancy. Above is a picture believed to be of the Duchess that the poem is based upon.

Line 33 reveals the duke's arrogance about his title and position. He talks about his nine-hundred-years-old name and clearly feels that his position and his title as Duke of Ferrara should have been given more respect by his wife. Note that he calls his name *My gift* – as though she should have been grateful that he married her.

In line 34 he starts to suggest that his attitude to all this was casual and relaxed. He calls her behaviour *trifling* and says he would not *stoop* to blame her. *Stoop* is an important word because it reminds us of his high social status and makes it clear that he regarded his wife as beneath him and inferior to him: it is a word that he repeats in the next few lines. And so it was that, even though his wife's behaviour disgusted him, he never said a word.

Browning allows the duke to say he is not good at speaking and so may not have been able to explain his misgivings to his wife – but this is sheer nonsense: every line of this poem shows that the duke (as Browning has created him) is a clever manipulator of words. He says that she might have argued with him: *plainly set her wits* against his; and that even if he could have explained, it would have been degrading for him to have done so

E'en then would be some stooping, and I choose

Never to stoop.

Once again we are reminded of his arrogance and superciliousness. It is interesting that he could not speak to his wife, but he takes 56 lines of the poem to talk to his visitor. She remained friendly to him – she smiled when she passed him, but she smiled at everyone and his sense of his own importance cannot allow that. And then we come to the heart, perhaps, of the poem

... I gave commands;

Then all smiles stopped together.

The duke gave some orders and had his wife murdered. This is quite clear. Browning said of the poem in an interview:

I meant that the commands were that she should be put to death....Or he might have had her shut up in a convent.

Now look back at line 19. It refers to the painter saying that he can never hope to reproduce in paint *the flush that dies along her throat* – that fades along her throat, but now we have read more of the poem and we know what the duke did to his wife, it is clear that Browning is preparing us verbally for the truth. Did she have her throat slashed? Or was she strangled? Either could be true. The flush in line 19 is the way that the Duchess blushed when she was flirting, perhaps, but the fact that Browning uses the verb 'dies' instead of 'fade' is a way of verbally prefiguring her fate. And his final sentence about his wife also suggests that she was murdered: *there she stands/As if alive.*

In line 47 he invites his visitor to stand and go downstairs with him to meet the company – the group of people who are waiting for them down below. Line 49 reveals that he has been talking to a servant of an unnamed Count (*your master*) whose *known munificence* means that he (the duke) expects a very large dowry. Having mentioned the dowry, the duke asserts that he doesn't really care about money – he is only interested in the count's daughter.

As they go down the stairs the duke points out a bronze statue, another of his pieces of art, sculpted by Claus of Innsbruck for him. The statue's subject matter is important: it shows the god of the sea, Neptune, taming a sea-horse. This demonstrates the relationship that the duke had with his first wife (he tamed her), with his servants and with his future wife – the daughter of the Count. Like Neptune ruling the sea, the duke likes to have power over people and beautiful objects like the painting of his wife and this statue. It is significant that the final word of this poem is *me* – because the duke's self-centredness has slowly been revealed the more we have read.

Browning writes in rhyming couplets of ten syllables, but his use of enjambment means that, because the lines are very rarely end-stopped, the poem drives onwards, just as the duke almost compulsively reveals what has happened to his wife. The enjambment also prevents the rhyming couplets from becoming too monotonous and make them sound more like real speech. The duke's hesitations and frequent interjections make him appear reasonable, although he is talking about the murder of his first wife. He has a very casual attitude to it all: he acquired a wife; she did not behave as he liked; he disposed of her. The naturalness of the sound of his speech, its casual, relaxed tone suggests that he does not see anything wrong in what he has done and expects his listener to find it normal too.

Although he claims he is not skilled in speaking, Browning ensures that the Duke gradually reveals the truth about what happened to his wife and the truth about his own character: he is possessive, jealous and likes the idea of controlling people. He is proud and arrogant about his aristocratic title and his family's history. He seems to prefer the painting of his dead wife to her living reality: he can control the painting, but he could not control his first wife. The poem ends on a note of dread – dread on behalf of his second wife who does not know what lies in store for her. He also seems to treat his wives like objects: objects are much easier to control than living human beings.

He seems more interested in being seen as a man of great taste than as a good husband. He draws the servant's attention to the painting and to the sculpture at the end. These objects are meant to demonstrate his taste and his wealth – he is connected to the great artists of his day. But his taste is limited to things he can control and totally possess – for example, he does not seem to be aware of the irony in the sculpture of Neptune and the fact that it might symbolize his relationships with other people, especially women.

Love and Power

The Duke of Ferrara exercises complete power in his palace and its grounds. His power is based on his aristocratic positon – his "nine hundred year old name", his money, and his possessive and jealous personality. There is a paradox here: despite all his money and power, he could not control the behaviour of his wife and – "I gave commands" – he gets rid of his troublesome wife. Now she exists as a painting, covered by curtains which only he can use, so he now has a measure of control over her. His power is also shown by the quick way in which his commands were acted upon and also by his collection of expensive and exquisite works of art. Because this is a dramatic monologue, Browning presents the Duke without comment – in marked contrast to the three preceding Romantic poems where the reader is left in no doubt about the poet's own views. With this poem Browning presents the Duke and allows the reader to make up their own mind about him. This is a poem about love as a means of control and ownership.

Why?

This casual-sounding but deeply sinister poem

- shows the pride and arrogance of the aristocracy.

- is a portrait of the psychology of a murderer.

- shows that money and status and power can corrupt.

- shows the domination of men over women.

- raises questions about the relationship between art and life.

- is superbly written by Browning so that the reader must read between the lines as the terrible truth dawns upon us.

'How Do I Love Thee' – Elizabeth Barrett Browning

Context

Elizabeth Barrett Browning was born into a wealthy family in 1806. At the age of 14 she suffered from a lung complaint and the following year damaged her spine in a riding accident, she was to be plagued with poor health for the rest of her life. Elizabeth had started to publish poetry anonymously and was starting to become famous. In 1838 her brother Edward drowned off the coast of Devon and for the next five years Elizabeth became a recluse, hardly leaving her bedroom in her father's house. However, she continued to write poetry and began a long correspondence with the poet Robert Browning, who began writing to her after reading her poems. Between 1844 and 1846 they wrote 574 letters to each other and finally ran away to Italy to get married. They had to flee to Italy because Elizabeth's father was violently opposed to the marriage. She and her father never spoke again and he disinherited her. Her health improved in Italy and she gave birth to a son in 1849. She died in her husband's arms in 1861.

'Sonnet 43' is from the sonnet cycle *Sonnets from the Portuguese* which she wrote during their correspondence and before their marriage. (*Sonnets from the Portuguese* is simply the title she chose – they are not translations and do not exist in Portuguese!). This sonnet cycle explores the development and growth of her love for Browning and, although she wrote many other poems, it is these sonnets for which she is mainly remembered today. What is interesting and rarely mentioned in guides like this, is that the earlier poems in the sonnet cycle were not as confident as 'Sonnet 43'. In the earlier sonnets she is afraid of the consequences of her love for Browning and unsure about her own feelings: 'Sonnet 43' is towards the end of the sonnet cycle and represents the achievement of a confident, mature love.

Thee- you

Grace – the Grace of God

My lost Saints – perhaps a reference to members of the poet's family who have died or to her former strong religious belief which has been replaced by love for Browning.

Who? The poet addresses her future husband.

When? From the period before they were married.

Where? The location is not specified.

What? The poet explores the many ways in which she loves her husband-to-be.

Commentary

Although this poem is a Petrarchan sonnet in form, it is unlike many sonnets because there is no turn in line 9 – there is no conflict or problem to be resolved because Barrett Browning's tone is assertive, confident and strong: she is expressing her love for Browning without doubt or hesitation.

The opening sentence – given more prominence by the poet's dramatic use of the caesura – asks a question which the following thirteen lines attempt to answer. In all there are eight different aspects of love identified. As the poem goes on each different type of love is introduced by the words *I love thee* – which is a very simple device of repetition, but may explain why so many readers find this a memorable poem. In the first quatrain the poet moves on to speak of the spiritual aspect of her love; the second quatrain deals with the love that enriches ordinary, everyday life. Her love is given *freely* she says in line 7 and *purely* – line 8: her love is given unselfishly and modestly, in the way someone might turn away from praise.

In the sestet the poet analyses her love in three more ways: she loves him with Passion – an emotion she once expended on grief and with the fidelity of a child. She loves him with the same passion she once reserved for religion. She then states that her love is completely overwhelming – it is like breathing and continues through good and bad times – *smiles, tears, of all my life*. The poem ends by stating that if it is God's will, then her love will continue after death and exist in the after-life – another answer to her opening question.

Apart from the lack of a turn or problem to be resolved, which sets it apart from many sonnets, Barrett Browning uses hardly any imagery, no metaphors or similes. She takes an abstract concept 'love' and defines it largely through other abstract concepts – Grace, Right. The words I love thee are repeated nine times in the course of the sonnet and this simple use of repetition has made the poem so well-known and popular. This repetition also shows the strength and confidence of her feelings.

So how does she love her husband?

She loves him with her soul when it is searching for the meaning of life (*the ends of Being*) and the mystery of God (*Ideal Grace*).

She loves him in an ordinary down-to-earth way – *the level of everyday's most quiet need*.

She loves him *freely* – in the same way that humans seek morality (*Right*).

She loves him purely and modestly (*as men turn from Praise*).

She loves him with the passion she once expended on *my old griefs*.

She loves him with the faith of childhood.

She loves him with the love she seemed to lose with her lost Saints (the siblings who had died when she was younger).

She loves him with the breath of all her life.

She will love him better after death.

This famous poem is very simple in its use of language – and perhaps that is its appeal. There are no metaphors to confuse or to analyze; the imagery is limited and where it occurs it is very simple – *sun, candlelight, smiles, tears*; it is clearly written in the Christian tradition and some readers may find her certainty and faith comforting.

Why?

In this famous sonnet, Barratt Browning

- asserts her unequivocal love and fidelity to her husband.
- uses simple language and hardly any imagery.
- expresses complete devotion to her husband.

'1st Date –She & 1st Date – He' – Wendy Cope

Author & Context

Poet Wendy Cope was born in Erith, Kent in 1945 and read History at St Hilda's College, Oxford.

She trained as a teacher at Westminster College of Education, Oxford, and taught in primary schools in London (1967-81 and 1984-6). She became Arts and Reviews editor for *Contact*, the Inner London Education Authority magazine, and continued to teach part-time, before becoming a freelance writer in 1986. She was television critic for *The Spectator* magazine until 1990. She received a Cholmondeley Award in 1987 and was awarded the Michael Braude Award for Light Verse (American Academy of Arts and Letters) in 1995. Her poetry collections include *Making Cocoa for Kingsley Amis* (1986), *Serious Concerns* (1992) and *If I Don't Know* (2001), which was shortlisted for the Whitbread Poetry Award. *Two Cures for Love* (2008) is a selection of previous poems with notes, together with new poems.

She has edited a number of poetry anthologies including *The Orchard Book of Funny Poems* (1993), *Is That The New Moon?* (1989), *The Funny Side: 101 Humorous Poems* (1998) and *The Faber Book of Bedtime Stories* (1999) and *Heaven on Earth: 101 Happy Poems* (2001). She is also the author of two books for children, *Twiddling Your Thumbs* (1988) and *The River Girl* (1991). Wendy Cope is a Fellow of the Royal Society of Literature and lives in Winchester, England. In 1998 she was the listeners' choice in a BBC Radio 4 poll to succeed Ted Hughes as Poet Laureate.

Her latest collection is *Family Values* (2011). She was awarded an OBE in 2010.

besotted – infatuated by, obsessed by, when applied to love.

Who? Two people who are going on their first date together.

When? Evening.

Where? A classical music concert hall.

What? Cope cleverly gives two accounts of the same experience from two different points of view. Both speakers seem lacking in confidence and anxious to create a good impression on their first date: this leads to some amusing misunderstandings.

Commentary

This comic poem has an unusual arrangement, because it is split into two columns, the first entitled 'Ist Date -She' and the second 'Ist Date – He' This enables Cope to give the two speakers their different thoughts on the date and what is going on.

The first funny thing for me is that neither of them are very keen on classical music, but they are both attending a classical music concert.

The woman says:

I said I liked classical music.

It wasn't exactly a lie.

I hoped he would get the impression

That my brow was acceptably high.

In other words, she says she likes classical music to impress him. He is similar in his self-delusion, saying *I implied I was keen on it too*, but he admits that although he rarely attends concerts *It wasn't entirely untrue*, which really means it is partly untrue.

In her second verse the woman writes that she mentioned *Vivaldi and Bach* and *he asked me along to this concert*. The man in his second verse reveals that he *looked for a suitable concert, / And here we are on our first date* – a date neither of them want to be on really given their minimal interest in classical music. They are attracted to each other and the concert is just a badly-chosen first date based on minor deception. The man is more concerned that the traffic that evening was *dreadful* and that he was *ten minutes late.*

In the woman's third stanza she admits that she was thrilled to be asked to the concert, but she couldn't care less what they play. Her attention is really on her date, the man she is attracted to, not the music at all:

But I'm trying my hardest to listen

So I'll have something clever to say.

This deeply ironic – the man knows very little about classical music and would not recognize if she had something clever to say or not.

Going to a concert on a first date is not a good idea because there are few opportunities to talk and get to know each other. In his third stanza the man looks at the woman's face and comes to the completely, laughably wrong conclusion:

She is totally lost in the music

And quite undistracted by me.

Cope then follows this with the woman's fourth stanza – which is hilarious given the man's observations:

When I glance at his face it's a picture

Of rapt concentration. I see

He is totally into this music

And quite undistracted by me.

This is funny partly because it echoes exactly the man's words, partly because, like the man's observation it is completely untrue and partly because the exact opposite is true – the man is attracted to her as his fourth stanza reveals.

The man's fourth stanza begins with his real interest – *In that dress she is very attractive* – and the second line refers admiringly to her neckline. However, as he has admitted in the third verse, he is a bit nervous and now, in stanza four, he tells himself

I mustn't appear too besotted.

Perhaps she is out of my league.

Clearly he IS besotted with her as a woman, but is held back, perhaps, by a lack of self-confidence and a fear of rejection... and, of course, by the formality of a classical music concert hall where they cannot speak to each other.

In the man's fifth stanza (the ninth stanza of the poem as a whole), he is unsure where they are in the programme of music: he does have a physical programme but has put his reading glasses away. He says to himself:

I'd better start paying attention

Or else I'll have nothing to say.

This is richly ironic because in her third stanza the woman had told herself to listen harder so that she would have something clever to say; she clearly wants to impress the man with her cleverness.

The poem as a whole presents a very funny situation: a man and a woman who are attracted to each other, but have not got the nerve to admit it, attend a classical music concert as a first date. They want to impress each other by having something to say about the concert, but they both misinterpret what the other is thinking. They are both thinking about each other, but, comically, each one is convinced that they are concentrating on the concert when nothing could be further from the truth. Although the poem is funny and highly ironic, there is a serious side, showing how difficult it is sometimes for would-be lovers to communicate their real feelings. The real joke is that neither of the speakers really wants to be at the concert at all and neither of them have any particular interest in classical music – they are much more interested in each other, but too wary to admit it and too keen to make a good impression.

Why?

In this amusing poem Wendy Cope:

- uses irony throughout by using dual narrators.
- shows both speakers to be reticent about what they really want to do.
- hints at a certain sadness because the would-be lovers are too self-conscious to be true to themselves.

'Valentine' – Carol Ann Duffy

Author & Context

Dame Carol Ann Duffy DBE FRSL (born 23 December 1955) is a Scottish poet and playwright. She is Professor of Contemporary Poetry at Manchester Metropolitan University, and was appointed Britain's Poet Laureate in May 2009. She is the first woman, the first Scot, and the first openly LGBT person to hold the position. Her collections include *Standing Female Nude* (1985), winner of a Scottish Arts Council Award; *Selling Manhattan* (1987), which won a Somerset Maugham Award; *Mean Time* (1993), which won the Whitbread Poetry Award; and *Rapture* (2005), winner of the T. S. Eliot Prize. Her poems address issues such as oppression, gender, and violence in an accessible language that has made them popular in schools.

Commentary

When we think of a Valentine's Day gift, our minds are apt to turn to clichés: red roses, chocolates, fancy lingerie, soft toys (usually teddy bears) holding little hearts – the conventional approach to Valentine's Day. Duffy dismisses all this tat in the first single-line stanza of her poem 'Valentine'.

Not a red rose or a satin heart.

Her gift for her lover is very different:

I give you an onion.

This is shocking, unsettling and funny at the same time.

She then uses a metaphor to describe the onion *as a moon wrapped in brown paper*. It has to be unpeeled and its unpeeling is like the way we unpeel our clothes as we prepare for sex. The moon is also a romantic image commonly associated with love, but this one comes wrapped in unromantic brown paper, Duffy again eschewing any of the romantic clichés of Valentine's Day.

Cutting onions makes you cry and Duffy goes on to promise that this onion will make her lover cry. Tears are associated with love in two ways: they can be tears of happiness and ecstasy or they can be tears of grief and sadness when love goes wrong or there are difficulties in the relationship. Duffy's onion offers both.

The next stanza certainly suggests there are problems in the relationship. Her lover will be *blinded by tears* and her reflection will become *a wobbling photo of grief.*

Duffy admits she is being *truthful* and again rejects the *cute card[s] and kissograms* of the conventional Valentine's Day celebrations.

Duffy claims that the onions

... fierce kiss, will stay on your lips,

Possessive and faithful

As we are,

For as long as we are.

The pungent aroma of the onion and its *fierce kiss* (indicative of fierce sexual passion) will always be on her lips – *for as long as we are*: for as long as their relationship continues.

In the final stanza Duffy is still urging her lover to accept the onion: *Take it.* The circular hoops of the onion get smaller and smaller and are white and

Its platinum hoops shrink to a wedding ring

If you like.

But Duffy's one-word line following this – *Lethal* – suggests she views marriage in a negative light, perhaps lethal to a relationship based on love. Certainly the earlier *for as long as we are* assumed that the relationship would one day come to an end.

Love, Duffy writes, as an onion *will cling to your fingers* – like the odours of sexual activity cling to one's fingers – and they will *cling to your knife* – an especially threatening way to end the poem, as if not only do you use a knife to cut an onion, but you might use it to break a relationship. Love can be a dangerous emotion if it is not returned.

Duffy's tone throughout the poem is scathing about the conventional rituals of Valentine's Day – and probably rightly so. Her use of single line stanzas, short sentences and simple vocabulary adds a harshness and honesty to her words. Elsewhere her brevity and the general shortness of her phrases suggests an honesty and no-nonsense approach to love – softened at points when she mentions the platinum wedding ring, only to dismiss it as *lethal*. Is she suggesting that marriage destroys love?

She conveys the reality of love – the tears of joy and happiness or of sadness and heartbreak. Above all, she delights and surprises the reader with her gift of an onion.

Why?

In 'Valentine' Carol Ann Duffy

- rejects the traditional symbols of romantic love.
- offers an onion as a Valentine's Day gift – and goes on to explain why it is an appropriate gift.

- shows how love can lead to heartbreak and tears when it goes wrong.
- shocks and amuses the reader by her choice of an onion.
- strongly suggests that marriage can result in the loss of love.

'One Flesh' – Elizabeth Jennings

Author and Context

Jennings was born in Boston, Lincolnshire. When she was six, her family moved to Oxford, where she remained for the rest of her life. There she later attended St Anne's College. After graduation, she became a writer.

Jennings' early poetry was published in journals such as *Oxford Poetry*, *New English Weekly*, *The Spectator*, *Outposts* and *Poetry Review*, but her first book was not published until she was 27. The lyrical poets she cited as having influenced her were Hopkins, Auden, Graves and Muir. Her second book, *A Way of Looking*, won the Somerset Maugham award and marked a turning point, as the prize money allowed her to spend nearly three months in Rome, which was a revelation. It brought a new dimension to her religious belief and inspired her imagination.

Regarded as traditionalist rather than an innovator, Jennings is known for her lyric poetry and mastery of form. Her work displays a simplicity of metre and rhyme shared with Philip Larkin, Kingsley Amis and Thom Gunn, all members of the group of English poets known as The Movement. She always made it clear that, whilst her life, which included a spell of severe mental illness, contributed to the themes contained within her work, she did not write explicitly autobiographical poetry. Her deeply held Roman Catholicism coloured much of her work.

She died in a care home in Bampton, Oxfordshire and is buried in Wolvercote Cemetery, Oxford.

flotsam - the wreckage of a ship or its cargo found floating on or washed up by the sea.

Who? The poet writes about her elderly parents who occupy the central place in the poem.

Where? In bed.

When? In the old age of Elizabeth Jennings' parents.

What? Jennings speculates about the state of their marriage now they are elderly and their youthful passion has disappeared.

Commentary

This poem is arranged in three stanzas, reflecting the three people in the poem: the poet, her father and her mother. Jennings uses a strict rhyme scheme which helps to show that her feelings, although deep, are restrained and under control – just as the language is under control. Each stanza follows the same rhyme scheme with some half-rhymes: ABABAA, although there is some variation in the last verse, which is ABABAB and does contain some half-rhyme.

The opening stanza is descriptive and reflective. Her parents are in bed – separate beds – and her father has a book, keeping the light on late. Her mother, by contrast, is

> ... *like a girl dreaming of childhood,*

All men elsewhere.

Jennings feels that

> ... *it is as if they wait*

Some new event: the book he holds unread,

Her eyes fixed on the shadows overhead.

But no new event is likely given their age and state. All that awaits them is death.

The second stanza begins with a simile – her parents are *Tosssed up like flotsam from a former passion*, but now the passion has disappeared and they *lie cool*. We are told that they *hardly ever touch* and if they ever do

> ... *it is like a confession*

Of having little feeling – or too much.

This is a deliberate paradox: perhaps they hardly ever touch because their feelings for each other have faded and withered; but perhaps they hardly ever touch because to do so is to recall their youthful, passionate days which are long gone – and it is painful to think about the past now they are old and decrepit.

The third stanza begins with a paradox they are *Strangely apart, yet strangely close together* – joined by their daughter and by decades of married life. They no longer talk much but the silence between them is *like a thread to hold* but *not wind in*: they are connected and perhaps content with the silence but it does not bring them closer together. Jennings then uses a very interesting metaphor:

And time itself's a feather

Touching them gently.

This is a beautiful and delicate image which suggests the frailty of old age and the gentleness with which they are touched by time; it may also refer directly to the physical frailty they both endure. Time has to be gentle with them.

In the final sentence Jennings asks a rhetorical question which reveals the real concern of the poem:

Do they know they're old,

These two who are my father and my mother

Whose fire from which I came, has now grown cold?

Here the contrast between the youthful passion they felt in their younger years has grown cold. Therefore, a poem which has a morose and melancholic tone throughout becomes a lament on the inevitable process of ageing and the loss of youthful vigour and energy.

Why?

In 'One Flesh' Elizabeth Jennings

- speculates on the state of her parents' marriage now that they are very old.
- presents her parents as almost leading separate lives in one house.
- speculates on the youthful passion that led to Jennings' birth and wonders what they have now to replace it.
- writes a rather melancholic poem, the tone of which is subdued and morose.

'i wanna be yours' – John Cooper Clarke

Author & Context

John Cooper Clarke (born 25 January 1949) is an English performance poet who first became famous during the punk rock era of the late 1970s when he became known as a "punk poet". He released several albums in the late 1970s and early 1980s, and continues to perform regularly. His recorded output has mainly centred on musical backing from the Invisible Girls, which featured Martin Hannett, Steve Hopkins, Pete Shelley, Bill Nelson, and Paul Burgess.

Commentary

John Cooper Clarke is a performance poet and I would strongly recommend that you watch some of his performances on Youtube before you read the commentary that follows.

'i wanna be yours' is a funny poem, even funnier, I would suggest, in performance. It relies on repetition, simple rhymes and unusual metaphors for its comic effect. The opening is typical of the whole poem:

let me be your vacuum cleaner

breathing in your dust

let me be your ford cortina

i will never rust

The humour here is two-fold. Firstly, everyday objects like vacuum cleaners and Ford Cortinas do not often appear in love poems – so there is the shock of the bizarre and the unusual. Secondly, while love poetry is full of poets offering to perform actions for their loved ones, the thought of a human being transformed to a vacuum cleaner or a type of car borders on the surreal.

The second half of the first stanza continues in similar vein:

if you like your coffee hot

let me be your coffee pot

you call the shots

i wanna be yours

The last two lines are slightly shorter than the others and break the pattern of the previous six.

In the second stanza he offers to be her raincoat, her dreamboat and her teddy bear which she can

take... with you anywhere

i don't care

i wanna be yours

The metrical pattern of the second verse is exactly the same as the first and the effects are just as amusing.

The third stanza begins as the first two do with surreal offers to prove his love and devotion:

let me be your electric meter

i will not run out

let me be your electric heater

you get cold without

He then expresses a desire to be her setting lotion and this starts a riff on words that rhyme with lotion: he will hold her hair

with deep devotion

deep as the deep

atlantic ocean

that's how deep is my devotion

deep deep deep deep de deep deep

i don't wanna be hers

i wanna be yours

Throughout the poem Cooper Clarke uses simple vocabulary to convey straightforward emotions in a funny and engaging style.

Why?

In this funny performance poem John Cooper Clarke

- rejects the traditional clichés of romantic love.
- uses everyday language and objects in interesting, amusing and new ways.
- expresses complete devotion and love in a humorous way.

'Love's Dog' – Jen Hatfield

Author & Context

Jen Hadfield was born in Cheshire, England, to Canadian and British parents. She earned her BA from the University of Edinburgh and MLitt in creative writing from the University of Strathclyde and the University of Glasgow, where she worked with the poet Tom Leonard. Hadfield's first collection, *Almanacs* (2005), explored Canadian and Scottish topography, in particular the Shetland Islands where Hadfield still lives, paying special attention to how dialects and local languages emerge from landscapes, labour, and encounters with other cultures. For her second book, *Nigh-No-Place* (2008), Hadfield won a T.S. Eliot Prize, making her the youngest poet ever to do so. Of both books Hadfield has written, "the poems are united by my fascination with spoken language and by themes of wildness and subsistence; fretting over what it means to be 'no-place' and what it means to make yourself 'at home.'"

Hadfield is also a visual artist and bookmaker. In 2007, she received a DeWar Award to travel to Mexico and study Mexican devotional folk art. She is a member of the artists' collective Veer North and provided photographs for the collaborative artists' book *The Printer's Devil and the Little Bear* (2006). Hadfield's honours and awards include an Eric Gregory Award, a Scottish Arts Council Bursary Award, and residencies with the Shetland Arts Trust and the Scottish Poetry Library. In 2014, she was named one of 20 poets selected to represent the Next Generation of UK poets. Hadfield currently lives in the Shetland Islands, where she is reader in residence at Shetland Library.

The poem was inspired by 'A View of Things' by the Scottish poet Edwin Morgan which contains the line *What I hate about love is its dog*.

Who? There is one speaker, probably the poet.

When? No specific time is mentioned.

Where? There is no specific location.

What? The poem is a list of the things the poet loves and hates about love.

Commentary

This is an anaphoric poem – that is to say that the lines begin with the same words (with some variations). Generally, in this poem each line begins *What I love about love is its...*, although *hate* and *loathe* are used to replace *love*. The poem consists of eight two line stanzas with occasional rhyme and half-rhyme. I think this poem would cause laughter at a poetry reading and I hope to explain why.

The first verse makes perfect sense

What I love about love is its diagnosis

What I hate about love is its prognosis

The *diagnosis* may well refer to the fact and realization that you are in love, while the *prognosis* may refer to the future of the relationship and a possible future break up.

Usually the words at the end of the line relate to each other in one way or another, as in stanza three

What I love about love is its petting zoo

What I love about love is its zookeeper – you

From this point on in the poem the things mentioned are increasingly random, as in the fifth stanza:

What I love about love is its doubloons

What I love about love is its bird-bones.

In the following stanza she hates love's boilwash, but loves its spin cycle:

112

these domestic details are bizarre and random, and the poem is deliberately and playfully descending into nonsense. There is a long tradition of nonsense verse in English Literature.

The penultimate stanza is wholly negative:

What I loathe about love is its burnt toast and bonemeal

What I hate about love is its bent cigarette

These domestic details keep the poem grounded in reality, but their yoking together at the end of the lines introduces a surreal element – which is true of all the line endings.

The final stanza continues this surreal and amusing tone:

What I love about love is its pirate

What I hate about love is its sick parrot

An amusing and bizarre end to this funny poem. The humour lies at the end of the lines where disparate objects are joined together or juxtaposed. In addition, the objects singled out have very little to do with traditional images of love. Only in stanza three does Hatfield admit to another person to whom these lines are addressed.

Why?

In 'Love's Dog' Jen Hatfield

- writes a funny poem by juxtaposing unusual things, not normally associated with love.
- the poem is given structure by its anaphoric nature.
- creates humour through the often bizarre juxtaposition of things at the end of each line.
- acts as a homage to Edwin Morgan whose line inspired the poem.

'Nettles' – Vernon Scannell

Author & Context

Vernon Scannell (1922 – 2007) was born in Spilsby in Lincolnshire and led a very interesting life, working as both a teacher and a boxer before becoming a full-time writer. The defining experience of his life was being a soldier in the British Army in the Second World War. He fought in North Africa and took part in the 1944 invasion of Normandy, during which he was wounded. Time and time again in his poetry he returns to the war and his memories of it and how they have altered his life.

nettle bed – an area of neglected land on which lots of nettles grow.

hook – scythe, for chopping down tall plants.

Who? Scannell, his son and the mother (*us* in line eight)

When? When Scannell's son was three.

Where? In the back garden, behind the shed where the nettles grow.

What? The poet's son has fallen in the nettle bed and runs to his parents for comfort. His parents soothe him and then Scannell takes his scythe and cuts the nettles down, before burning them. In two weeks they have grown again.

Commentary

In this poem Scannell explores his feelings of care, gentleness and compassion for his son, taking an incident from his son's childhood as a starting point, it reflects on the relationship between father and son. It is tightly structured in rhyming quatrains, but Scannell uses enjambment extensively to make the poem sound almost like real speech and to draw attention away from the rhyme scheme – except at the very start and end of the poem where he uses end-stopped lines.

The blunt opening line, expressed in very simple language, tells us all we need to know about the situation:

My son aged three fell in the nettle bed.

This simple statement of fact is then followed by a detailed description of the incident. Scannell then reflects on how inappropriate that word *bed* is for something which causes so much pain. Bed is a place where we rest, but his son is clearly very distressed – he rushes to his parents in sobs and tears and Scannell sees *blisters beaded* on his son's skin. His pain is raw and after a while he has *a watery grin* – he is grinning through the tears. Scannell's reaction then is one of rage and protective anger. He hacks the nettles down – *slashed in fury* – and then burns the nettles in order that his son will not be hurt again. Scannell makes extensive use of alliteration, especially sibilance, to emphasise the strong feelings which this incident provoked as well as strong and vivid verbs like *slashed* and words like *fury* and *fierce*.

Scannell uses an extended metaphor to describe the nettles in military terms, suggesting he has had first-hand experience of warfare and that the nettles are violent and aggressive and opposed to human life: *spears, regiment, parade, the fallen dead, recruits*. This metaphor also personifies the nettles (even the word *pyre* is normally associated with humans), but Scannell also personifies *the busy sun and rain* who in two weeks had *called up tall recruits behind the shed* – more nettles which may hurt his son. The final line is full of foreboding and, like the opening line, makes complete sense on its own:

My son would often feel sharp wounds again.

It is tempting, isn't it, to see in this line not just a warning about the nettles behind the shed which have grown back so quickly, but a warning about the future in general. Then the poem becomes something else: it is grounded in a clearly remembered event from his son's childhood, but it is a lament for the human condition – just by being alive, Scannell's son will feel sharp wounds again. You might be tempted to go even further and see the military imagery used about the nettles as a warning of what happens to young men in wars – they die – and Scannell knew this from his own experience in the Second World War. Nature too is very hostile in this poem (it isn't in all the poems in the Anthology): the nettles are obviously dangerous and cause pain, but they are helped to grow by the sun and the rain. And what about the bed? Bed is a place of rest, but it can also be the place where you die.

Why?

This poem, based on an everyday incident:

- is a moving poem about a father's love for his son.

- is a warning about his son's future suffering and regrets that the father will not be able to protect his son forever.

- nature is seen as hostile and threatening to human welfare.

- suffering is an inevitable part of being human.

- future wars will also cause pain and suffering.

'The Manhunt' (Laura's Poem) – Simon Armitage

Context

Simon Armitage was born in 1963 in the village of Marsden in West Yorkshire and has spent most of his life in that area. He is a very successful and highly-regarded poet, celebrated for his down-to-earth language and subject matter. Several of his poems are in the Anthology. His poetry often (but not always) deals with the ordinary incidents and events of modern life and appear to be based on personal experience. '

This poem was originally written for a television documentary (Channel 4 – *Forgotten Heroes: The Not Dead*) about soldiers who live with the long-term effects of being involved in warfare and suffering from post-traumatic stress syndrome. In the documentary the poem is read by Laura Beddoes, whose husband Eddie had served as a peace-keeper with the British Army in Bosnia. For this reason, the poem is sometimes called 'Manhunt: Laura's Story'. Eddie was discharged because of injury and depression and the poem explores the impact this had on his marriage. Armitage listened to many accounts by soldiers of their experiences in order to get the inspiration for this poem. He has said:

Never having been to the front line, turning the words, phrases and experiences of these soldiers into verse has been the closest I've ever come to writing 'real' war poetry, and as close as I ever want to get.

Bosnia was once part of Yugoslavia. When the Communist system all over Eastern Europe fell, in Yugoslavia ethnic and religious tensions which had been controlled and suppressed under communism came to the surface. By the mid-1990s the different ethnic groups began fighting each other and committing acts of genocide. The United Kingdom and other NATO countries responded by sending troops to the region to act as peace-keepers and to keep the warring factions apart. In particular, they were attempting to protect Bosnia from attacks by its more powerful neighbour – Serbia.

Who? Armitage adopts the voice of Laura who narrates the poem in the past tense.

When? After Eddie has returned injured, physically and mentally, from war.

Where? No specific location.

What? Laura explains how she very slowly re-discovered the man that Eddie had become.

Commentary

This poem is written in free verse with frequent use of rhyme and half-rhyme. On the page it is divided into separate two line couplets but the lines are of unequal length. This immediately suggests that it looks like a normal poem but it isn't. In the poem we will find that Eddie's mental wounds are much worse than his physical ones – so he may look normal but underneath the surface he is suffering a terrible trauma because of what he has seen in war. Note the deliberate ambiguity of the title: if you are looking for an escaped soldier or airman you 'launch a manhunt'. Laura is on a manhunt but for the man she used to know before he went to war.

The repetition of *then* and *and* is very important in the poem: it suggests that each step in renewing her love for Eddie, in trying to find him again, in trying to understand what he had suffered, is a step in a very slow process. They quickly re-establish a physical relationship with

... passionate nights and intimate days

And she then starts to explore his physical wounds by touching his wounds and scars. In these lines the human body's fragility is emphasized in the metaphors – *porcelain collar-bone, parachute silk* – and his body is seen in terms of machines which do not quite work - *broken hinge, fractured rudder*. In some ways these images are re-assuring because broken hinges can be fixed.

But line 16 mentions Eddie's *grazed heart* and the rest of the poem becomes more difficult in the sense that his mental wounds are invisible and more permanent. Does his *grazed heart* suggest he has lost the ability to love? The fragments left by the bullet are a *metal foetus* – a metaphor that suggests something is growing inside him. Laura then widened the search (remember she is still on a manhunt for the man she used to know) – and finds

... a sweating, unexploded mine

buried deep in his mind, around which

every nerve in his body had tightened and closed.

And this confirms that what really makes Eddie so distant is his mental trauma at the sights and sounds of war, the suffering he witnessed that he now cannot forget. And

Then, and only then, did I come close.

And so the poem ends with the manhunt unsuccessful: Laura does not find him – she only comes close. And comes close to what? The man that Eddie now is? An understanding of what he has been through? What he has seen and heard in Bosnia?

Armitage gives Laura a voice of incredible sensitivity and feeling in this poem. She remains loyal to her lover, despite the difficulty she has in renewing her relationship with him. Eddie remains throughout the poem passive, silent and unknown – which actually makes his mental torments more terrible because they remain hidden and unknown, perhaps unknowable.

This contemporary poem raises with powerful sensitivity

- the long-term effects of warfare on soldiers and their loved ones.
- how the human mind can cope with images and memories of suffering.

- the traumatizing mental scars that ex-soldiers carry with them and which affect their relationships.

'My Father Would Not Show Us' – Ingrid de Kok

Author & Context

Ingrid de Kok grew up in Stilfontein, a gold mining town in what was then the Western Transvaal. When she was 12 years old, her parents moved to Johannesburg. In 1977 she emigrated to Canada where she lived until returning to South Africa in 1984. She has one child, a son. Her partner is Tony Morphet. Ingrid is a Fellow of the University of Cape Town, an Associate Professor in Extra Mural Studies and part of a team of two that designs and administers the public non-formal educational curriculum that constitutes the Extra-Mural Programmes at the University of Cape Town. She has also designed and co-ordinated national colloquiums and cultural programmes, such as one on Technology and Reconstruction and on Equal Opportunity Policy and At the Fault Line: Cultural Inquiries into Truth and Reconciliation and runs various capacity building, civic and trade union programmes. She alternates in the role of Director.

She has acted as a consultant for various adult educational courses or events, (for example, for writers' seminars, cultural forums, and Northwestern University and the University of Chicago's Study Abroad programmes). She has also co-ordinated schools and public programmes devoted to the development of a reading culture. She is a member of PEN, South Africa and a Trustee of Buchu Publishing Project. She was a member of the committee of the National Arts Festival in Grahamstown, South Africa with responsibility for convening the Winter School from 2000 - 2005 and is currently on the National Arts Council Literary Advisory Committee. She is the Chair of the South African Association of Canadian Studies.

Between 1977 and 2006 Ingrid's poems have been published in numerous South African literary journals, including *Upstream*, *Sesame*, *Staffrider*, *Contrast*, *New* Contrast, *New Coin*, Carapace. Occasionally poems have also appeared, translated into Afrikaans, in various South African Afrikaans newspapers.

counterpane – a bed cover.

Who? The poet speaks for herself about her father's death. She has siblings.

When? After her father's death.

Where? At the undertakers and at the family house.

What? De Kok laments her father's death and reflects on what he was like when he was alive.

Commentary

The poem begins with an epigraph by the German poet Rilke: *Which way do we face to talk to the dead?* suggesting perhaps that De Kok wants to talk to her dead father, but now she cannot – except in this poem. The poem is organised into seven stanzas and is written in free verse, although De Kok uses some rhyme towards the end of the poem which suggests a resolution of her feelings.

In the first stanza she visits the undertaker's to see her father's corpse. He has been dead for five days. His face *is organised for me to see* – which suggests a certain artificiality. The second stanza continues with this sense of artificiality: the room is cold (to stop the body decaying) and the *borrowed coffin* he is lying in *gleams unnaturally*. He will be buried in a cheaper pine coffin.

The poet is clearly at the head of the coffin looking down its length which is why her father's face is inverted. She had not expected to see him wearing

…the soft, for some

reason unfrozen collar of his striped pyjamas.

The sight of his pyjamas leads to a stanza of reflection on her childhood. The fourth stanza begins:

This is the last time I am allowed

To remember my childhood as it might have been.

The key words here are *as it might have been*: what follows is not a description of her childhood as it actually was, but as it might have been had her father been a different man. De Kok imagines her home as

a louder, braver place,

crowded, a house with a tin roof

being hailed upon, and voices rising,

my father's wry smile, his half-turned face.

But this is not what her childhood was like. Far from being loud and brave, her father was taciturn and distant as the opening to the next stanza suggests: *My father would not show us how to die* – just as he has not shown them many things. Faced with the fact of dying her father *hid, he hid away / behind the curtains where his life had been... he lay inside he lay.* De Kok's father's reticence extends to the fact of his dying: perhaps he wants to protect his family; perhaps he wants to show courage and stoicism in the face of death.

The next stanza deals with things he remembers on his death bed. His memory of his childhood is very clear:

He could recall the rag-and-bone man

passing his mother's gate in the morning light.

now the tunnelling sounds of the dogs next door....

Towards the end of life, we begin to lose our faculties and her father can no longer hear properly: *everything he hears is white* – a complete blank.

The final stanza begins with a subtle change of word: *My father **could** not show us how to die* [My emboldening]. Perhaps he could not show them how to die, because he does not know himself. We face death alone – even if we are surrounded by family and friends, we have to face the final days knowing the inevitable will come. De Kok's father retreats from his family as if to protect them from his death:

He turned, he turned away.

Under the counterpane, without one call

or word or name,

face to the wall he lay.

He dies alone which is tribute to his courage and stoicism, but also to protect his family from the fact of death. He is isolated in death and we get a sense of De Kok's sorrow in the repeated *turned away* in the final stanza.

Why?

In this poem Ingrid De Kok

- presents a lament for the death of her father.

- the epigraph suggests there are still things she would like to talk to him about.

- the poem presents her father as a reticent and taciturn man, not used to expressing emotions.

- her father also shows great courage and selflessness in facing death alone.

CONFLICT

Introduction

Before we look at any of the poems from the anthology, I want to briefly examine some poems which deal with conflict to give you a taste of the approach that will be followed throughout the rest of the book. So we will start by looking at two completely different poems. I am not going to subject either to a full analysis, but I will demonstrate with both poems some crucial ways of reading poetry and give you some general guidance which will stand you in good stead when we deal with the poems in the anthology itself. This is not meant to confuse you, but to help. I cannot stress enough that these two poems are not ones that you will be assessed on. They are my choice – and I would use the same method in the classroom – introducing a class very slowly to poetry and 'warming up' for the anthology by practising the sorts of reading skills which will help with any poem. Besides, you may find the method valuable in your preparation for answering on the unseen poem in the exam.

Here is the first poem we will consider. It is called 'Futility' and was written during the First World War by Wilfred Owen about life in the trenches. It links well with his poem 'Exposure' which is in the Anthology.

Move him into the sun—
Gently its touch awoke him once,
At home, whispering of fields half-sown.
Always it woke him, even in France,
Until this morning and this snow.
If anything might rouse him now
The kind old sun will know.

Think how it wakes the seeds,—
Woke, once, the clays of a cold star.
Are limbs, so dear-achieved, are sides,
Full-nerved—still warm—too hard to stir?
Was it for this the clay grew tall?

—O what made fatuous sunbeams toil
To break earth's sleep at all?

Context

Wilfred Owen (1893 – 1918) is widely regarded as the leading British poet of the First World War. He died in action on November 4th 1918 – just seven days before the war finally came to an end. Owen was an officer and was awarded the Military Cross for leadership and bravery in October 1918. The shock of what he saw in the front-line moved him to produce a great many poems in a very short time – most of which were not published until after his death. He seems to have been particularly keen to ensure that the British public was told the horrific truth about the war. He developed his own use of half-rhyme which was to influence other poets for the whole of the 20th century.

It is over a hundred years since the First World War began, and, because of the many commemorations, many readers will have a visual sense of what that war was like. In fact, it was a world war with fighting taking place on almost every continent, but the abiding memory of the war – a memory based on photos, documentaries and even poems like this one, is of the trench warfare on the Western Front in Belgium and France. There are clear reasons for this. The war waged in the trenches resulted in battles with enormous loss of life with very little ground gained: on the first day of the Battle of the Somme the British army suffered 70,000 casualties, 20,000 of whom were killed. I think the other reason the Western Front holds such an important place in our image of the First World War is the trenches themselves and trench life: hundreds of thousands of soldiers living very close to each other in holes in the ground and suffering terrible, barbaric conditions, plagued by rats, lice and the cold. So the futility and loss of life in the battles, as well as the appalling conditions make the war in the trenches especially memorable.

'Futility' is one of only five poems that were published when Owen was alive. It was published in a magazine called *The Nation* in June 1918. The compassion that Owen reveals in this poem for the suffering of the ordinary soldier is typical of his work; some of his other poems though, are more brutal and horrific in their realism.

Owen was one of many British writers who felt moved to describe what they saw of the war in the trenches of France and Belgium – and it is a subject to which British writers have returned again and again. Why? Most people would agree that all wars are horrific and cause death and terrible injuries, so what was it about the First World War that so captures the imagination of writers generation after generation? It seems that the First World War was unique because it caused huge numbers of deaths on all sides without any obvious effect on the course of the war; infantry troops were sent from their trenches to almost certain death and battles lasted for months with only a tiny movement of the front-line – so there was huge loss of life with no clear objective: it began to seem pointless to those involved in it and that pointlessness is echoed by this poem's title. Added to that, the conditions in the trenches – where the men lived and fought and often died – were appalling.

Futility – uselessness.

the clay – humanity. In the Bible God creates man from a lump of clay.

fatuous – foolish.

Who? Owen speaks as himself.

When? In the present – *this morning, this snow*. But we know from the biographical context that this poem is set during the First World War – the poem itself contains no military detail at all.

Where? From the poem, we know it is set in France; from our knowledge of Owen, we know that this is set in the trenches of the front-line.

What? A soldier has died. The speaker wants to move him into the sun, since that surely will bring him back to life. It doesn't, and the speaker reflects on the sadness and pity of the death as well as thinking about the bigger questions of human existence.

Commentary

The poem begins with an order - *Move him into the sun* - perhaps given by an officer. A soldier has died in the night – frozen to death in the snow it seems. In a sense, *how* he has died is irrelevant – it is the fact that he has died that Owen finds so shocking. He comes from the countryside and has always woken at dawn. Furthermore, *whispering of fields unsown* suggests that in Britain he worked on the land and had to sow seeds in fields, but this might also suggest the promise for the future growth that seeds contain. Because the sun had always woken him and had woken him *gently*, the speaker articulates an innocent trust that the *kind old sun* will wake him now. But, of course, it won't. The tone of this opening stanza is gentle with soft sounds, even the personified sun used to whisper to the young man.

The second stanza begins by pointing out that our solar system and our planet only exists because of the sun. Owen ends the stanza with three questions that simply cannot be answered without calling into doubt any religious faith and our very existence. Human beings are seen as the summit of evolution – *so dear achieved* – but the poet wonders why Creation occurred at all, if it will end in tragic deaths like this one: the sunbeams that helped create life on earth are *fatuous* and powerless. And this makes Owen question the whole point of human existence. Here in the second stanza the rhythm is broken up by the dashes and question marks which give a faltering, uncertain mood to the poem. Is Owen bitter or simply puzzled and confused about why we are here on this planet?

This is a very memorable poem in all sorts of ways. It uses half-rhyme to suggest that something very profound is wrong with what Owen describes, but it has no specific references to the First World War – apart from the word *France*. This perhaps gives the poem a timeless quality – it could apply to all deaths in all wars and the sense of futility that Owen feels could be applied to every death of a young person. It fits the definition of freshness of ideas because Owen uses one individual death to question the very nature of our existence on earth, the point of human existence and the nature of God – and he does so in only 12 lines – a remarkable feat of compression. This is a poem that is not just anti-war – it is also, one might say, anti-God because it questions why we are on earth if all that is going to happen is that we will die. It is a tender, poignant and gentle poem, full of a profound sadness at the thought of anyone dying before their time. Nature is important in the poem too: the dead soldier is at home in nature and at ease with the rhythms of nature but that does not help him escape death.

Why?

This short gentle poem raises important issues:

- Life on earth seems pointless when we are faced with the death, especially of young people.

- The sun (which might be symbolic of God as the creator of the planet) can create a whole world but cannot bring one young man back to life.

- What is the purpose of human life on earth? The poet cannot accept that it is to kill each other in war.

- God – given the questions in the second stanza – seems not to exist or at least not to care about individual human deaths.

Here is the second poem that we will look at as an unseen:

The Falling Leaves

BY MARGARET POSTGATE COLE

November 1915
Today, as I rode by,

I saw the brown leaves dropping from their tree

In a still afternoon,

When no wind whirled them whistling to the sky,

But thickly, silently,

They fell, like snowflakes wiping out the noon;

And wandered slowly thence

For thinking of a gallant multitude

Which now all withering lay,

Slain by no wind of age or pestilence,

But in their beauty strewed

Like snowflakes falling on the Flemish clay.

Context

Born in 1893 into a firmly Anglican family, Margaret Postgate began to question her religious beliefs as a student at Cambridge. She became a socialist, a feminist and an atheist. Her brother, Raymond, was put in prison during the First World War because he was a conscientious objector – someone who refused to fight because it is against their principles of pacifism. He was eventually forced to sign up, but was declared medically unfit to be a soldier. Nonetheless, her brother's stand influenced Margaret and she became a pacifist and began to campaign against conscription or forced enlistment. It was through this work that she met her husband, G D H Cole.

The date of the poem is important. The early summer of 1915 saw the Second Battle of Ypres in Flanders, a region of Belgium. In the battle it became clear that the First World War battles would produce many casualties as men armed with rifles and bayonets were sent to take enemy positions guarded by rapid-fire machine guns and artillery. It was also during the Second Battle of Ypres where the German Army used poison gas in battle against British, Canadian and French soldiers for the very first time (the Germans had already used it against the Russian army in the east). The battle lasted a month, but resulted in over 105,000 men from both armies being killed or wounded.

It was not only the men who suffered during the First World War. The women at home were the mothers, wives, sweethearts and sisters of the men dying in such huge numbers in France and Belgium, and many women poets responded to the war by writing poems.

thence – from that place

gallant – brave, courageous

multitude – a great many

pestilence – a plague

strewed – scattered loosely

Flemish – of or belonging to Flanders

Who? The poet writes in the first person and the present tense.

When? November 1915.

Where? The poet is riding on a horse in the English countryside.

What? She sees the leaves falling from the trees and this makes her think about the dead soldiers in Belgium.

Commentary

This is a peaceful and gentle poem, full of a tender sadness at the sheer number of deaths occurring in the First World War. The scene of the

English countryside on a still afternoon is in contrast to what must be happening in Europe on the battlefields. The falling leaves are symbolic of all the young men dying in France and Belgium. It is written as one long verse paragraph which is one long sentence, but with lines of unequal length, suggesting that the thoughts of the poet are uneven or with the short lines suggesting the short lives of the soldiers which have literally been cut short. There is a rhyme scheme too, but it is unobtrusive because of the irregular line length and enjambment.

Autumn is often used as a time of reflection by poets on the inevitability of death and decay – the season shows that the year is dying and the use of snowflakes twice as a simile re-enforces the sense that winter is coming and perhaps that there will be more deaths as the war continues. But the poem is gentle in tone because of the frequent use of words beginning with *w* and *l* and *f* – all very soft consonants. These mean that the combined effect of the alliteration is to create euphony and a mood that is wistful and elegiac. The poet has no experience of warfare and there is no first-hand detail of warfare in the poem. The dead are praised – they are *gallant* and have *beauty* - and there is no distinction between British and German soldiers. The leaves are so numerous that they are like snowflakes *wiping out the noon* – that phrase *wiping out* being especially appropriate to the deaths in the war, but it also emphasizes through hyperbole the staggering number of deaths that can wipe out the sun; this seems to be connected with the autumnal mood and the sense of everything ending as the year draws to its close and is an example of pathetic fallacy. The leaves, like the soldiers, are *withering* – but the poet makes clear they have not been killed by something natural like *age* or *pestilence* – this slaughter is man-made. The final line

Like snowflakes falling on the Flemish clay

is astonishingly beautiful and poignant. The alliteration on *f*, the fragility of the leaves and the snowflakes and the reference to *clay* (remember God created man out of clay according to Christian myth) all give a sense of sadness and pointless loss which ends the poem on a note of gentle compassion and pity.

Why?

This poem is a lament for the many deaths caused in the First World War.

- It expresses great compassion and pity for the *gallant multitude*.

- Its tone is sad and elegiac.

- It uses pathetic fallacy.

- It reminds us of the inevitability of death through its use of natural imagery.

- Its imagery is soft and gentle which suggests the sympathy and compassion the poet feels for the dead soldiers.

Here is the final poem we will consider on the theme of conflict.

Anthem for Doomed Youth

BY WILFRED OWEN

What passing-bells for these who die as cattle?
    — Only the monstrous anger of the guns.
    Only the stuttering rifles' rapid rattle
Can patter out their hasty orisons.
No mockeries now for them; no prayers nor bells;
    Nor any voice of mourning save the choirs,—
The shrill, demented choirs of wailing shells;
    And bugles calling for them from sad shires.

What candles may be held to speed them all?

Not in the hands of boys, but in their eyes
Shall shine the holy glimmers of goodbyes.
    The pallor of girls' brows shall be their pall;
Their flowers the tenderness of patient minds,
And each slow dusk a drawing-down of blinds.

Author & Context

Wilfred Owen (1893 – 1918) is widely regarded as the leading British poet of the First World War. He died in action on November 4th 1918 – just seven days before the war finally came to an end. Owen was an officer and was awarded the Military Cross for leadership and bravery in October 1918. The shock of what he saw in the front-line moved him to produce a great many poems in a very short time – most of which were not published until after his death. He seems to have been particularly keen to ensure that the British public was told the horrific truth about the war. He developed his own use of half-rhyme which was to influence other poets for the whole of the 20th century. Owen famously wrote that his subject was not war, but the pity of war – a feeling that is especially apparent in this poem. "Above all I am not concerned with Poetry. My subject is War, and the pity of War. The Poetry is in the pity."

It is over a hundred years since the First World War began, and, because of the many commemorations, many readers will have a visual sense of what that war was like. In fact, it was a world war with fighting taking place on almost every continent, but the abiding memory of the war – a memory based on photos, documentaries and even poems like this one, is of the trench warfare on the Western Front in Belgium and France. There are clear reasons for this. The war waged in the trenches resulted in battles with enormous loss of life with very little ground gained: on the first day of the Battle of the Somme the British army suffered 70,000 casualties, 20,000 of whom were killed. I think the other reason the Western Front holds such an important place in our image of the First World War is the trenches themselves and trench life: hundreds of thousands of soldiers living very close to each other in holes in the ground and suffering terrible, barbaric conditions, plagued by rats, lice and the cold. So the futility and loss of life in the battles, as well as the appalling conditions make the war in the trenches especially memorable.

passing-bells – the single tolling bell rung at funerals.

orisons – an archaic word for prayers.

shires – British Army infantry regiments were based on the counties and shires, so if you came from Lincolnshire you fought in the Lincolnshire regiment.

pallor – extreme paleness, here out of grief.

pall – the cloth used to cover the coffin; in a formal military ceremony this would be the Union Jack.

a drawing down of blinds – it was tradition, when there was a death in the family to draw all the curtains.

Who? Owen writes as himself to a general audience.

When? The First World War, probably 1917.

Where? On the Western Front.

What? Owen compares and contrasts the funerals the dead soldiers would receive if they were buried at home in England with the hasty, makeshift funerals they receive on the battlefields in France.

Commentary

'Anthem for Doomed Youth' is probably the best poem wrote about the war, and it is possibly the best poem to be written about the war. It is a Petrarchan sonnet – which for me adds to its emotional impact. The sonnet is considered by many to be the highest form of poetry (because of the difficulty of composing one): that such a beautiful form should be used to write about the tragedy of the war increases its impact.

The poem is based on an extended contrast with a conventional funeral, so Owen gives aspects of a funeral their sad, heart-rending parallel in the terrible conditions of the battlefield. Because of the war, there was not time to bury bodies properly – indeed, many were buried in mass graves and some bodies were simply never found, leading the soldier to have no known grave. The Thiepval Monument lists the 72,000 British soldiers who died on the Somme but who have no known grave.

The doomed soldiers have no passing bells, only the *monstrous anger of the guns*: the guns are transformed into monsters and there is a hint of onomatopoeia in *monstrous anger*. The third line uses alliteration and onomatopoeia to give a sense of the sounds of battle – and asserts that this is what the soldiers will have instead of their final prayers to God. The *stuttering rifles' rapid rattle* imitates the sound of gunfire in battle.

Line 5 insists there be *No mockeries for them; no prayers or bells*. Owen seems to be implying that to have a proper, funeral service would be a mockery, given the way these men have fought and died, in huge numbers and horrific conditions. They will have no choirs to sing at their funerals only the

The shrill, demented choirs of wailing shells;

And bugles calling from them from sad shires.

Note the onomatopoeia in *shrill* and *wailing* – this poem is rich in literary techniques. They will be missed in their native counties where bugles will call - in vain - for them.

There is a turn or volta in line 9 at the start of the third quatrain as Owen turns his attention to the friends and loved ones the soldiers will leave behind. There will be no candles held in the hands of boys for these dead soldiers

...but in their eyes

Shall shine the holy glimmers of goodbyes.

Their comrades' eyes will be filled with tears which will shine. Their coffins will have no pall which will be replaced by *The pallor of girls' brows* – pale from the shock and sadness at the news of their husbands' or boyfriends' deaths.

The final couplet is especially moving:

Their flowers the tenderness of patient minds,

And each slow dusk a drawing down of blinds.

They will have no flowers at their funerals. They will be replaced by *tenderness* – the emotion which is the exact opposite of their experiences as soldiers and as corpses; it is unclear who the *patient minds* belong to – perhaps their surviving companions, perhaps their loved ones at home. In the final line the slowness created by *each slow dusk* emphasizes the action it describes, while in the final phrase the repeated 'd' sounds give an aural harmony to the end of the poem.

Conflict

The conflict that was the First World War forms the background to the poem and Owen conveys superbly the sounds and horrors of that war. However, the main conflict in the poem is the disparity between the funerals the dead soldiers would expect to get at home in normal circumstances and the rushed, undignified funerals they receive on the battlefield. That is where the pity of the poem lies.

Why?

In 'Anthem for Doomed Youth' Owen has

- written an elegy for a generation and evoked pity for them all.

- written a perfect Petrarchan sonnet.

- written a poem rich is assonance, alliteration and onomatopoeia which adds greatly to its emotional impact.

- used a comparison throughout the poem – the burial the soldiers do get on the battlefield compared with the funerals they would expect at home.

- ended the poem on a note of tenderness, pity and compassion.

'A Poison Tree' – William Blake

Author and Context

William Blake (1757 – 1827) is now seen as the foremost artist and poet of his time, but his work was largely unknown during his lifetime. He was a painter as well as a poet and you can see some of his paintings in art galleries like Tate Britain in London or the Fitzwilliam Museum in Cambridge. 'London' comes from a collection called *Songs of Innocence and of Experience*, which appeared together for the first time in 1794. *The Songs of Innocence* (which originally appeared on their own in 1789) are positive in tone and celebrate unspoilt nature, childhood and love. *The Songs of Experience* (from which 'A Poison Tree' comes) depict a corrupt society in which the prevailing mood is one of despair, children are exploited and love is corrupted.

Blake was writing at a time when Britain was the wealthiest country in the world because of its global empire and because of the Industrial Revolution which produced goods which were exported all over the world. But not everyone shared in this enormous wealth; the gap between rich and poor was huge, with the poor suffering really terrible living and working conditions. *The Songs of Innocence and of Experience* first 'appeared' (this term will be explained below) in 1794. The date of publication is crucial: Blake is partly seeing London in this way because of events in France. In 1789 the French Revolution began, changing French society forever and ushering in a new age of freedom, equality and brotherhood. Many English people saw what was happening in France and thought it was good to have a society based on greater equality; they looked critically at British society and saw appalling inequalities and injustices. For example, you may be aware that this was the period in British history that some people campaigned against slavery in the British Empire: what is less well-known is that forms of slavery existed in London. There are recorded cases of parents selling their sons to master chimneysweeps in London. The life of a chimney sweep was likely to be short: they were sent up the chimneys of large houses to clean them. Some suffocated; others were trapped in the confined space and died; sometimes their masters would light fires below them to encourage them to work faster – they sometimes were burnt alive. For those who survived, their health was affected: they suffered from terrible lung complaints as a result of breathing in coal dust and, because of poor hygiene, might also succumb to testicular cancer brought on by the accumulated layers of biting coal dust. Apart from being in favour of the slogans of the French Revolution, evidence from his other writings would suggest that Blake was in favour of openness and honesty. Think back to 'The Sick Rose' discussed in the introduction: the rose harbours a *dark, secret love* and is annihilated by *the invisible worm*.

Blake had produced *Songs of Innocence* on its own in 1789, although we can tell from his surviving notebooks that he always intended to write *Songs of Experience*. I have used the term 'appeared' because they were not published in a conventional sense. Blake produced each copy of *Songs of Innocence and of Experience* at home by hand and copies were then given to friends and acquaintances. Part of this was Blake's own choice, but we can easily see that his views about Britain and its government would have been highly controversial, so open publication of them may have led to charges of sedition or treason. The British government at the time was terrified of a revolution here, like the one in France, and was doing everything it could to silence people like Blake who were critical of the society in which they lived.

Blake earned his living as an engraver. Before photographs and modern ways of reproducing images, engravings were the cheapest and easiest way of illustrating a book. Blake produced illustrations for other people's books throughout his life – that was how he earned a living. To create an engraving, the engraver has to carve, with a specialist knife, lines on a metal plate; when the plate is then covered in ink and pressed on paper the lines appear on the paper.

On page 31, you can see (in black and white) Blake's illustration for 'a Poison Tree'. Many of the illustrations to Songs of Experience are quite dark in tone and atmosphere, but the overall impression of 'A Poison Tree' is one of light, which, as we will see below, may be connected with the poem's themes and message

Blake used the same technique for reproducing his own poems. After coating the metal plate with ink and producing the outline, Blake coloured each page of each copy of *Songs of Innocence and of Experience* by hand with water colour paint. It is estimated that only 25 copies were produced in his lifetime. If you go to the British Museum you can see one copy: it is tiny and exquisitely detailed and, of course, very personal, because Blake coloured it by hand himself. In addition, to produce his poems in this way was time-consuming and arduous, since in order for the words to appear the right way round when the page was printed, they had to be written in mirror hand-writing on the plate – a painstaking process that must have taken hours and shows not only Blake's artistry but also his devotion to hard work.

wrath – anger

foe – enemy

wiles – tricks and deceit

stole – crept

When the night had veiled the pole – when clouds had darkened the night sky so that even the Pole Star could not be seen.

Who? The speaker tells a simple story about how his untold anger for an enemy grew and grew until it killed the enemy.

When? No specific time: the poem appeared first in 1794.

Where? No specific location but the metaphor of the tree symbolizing his anger suggests a garden setting.

What? Blake is angry with a friend but tells him so and the anger passes away. He is also angry with an enemy but says nothing. His anger for his enemy grows and grows; Blake uses the metaphor of a plant to describe his growing anger – an anger which he feeds with his hypocritical reactions to his enemy. The tree becomes an apple tree and one night his enemy steals into his garden and plucks the apple. This action ends in his death.

When you first read Blake's 'A Poison Tree' you may be astonished at its simplicity, but, as we will see, Blake uses a simple form and simple language to make a complex statement about how we deal with anger and its effects.

In the first stanza, the situation is clear: the speaker was angry with a friend with whom he was open about his anger and their disagreement and his anger subsided. He was also angry with his foe, but said nothing, kept his anger hidden and, once it is hidden, it grows. The two couplets are perfectly balanced in terms of rhyme, the number of syllables, the repetition of words and even the exact placing of the caesura in lines 2 and 4.

In the next two stanzas, Blake uses anaphora: seven of the eight lines begin with 'and', as he excitedly describes what happens to his wrath. In the second stanza he introduces a metaphor: his wrath is a plant and he *water'd it in fears* and *sunned it with smiles/ And soft deceitful wiles*. The speaker's disagreement with his friend makes him fearful, makes him cry with rage and frustration, but he still appears outwardly friendly, showering his enemy with *smiles*, showing him to be hypocritical and deceitful.

The third stanza fleshes out the metaphor of the plant which now *grew day and night*. The anaphora of *and* does create a sense of excited enjoyment – this is a process which not only involves hypocrisy but the enjoyment of that hypocrisy. The tree grows an apple and Blake tells us:

And my foe beheld it shine,

And he knew that it was mine.

In the final stanza, the foe creeps into the garden, steals the apple and dies – a sacrifice to secrecy, hypocrisy and deceit. What is most disturbing is that the speaker is glad. To be glad at someone's misfortune – let alone death – shows an evil and unhealthy attitude.

The poem consists of four quatrains with each quatrain made up of two rhyming couplets. Basically the poem is written in trochaic tetrameters. 'Tetrameter' simply means there are four stressed syllables in each line; trochaic means that the pattern of stresses is a stressed syllable followed by an unstressed syllable; however, Blake uses variations on this basic pattern to reflect what is happening in the poem. Normally we would expect a tetrameter line to have eight syllables – four stressed and four unstressed – but Blake only writes three lines with eight syllables: lines two, four and the last line of the poem. So what? I hear you say. Well, it means that each line, which is short, seems a little incomplete and it is masterful of Blake to utilise these short lines in most of the poem – he is describing an incomplete process (the slow and steady growth of his anger (the tree) so he is describing an ongoing, incomplete process – just as the lines themselves are incomplete by being one syllable too short. To further vary the metrical pattern lines two, four and the last line are perfect iambic tetrameters. Why? Because they describe a situation or action which is complete or has been resolved.

The original draft of 'A Poison Tree' in Blake's Notebooks had the title

'Christian Forbearance' suggesting that tolerance for something or someone you disagree with is a good thing, but might also be covering up anger or disapproval. Blake felt that traditional Christians who were taught to be pious could easily be hypocritical, masking their true feelings beneath superficial friendliness. In the poem, the speaker's hypocrisy leads to the death of his enemy.

The main theme of 'A Poison Tree' is not anger in itself (we are given no reason for the speaker's anger) but how the suppression of anger is harmful and dangerous. Repressing anger rather than being honest and open about it transforms anger into a seed, which will grow into a tree. The growth of the seed is made possible by the energetic anger of the speaker into a destructive force. Blake pursues the metaphor of a growing plant when he writes *and I water'd it in fears/Night and morning with my tears* his foe makes him fearful and cry tears of rage. The speaker also says *I sunned it with smiles*: on the surface he is polite to his foe and smiles at him. The metaphor works because plants need water and sunlight to thrive. But this deceit and hypocrisy must take its toll on the speaker.

The tree in 'A Poison Tree' is meant to remind the reader of the Tree of the Knowledge of Good and Evil in the Biblical story of the Fall of Man. God forbids Adam or Eve to eat the fruit of that tree, but Eve disobeys and Adam and Eve are expelled from the Garden of Eden. This event is known as the Fall of Man and is responsible (in Christian belief) for bringing death and sin into the world. As far as the poem is concerned, the speaker takes the wrathful, vengeful attitude to his enemy – acting in a way that is reminiscent of the God of the Old Testament. [Blake was a devout Christian but his views were rather unorthodox: basically, he thought the God of the Old Testament was evil, but the God of the New Testament – Jesus – was the true God.] In this poem, we can say that Blake gives his speaker the attitudes and outlook of the wrathful God of the Old Testament. It may be significant here that the foe is lying on the floor with his arms outstretched – very like the crucified Christ.

If the poem has a message it is not only the importance of expressing your anger and not stifling it. It also demonstrates that the suppression of feelings of anger will lead to a corruption of those feelings, through secrecy and deceit, to a corruption of innocence.

Conflict

The obvious source of conflict in the poem is that between the speaker and his enemy, but there are other more subtle conflicts at work in the poem. Firstly, there is the speaker's own division of the people he knows into friends and foes – we have no knowledge about how he makes this distinction, but it is built into characterising the people we know as friend or foes. More egregiously there is conflict within the speaker himself, due to his lack of honesty and his superficial friendliness towards his foe – the 'smiles' that he gives the foe and which, in the poem, allow the tree to grow. The effort to be nice to someone he loathes causes the speaker to cry tears which also help the tree and the resentment grow. Therefore, the theft of the apple not only kills the foe, the process leading up to it – the strain and hypocrisy of pretending to be nice to your enemy – takes a psychological toll on the speaker, so that he has lost all human empathy and is glad to see his foe dead alongside the tree.

A Romantic Poem

Blake's work is very different from the poetry of the other Romantic poets. However, the simplicity of language marks this out as a Romantic poem: Wordsworth had experimented with simple language in *Lyrical Ballads*, first published in 1798, and in that collection Samuel Taylor Coleridge's famous poem 'The Rime of the Ancient Mariner' had made use of Christian symbolism as Blake does here. More generally, Blake's call for openness and his criticism of authoritarian power and hypocrisy places this poem firmly within the Romantic poetic spectrum.

Why?

In this short but complex poem, Blake:

- attacks hypocrisy.

- attacks secrecy.

- shows how the suppression of anger can have worse consequences than its expression.

- praises openness and honesty in personal relationships.

- by implication attacks the Old Testament God for his harsh, forbidding attitude to humanity.

'The Destruction of Sennacherib' – Lord Byron

Author and Context

Byron was the ideal of the Romantic poet, gaining notoriety for his scandalous private life and being described by one contemporary as 'mad, bad and dangerous to know'.

George Gordon Noel, sixth Baron Byron, was born on 22 January 1788 in London. His father died when he was three, with the result that he inherited his title from his great uncle in 1798.

Byron spent his early years in Aberdeen and was educated at Harrow School and Cambridge University. In 1809, he left for a two-year tour of a number of Mediterranean countries. He returned to England in 1811, and in 1812 the first two cantos of 'Childe Harold's Pilgrimage' were published. Byron became famous overnight and very wealthy from the high sales his poetry achieved. He achieved what we would now term 'celebrity status', but public opinion was soon to turn against him.

In 1814, Byron's half-sister Augusta gave birth to a daughter, almost certainly Byron's. The following year Byron married Annabella Milbanke, with whom he had a daughter, his only legitimate child. The couple separated in 1816.

Facing mounting pressure as a result of his failed marriage, scandalous affairs and huge debts, Byron left England in April 1816 and never returned. He spent the summer of 1816 at Lake Geneva with Percy Bysshe Shelley, his wife Mary and Mary's half-sister Claire Clairmont, with whom Byron had a daughter.

Byron travelled on to Italy, where he was to live for more than six years. In 1819, while staying in Venice, he began an affair with Teresa Guiccioli, the wife of an Italian nobleman. It was in this period that Byron wrote some of his most famous works, including 'Don Juan' (1819-1824).

In July 1823, Byron left Italy to join the Greek insurgents who were fighting a war of independence against the Ottoman Empire. On 19 April 1824, he died from fever at Missolonghi, in modern day Greece. His death was mourned throughout Britain. His body was brought back to England and buried at his ancestral home in Nottinghamshire.

Much of the Old Testament in the Christian Bible, from which Byron took the bare bones of this story, concerns the efforts of the Israelites or Jews to withstand enemies who wanted to conquer their land or take them into captivity as slaves. This story is no exception. In the Bible, the Second Book of Kings, Chapter 18, verse 13 the story begins:

Now in the fourteenth year of King Hezekiah did Sennacherib King of Assyria came up against the fenced cites of Judah and took them.

There then follows an extremely long account of negotiations and diplomacy – which Byron judiciously omits – and the story comes to an end in the Second Book of Kings, Chapter 19, verse 35:

And it came to pass that night that the angel of the Lord went out and smote in the camp of the Assyrians an hundred four score and five thousand: and when they arose early in the morning, behold, they were all dead.

It is this miraculous divine intervention that forms the inspiration for Byron's poem.

If you want to read this poem in context *Hebrew Melodies* is available in a cheap paperback version.

Sennacherib – the main god worshipped by the Assyrians and the name of one of their emperors whose reign was from 705 BCE to 681 BCE.

Assyrian - Assyria was a major Mesopotamian East Semitic kingdom, and empire, of the Ancient Near East, existing as an independent state for a period of approximately six centuries from c. 1250 BCE to 612 BCE, spanning the Early Bronze Age through to the late Iron Age. For a further thirteen centuries, from the end of the 7th century BC to the mid-7th century AD, it survived as a geo-political entity. It covered most of what is now Syria and Iraq.

fold – a fenced enclosure usually holding sheep.

cohorts – troops of soldiers.

host – army.

on the morrow – on the next day.

strown – disordered

waxed – became.

steed – horse.

mail – chain mail armour.

Ashur – another god worshipped by the Assyrians and also the name of one of their major cities and one-time capital.

Baal – another God worshipped by the Assyrians.

The Gentile – 'Gentile' is a Jewish term used to cover all those who are non-Jews, in this case the defeated Assyrian army.

unsmote – 'unhit' by human swords, arrows, lances and other weapons.

Who? Sennacherib besieged Jerusalem in 701 BCE. The speaker narrates a story which is well-documented in the Old Testament. He speaks directly to the modern reader and assumes an air of authority.

When? Byron published the poem in 1815, as part of a collection called *Hebrew Melodies*. The collection was published twice – as a book of poems and also as a book of songs with the music written by the Jewish composer Isaac Nathan.

Where? In Judea, the historic land of the Jews, now roughly covered by the state of Israel and Palestine.

What? The mighty Assyrian army attacks Jerusalem but is destroyed by divine intervention – the angel of the Lord.

Commentary

The Assyrian Empire was very militaristic and aggressive in expanding their empire. Byron's opening simile *like the wolf on the fold* – suggests an evil, animalistic aggressor quickly bearing down on an innocent and defenceless innocent. Their troops present an impressive sight: *gleaming in purple and gold*. Then, in the third line of the first stanza, Byron uses sibilance to give the line cohesion, but the fact that *their spears were like stars on the sea* suggests the sheer size of the army.

In the second stanza, it contains an abrupt contrast between the two couplets: in the first couplet the Assyrian army looks grand and magnificent: *Like the leaves of the forest is green*, but in the second couplet

and on the morning of the next day the army has been transformed –
Like the leaves of the forest when Autumn has blown.

In the third stanza, Byron reveals what has happened to the once-mighty
army. The Angel of Death has *breathed in the face of the foe as he passed* and
the Assyrians are all dead:

… the eyes of the sleepers waxed deadly and chill,

And the hearts but once heaved, and for ever grew still.

The next two stanzas emphasise the complete destruction of the
Assyrian army. In the fourth stanza, the horses that carried the Assyrians
into battle are foaming at the mouth and as *cold as the spray of the rock-
beating surf.* In the fifth stanza, the Assyrian soldiers lie dead with *the dew
on his brow, and the rust on his mail.* The mighty army is now all dead and
their encampment is destroyed and Byron emphasises this by describing
their camp:

… the tents were all silent, the banners alone,

The lances unlifted, the trumpet unblown.

Despite their military superiority and their wonderful appearance (as
suggested in the first stanza) the Assyrian army has been destroyed by
the Angel of Death sent by God.

The final stanza describes the reaction in Ashur, the Assyria capital is
shown: the widows of the dead soldiers are *loud in their wail* and the
statues of Baal are destroyed in their temples. The Assyrians worshipped
several Gods and worshipped idols of them – unlike the Jews who
worshipped a single God and who were banned from worshipping
statues or idols of him in the Ten Commandments. The materialistic
Assyrians have been defeated by the true God – they *Have melted like snow
in the glance of the Lord!*

'The Destruction of Sennacherib' is a very regular poem, consisting of
six stanzas each with four lines. Each line has twelve syllables and Byron

chooses to write in anapaestic tetrameters. Tetrameter means that there are four stressed syllables in each line. Anapaestic refers to the arrangement of stresses in each line of the poem. An anapaest consists of two unstressed syllables followed by a stressed syllable:

And his *co*horts were *gleam*ing in *pur*ple and *gold*

Here I have italicised the stressed syllables. But why? What is the effect of this metrical patterning? Firstly, when read aloud the poem generates a quick speed which is very appropriate for a narrative poem – the rhythm pushes us on to the next stage of the story. Secondly and more importantly, the speed mimics the speed of the Assyrian army as it approaches Jerusalem – it may even be said to mimic the speed and rhythm of the horses of its army approaching. Thirdly, and perhaps most important of all, the rhythm and its speed suggest the speed of the Assyrian defeat and devastation at the hands of the Angel of Death. In general, the rhythm helps give us an aural sense of the urgency of the situation facing Jerusalem and the speed at which the events unfold.

The rhyme scheme is AABB: the first two lines in each stanza rhyme with each other as do the third and fourth lines. This apposition of lines is powerful and suggests the opposition between the invading Assyrian army and Jerusalem and its defenders. Byron also uses anaphora at the start of many of his lines – *like*, *the* and *and* – *then* and *and* are especially appropriate in a narrative poem describing a quick series of events.

Conflict

The conflict in this poem is straightforward between Judea and Jerusalem and the powerful conquering army of the Assyrians. The tone of the poem is one of triumph and celebration at the deliverance from military conquest of Jerusalem and the Jewish people.

A Romantic Poem?

Before he published *Hebrew Melodies* Byron was best known for long narrative poems, so to publish a collection of short lyric poems was not typical of him. Byron was also known as a radical free thinker, so it is ironic that he should choose a story from the Old Testament. Indeed, this poem is the most famous poem on a Biblical subject to be produced by any English Romantic poet. Coleridge and Wordsworth were avowedly Christian but neither produced a poem like 'The Destruction of Sennacherib'. Blake, as we have seen, was a Christian but held esoteric and unconventional ideas about God, especially the God of the Old Testament.

And so the poem is not typical of Byron and is an oddity when judged against the work of the other English Romantic poets.

Some readers argue that the arrogance and might of the Assyrian army is analogous to the power and threat to peace posed by the French emperor Napoleon. However, Byron was a political radical and the government of Britain at the time was increasingly tyrannical and oppressive, so if the poem has any contemporary significance, it is probably a reminder to British conservative politicians that their days are numbered.

Why?

In this fast and dramatic narrative poem, Byron:

- makes brilliant use of metre and rhythm to capture both the quick approach of the Assyrian army and its quick and ruthless destruction by the Angel of Death.

- takes a fairly obscure story from the Bible and writes an exciting, thrilling poem whose speed gives the whole poem narrative verve and purpose.

- uses similes well to describe the invading army.

- at the end paints a vivid picture through words of the desolation of the Assyrian camp.

'The Prelude' (stealing the boat) – William Wordsworth

Author and Context

William Wordsworth was born in 1770 in Cockermouth on the edge of the English Lake District. He had a life-long fascination with nature and it is from the natural world that he took much of his inspiration. He died in 1850, having been made Poet Laureate in 1843. Wordsworth began to write *The Prelude* in 1798 and kept working on it and revising it until his death. It was not published until 1850, three months after his death. He published many poems during his own lifetime, but many readers feel that *The Prelude* is his finest work.

This extract is from *The Prelude*, a long autobiographical poem first finished in 1805. It is subtitled *The Growth of the Poet's Mind* – and Wordsworth tells the story of his life but with the intention of showing his psychological development and also how he came to be a poet. Central to his development, he claims, was the influence of nature: Wordsworth grew up in the English Lake District – a national park and an area of outstanding natural beauty even today. It is not just that Wordsworth liked the beauty of nature – we perhaps all do that because we associate it with peace, away from the hustle and bustle of urban or suburban life; he also believed that nature had a moral influence on him and had made him a better human being. He is at pains throughout *The Prelude* to try and prove this connection – that his experiences in the natural world made him a better person and a poet. You may elsewhere read references to Wordsworth's pantheism. Pantheists worship nature and feel that if there is a God then that God exists in every living thing, every part of the natural world: God is a spirit of the universe which exists in a rock or a daffodil as much as it does in a human being.

her – Nature.

elfin pinnace – a pinnace is a small boat; elfin means small and charming.

covert – secret.

bark – boat.

Who? The poet narrates in the past tense an incident from his childhood.

When? 1805. Wordsworth was a child in the late 18th century but is recollecting this experience as an adult.

Where? On a lake in the English Lake District, generally thought to be Ullswater.

What? Wordsworth steals a boat and goes for a row on the lake. He explores the ramifications of this incident on his conscience.

Commentary

This extract is written in blank verse. It narrates an incident. This extract comes from Book II of *The Prelude* which is entitled *Childhood and School-Time*.

One evening the poet find a shepherd's boat moored at the edge of the lake. The poet proceeds to unchain the boat and take it for an illicit row on the lake. In effect, Wordsworth is stealing the boat: he describes it as *an act of stealth* (he doesn't want to get caught) and uses an oxymoron – *troubled pleasure* – to show us that he has mixed feelings about what he is doing: he knows it is wrong. Lines 8–11 use a variety of sound effects and very positive vocabulary to present the initial experience of this escapade. He says the boat left behind her

still, on either side,

Small circles glittering idly in the moon,

Until they melted all into one track

Of sparkling light.

Listen to those lines: Wordsworth uses no figurative language, but there is a preponderance of *s*, *l* and *m* sounds which give a gentle, restful feeling which reinforces the meanings of the words. The lines are given more aural coherence by assonance: *side/idly/light* and by consonance - track/sparkling. Wordsworth has decided to row across the lake and has picked out a craggy ridge as his landmark towards which he is heading.

This positive tone and atmosphere continues up to line 20. The boat is an *elfin pinnace* – playful, mischievous (like an elf) – and the boat moves through the water *like a swan* – a beautiful, majestic bird.

And then the whole tone changes. By a trick of perspective, as Wordsworth rows across the lake, a huge peak comes into view. When you row, you face the direction you started from and the further Wordsworth rows from the shore of the lake, the mountains behind his starting point start to appear. Look at how the poet describes it and his response to it:

a huge peak, black and huge,

As if with voluntary power instinct,

Upreared its head. I struck and struck again,

And growing still in stature the grim shape

Towered up between me and the stars, and still,

For so it seemed, with purpose of its own

And measured motion like a living thing,

Strode after me.

Like nature, like the boat, the peak is personified and takes on a life of its own, but note also the way a sense of panic in the poet is created by simple repetition of *huge* and *struck*; these lines are full of sibilance too, which creates a sinister, hissing sound. Wordsworth's reaction is one of guilt and shame:

With trembling oars I turned,

And through the silent water stole my way.

He puts the boat back where he found it and then finds he is haunted by this experience for many days afterwards. He does not fully understand what has happened to him:

my brain

Worked with a dim and undetermined sense

Of unknown modes of being.

He is also depressed by the experience:

o'er my thoughts

There hung a darkness, call it solitude

Or blank desertion.

He cannot take his customary pleasure in nature – *No familiar shapes remained* – and his every waking thought and even his sleep is disturbed by:

huge and mighty forms that do not live

Like living men, moved slowly through the mind

By day, and were a trouble to my dreams.

How are we to interpret this poem? If some of the language towards the end of the extract seems a little vague, it is because Wordsworth himself – as a small boy – is struggling to make sense of what happened to him.

What is certain is that this experience is a formative one and leads to an epiphany: the poet is made to feel guilty for taking the boat and in that sense it is an important part of Wordsworth's intention – to show that we can learn morality from nature – not just from books or other people. And so nature is presented as beautiful and inspiring but also frightening if you do something wrong or immoral. The huge and mighty forms that haunt the young boy's mind in the days that follow the incident seem to suggest that there is a divinity in nature, that the natural world (as Wordsworth sees it) is an expression of the existence of God and one which punishes us when we commit immoral acts – like stealing someone else's boat.

We can also see this extract as charting the passage from innocence to experience, from childhood to adulthood. In the first part of the extract Wordsworth is totally in control – of the boat, the situation and his emotions. What he is doing may be wrong but it is clearly enjoyable for a brief period: this can be seen as showing how attractive it is to sin – we are tempted to do wrong because some sins are very attractive and pleasurable. But the sudden appearance of the mountain changes everything and shows the young poet that he is not in control: there is a higher power that watches over us. In simpler terms, we might say that the mountain symbolises his guilty conscience.

Conflict

This extract is remarkable for the power that Nature has over the young Wordsworth. Nature's influence makes him feel guilt for his casual theft of the boat and exerts a moral influence on him lasting for a long time after the incident. The long poem – *The Prelude* (from which this is an extract) – is full of examples of nature's influence on Wordsworth's spiritual and moral development, demonstrating Wordsworth's Pantheism. The conflict centres around the theft of the boat, and it really involves the internal conflict and guilt that Wordsworth feels and which is heightened by Nature and the looming crag that seems to rise up and overpower him. Wordsworth's personification, his animation of Nature, greatly aids the impression on the reader.

A Romantic Poem?

This extract is typically Romantic as is the whole of *The Prelude*. The very act of writing a long autobiographical poem about himself suggests that Wordsworth considers himself an exceptional individual with important truths to convey through his poetry. The supreme importance given to nature – in this passage and elsewhere in *The Prelude* – also marks it out as typically romantic, as does Wordsworth's pantheistic notion that Nature is a living force that can inculcate morality.

Why?

This very famous extract:

- shows nature as a moral and spiritual guide.

- explores the psychology of a young boy and his intense feelings of guilt.

- the importance it attaches to Nature make it a typically Romantic poem.

- explores the attractiveness of wrong-doing, but also the effects of a guilty conscience.

- demonstrates a deep love of and respect for nature.

- focuses very closely on the individual and his relationship with nature.

- depicts vividly the beautiful exuberance of rowing across the lake in the moonlight.

- focuses very closely on the individual and his relationship with nature.

- demonstrates the inner conflict Wordsworth feels after doing something wrong – stealing a shepherd's boat for a joy-ride on the lake.

- demonstrates the beauty of nature.

'The Man He Killed' – Thomas Hardy

Author and Context

 Thomas Hardy (1840 – 1928) is best known as a novelist. He wrote 15 novels, most of which are set largely in Dorset and the surrounding counties, and which deal with the ordinary lives of ordinary people in stories in which they struggle to find happiness and love – often battling against fate or their own circumstances. His final two novels *Tess of the D'Urbervilles* (1891) and *Jude the Obscure* (1895) both portray sex outside marriage in a sympathetic way and there was such a hysterical public outcry about the novels that Hardy stopped writing fiction and devoted the rest of his life to poetry. Although some of his poetry is intensely personal, this poem is also typical of his work in that it gives a voice to an ordinary man. Although Hardy trained as an architect, he came from a fairly poor family and, in both his novels and his fiction, he never forgets his roots – often making the rural poor central characters in his novels or giving them a voice in his poetry, as he does here.

Context

Who? The speaker of the poem is an ordinary, working class man who joined the army. The poem is a dramatic monologue.

When? Hardy wrote the poem in 1902 when Britain was fighting the Boers in South Africa in the Second Boer War. The Boers were settlers of Dutch descent who did not want to be subsumed within the British

Empire. British public opinion was divided on the issue of the Boer War – Hardy saw it as the British, motivated by South Africa's gold and diamond mines, meddling in the affairs of independent settlers who were simply trying to defend their homes and did not want to be part of the British Empire. Hardy opposed the war.

Where? There is no indication of where the speaker is (although given the poem itself and its contents, one can imagine the poem being part of an anecdotal pub conversation). The action of the poem takes place on an unnamed battlefield.

What? The speaker of the poem tells an anecdote about a man he killed during a war. The poem is a dramatic monologue, addressed seemingly to an acquaintance of the speaker and attempts to explain why the speaker killed a man in warfare.

inn – pub, public house.

nipperkin – a measure of beer roughly equivalent to a third of a pint and most common in the West Country.

foe – enemy.

'list – enlist in the army.

Off-hand – casually, without serious conviction.

sold his traps – the speaker assumes the man joined the army because he had sold his traps – presumably traps to catch rabbits and other game.

quaint – strange.

half a crown – an old unit of currency.

In the first stanza, the speaker admits that the man he killed and he would probably have enjoyed a drink together:

Had he and I but met

By some old ancient inn.

However, as they met in war-time as infantry soldiers *staring face to face*, they shot at each other and the speaker *killed him in his place*.

In the third stanza, the speaker tries to offer an explanation of why he shot the man:

I shot him dead because –

Because he was my foe.

The repetition of *because* suggests that the speaker is uncertain that this is a good enough reason, a point underlined by his statement in the third and fourth lines:

…my foe of course he was;

That's clear enough.

But the next word is *although* as the speaker and former soldier realises there is some fault in his logic; Hardy then uses enjambment from the third stanza to the fourth as the man's train of thought continues and he realises (despite the man being called his *foe*) that the man he killed probably had a lot in common with him: that the man enlisted *Off-hand like – just as I* or perhaps he was simply out of work.

The repetition of *because* also suggests hesitation and a lack of certainty, while the word *foe* (repeated twice) suggests that it is not the man's word: he has been told by propaganda that the men they are fighting are his *foe*. The phrase *my foe* is repeated too, which suggests perhaps that he is trying to convince himself of the justice of what he did or that he has heard the word used by a senior officer – both possibilities might be true. Hardy foregrounds the word *foe* not just through repetition but also through the internal rhyme with *so* in line three of the third stanza. The final line of the stanza is *No other reason why* and, although Hardy's speaker is too naïve to follow this thought to its logical conclusion, those simple words – *No other reason why* – explode all the myths about why men fight for their country: honour, glory, a sense of duty, patriotism, loyalty to one's King or Queen, loyalty to one's country or to one's flag. All these are exposed as lies by the simple words of Hardy's ex-soldier. Hardy's speaker cannot articulate these arguments but he does observe in the final stanza *How curious and quaint war is*, because it pits men who might have much in common – who, indeed, might have shared a beer together - but calls them the *foe* who must be killed. This is a profoundly anti-war poem.

The other reason war is shown to be less than heroic are the reasons the speaker tells us for joining the army: being out of work or having sold one's traps – *No other reason why* – which completely undercuts all the patriotic reasons for which men supposedly joined.

Hardy chooses to use the ballad stanza in the poem: a simple quatrain with a rhyme scheme of ABAB in each stanza. This ancient, egalitarian form is appropriate to his speaker. Hardy's language is also appropriately chatty and colloquial: there are no metaphors or similes – Hardy is imitating the voice of a working class soldier.

The structure of the poem is significant. The first stanza opens with a positive tone; the picture of two men perhaps enjoying a beer together at a traditional English inn is a positive one. The second stanza shatters this by revealing that the speaker killed the man. The third stanza attempts to provide a justification for the killing his *foe*, while the fourth speculates that they had *perhaps* some shared reasons for enlisting in the army – such as being out of work. The final stanza ends the poem, but all Hardy's working class soldier can conclude is that war is *quaint and curious*. Hardy's use of a relatively inarticulate common soldier is important: the reader can see that war (put in the soldier's terms) is absurd and futile but these are words his speaker would never use. Therefore, the structure of the poem (we might say) moves from casual and light to casual and dark – a human being has died. It remains casual because of the speaker's colloquial language and his simple explanation for what he did.

Neither soldier is named nor are the armies they are fighting for identified. It is clear that the speaker is intended to be English, but the poem arguably has a universal feel to it – that it could apply to any war in any century. The dashes in the fourth stanza are important too: they are examples of ellipsis: the words they separate are shortened forms and help to give an impression of a real speaker. However, coming after *perhaps* in the first line of the stanza it is also as though the speaker is hesitantly realising that he and the man he killed had a lot in common. The poem uses several parallel structures and repetition – *I shot at him as he at me, face to face* and *off-hand like just as I*. The most important parallel structure – that the two men are essentially very similar is implied throughout the poem.

Hardy's use of a working class soldier is absolutely vital to the effect of this poem. Both the speaker and the man he killed have been following orders given to them by their officers from higher classes. If a state of war did not exist, then they would have enjoyed a beer together. And where does the word *foe* come from: it would appear to be a word the soldier has heard from a superior officer or perhaps read in a newspaper, which are so keen to whip up jingoistic sentiment in a time of war.

Conflict

The war and the man the speaker kills are the obvious conflict in the poem; however, there is another conflict – within the speaker himself. Although he attempts to justify the killing – he was his *foe* and they were *ranged as infantry/And staring face to face* – his efforts to do this are rather naïve. The man he killed is still someone with whom he could have enjoyed a few beers. His conclusion – *How quaint and curious war is* – is naïve because, as we are well aware, wars do not simply happen, politicians decide that they should happen and send men to their deaths. Therefore, because of the speaker's lack of understanding, there is likely to be a conflict between his stated view of war and the readers'.

This short but powerful poem by Hardy:

- uses a working class soldier to expose the futility and absurdity of war.

- shows that the demonisation of the enemy as the *foe* is an important device to justify murder.

- demonstrates that the working classes of different countries have more in common than their rulers or those (the government) who choose to go to war.

- demonstrates the dreadful randomness of warfare: the two men were "staring face to face" and one was lucky enough to live.

- uses colloquial language throughout the poem to give a realistic sense of the speaker's voice.

'Cousin Kate' – Christina Rossetti

Author and Context

Christina Rossetti was born in 1830 into a highly talented family, all of whom wrote or painted. Rossetti was encouraged by her family to pursue her artistic talents from an early age. Her father: a poet and translator, lived in exile, and the family were held together by the mother who had a very strong Christian faith. Rossetti's mother was Francis Polidori, the sister of John Polidori who wrote an early Gothic story called *The Vampyr*. He wrote it while on holiday in 1816 with Percy and Mary Shelley and Lord Byron. They decided to have a competition to tell the scariest story: it is from this same party game that Mary Shelley's famous novel *Frankenstein* emerged.

Rossetti's poetry revolves around the themes of love and death, and there is often a strong religious dimension to her work. Love in her poems is often presented as problematical, unrequited, unreturned or unfulfilled. As she grew older her work became increasingly religious in tone and subject matter. She also wrote many poems for children.

Her own life was increasingly unhappy: she was engaged to be married twice but broke off both engagements. She suffered terrible ill-health, although she continued to write, and her final years were darkened by the deaths of most of her family and her two previous lovers. She died in 1894, having achieved much acclaim for her writing. Her brother was Dante Gabriel Rossetti who was a poet, a painter and a member of a group of painters known as the Pre-Raphaelites. The Pre-Raphaelites took much of their inspiration from the Middle Ages; it is possible to see the same tendency in some of Christina Rossetti's work.

maiden – young woman but with the implication she was a virgin.

flaxen – very blonde.

Woe's me for joy thereof – woe (sadness) to me for the happy time I lived in his palace.

knot – a true lover's knot, often made from thread and worn sometimes as a ring.

mean estate – poor, working class background.

coronet – small crown, which shows that the man is a member of the aristocracy.

fret – worry.

Who? Rossetti adopts the voice of a simple country girl who has been seduced by the Lord of the manor and then rejected in favour of her own Cousin – the Cousin Kate of the title. Rossetti also gives us a strong sense of the community looking on and judging these events, though none are named. The poem is a dramatic monologue, spoken by the rejected woman and directly addressed to her rival in love – her cousin Kate.

When? This is a hard question to answer. Of course, it could be contemporary to Rossetti in some remote rural part of the British Isles, but other factors suggest it is located in an unidentified past. The serious points it makes are probably true of all societies at all times – it is still traumatic to have one's love betrayed. Moreover, Rossetti's use of what is essentially the ballad form (as we will see below) gives a timeless atmosphere to the poem.

Where? In a small rural community which is dominated by the Lord of the manor's palace.

What? The speaker tells us that she was seduced by the Lord of the manor and lived with him in his palace but did not marry him even though he made her pregnant. Her place is taken by her Cousin Kate who is "pure" (i.e. a virgin) and whom the Lord does marry. The speaker's anger and rage at her cousin are only mollified by the fact that Kate does not seem able to conceive and, therefore, cannot give the Lord of the manor the thing he most craves – an heir – which ironically the speaker has provided – albeit illegitimately.

Commentary

The earliest surviving ballads in English date from the Middle Ages and are anonymous. They use the ballad stanza – a quatrain with a rhyme scheme of ABCB, but some six line ballads exist (the last two lines often being a repeated refrain) and there are some eight line ballads – formed (as Rossetti's poem is) by combining two quatrains to form an octet. The odd lines have 8 syllables generally; the even lines have 6.

Traditional ballads are usually set in an unidentified rural landscape and they always tell a story. The stories that traditional ballads tell are full of the most basic of human emotions: death, betrayal, revenge, and love in all its forms: unrequited, unfulfilled, unreturned, unwanted. The language is usually very simple and the narrative impels the ballad forward. Ballads often used repetition and were originally written to be sung or read aloud. In Rossetti's poem the language is simple (she is adopting the persona and voice of a simple country girl) and all the even lines rhyme. This background is important: Rossetti is writing in a long-established tradition and is, in a sense, writing her own Medieval ballad. She joins two quatrains together to come up with an eight line stanza. It is certainly written in the spirit of the ballad tradition and has an almost timeless quality to it as though the events of the poem could have taken place at any point over the previous four or five centuries, or even contemporary to Rossetti's writing of the poem.

In the opening stanza, the speaker (whose name we never know) tells us the past when she was happy (*Contented with my cottage mates*) and unaware that she was an attractive woman (*Not mindful I was fair*). The stanza ends with two rhetorical questions:

Why did a great lord find me out,

And praise my flaxen hair?

Why did a great lord find me out

To fill my heart with care?

Note the simple repetition in lines five and seven. The rhetorical questions are full of pain and anguish when we read the rest of the poem: she had been perfectly content before the *great lord* noticed her, but now her "heart is full of care" for reasons which we can only guess at this point in the poem.

In the second stanza, the Lord sets her up as his mistress in his palace – a contrast to the poor cottage she has lived in. There she leads a *shameless shameful life*. The apparent paradox is simple; her life was *shameless*: she and the great Lord enjoyed great physical intimacy and she felt secure in his palace but she is aware that their relationship is *shameful* because they are not married. The Lord's attitude to the speaker is presented as casual: she was his *plaything* and he *changed me like a glove* which suggests his feelings for her are superficial –

So now I moan, an unclean thing,

Who might have been a dove.

She is now considered *unclean* by her community because she is no longer a virgin and has lived a *shameful life* in the Lord's palace. The image of the glove shows the ease with which the Lord casts her aside and breaks their relationship. The image of the dove is a traditional symbol of innocence; the person the speaker might have been had she not been seduced by the Lord.

The third stanza addresses Kate directly for the first time and by addressing her as *Lady Kate* foreshadows what is about to happen. Cousin Kate grew more beautiful than the speaker, the Lord sees her, casts the speaker aside and marries Kate, thus changing her social class:

He lifted you from mean estate

To sit with him on high.

He is able to get away with such egregious behaviour because of his high social status.

The opening of the fourth stanza shows enormous hypocrisy on the part of the Lord and the community:

Because you were so good and pure

He bound you with his ring:

The neighbours call you good and pure,

Call me an outcast thing.

But she is only an *outcast thing* because the Lord took her virginity: the speaker was good and pure once and the fact that she is no longer is purely the Lord's doing. The speaker's sadness, trauma and despair are well-captured in the way she sits and howls in dust. The stanza ends with the line, addressed to Kate – *You had the stronger wing*: this may refer back to the image of the speaker as a dove, but it also looks forward to the next stanza. Kate with a *stronger wing* is able to fly higher socially.

In the fifth stanza, the speaker insists that *my love was true*, while she accuses Kate of not really loving the Lord – *Your love was writ in sand*. The speaker vehemently asserts that – had their positions been reversed and Kate had been his mistress – the speaker would have rejected the Lord's offer of marriage: *He'd not have won me with his love*. She accuses Kate of having mercenary values and suggests that the Lord *bought [Kate] with his land*. The bitter vehemence of the speaker is clearly demonstrated in her alleged reaction to the Lord, had her and Kate's positions been reversed – *I would have spit into his face*. The speaker does not tell us but we might infer she is claiming that she would have shown greater family loyalty than her Cousin Kate has done. She also alleges that Kate is only interested in the Lord's land and the social position that goes with it.

The final stanza is the climax of the poem and the zenith of the speaker's revengeful feelings. The stanza opens cryptically – *Yet I've a gift you have not got*. Kate may have many fine *clothes and [a] wedding ring*. But the speaker has a *fair-haired son* while the Lord and Kate remain childless. The speaker's description of her son as *my shame* and *my pride* makes perfect sense: he is her shame because he is evidence that she had sex outside marriage with the Lord and is now treated as an outcast by her community; however, he is also her *pride* because she is full of maternal love for him.

Rossetti uses structure cleverly. We know by line 11 that the narrator is moaning and thinks of herself as an "unclean thing", but Cousin Kate's part in all this is delayed until stanza three. The final twist or reveal – that the speaker has a son by the Lord and that Cousin Kate is childless – is left to the final stanza. The speaker has her perfect revenge for her betrayal and the terrible feelings she has suffered.

There is a strong sense of injustice in this poem – or rather Rossetti presents the speaker as having a strong sense of injustice – directed at the Lord and at her cousin Kate. As readers, however, we can see that there is a wider injustice at work: both women are very passive and both, in a sense, are victims of a patriarchal society where men take what they want with little thought of the human consequences.

Conflict

There is a bitter conflict between the narrator on the one hand and the Lord and the speaker's Cousin Kate on the other. On the surface, this is to do with love; the Lord's betrayal of the narrator and his choice to marry Cousin Kate. However, there is further conflict caused by gender inequality and by class inequality: all the way through the poem we are reminded that the narrator comes from a cottage while the Lord lives in his palace home.

Why?

This bitter ballad by Rossetti:

- demonstrates the anger and rage that can arise from rejection of love and the failure of relationships.

- reveals the gender inequality at the heart of the society it describes.

- shows the sexual hypocrisy in society over the different attitudes to male and female sexuality.

- shows the deference of ordinary people towards their so-called social betters.

- shows the importance and malign influence of class in society.

- seethes with a desire for revenge on the part of the speaker. The final stanza is redolent with schadenfreude (the pleasure you take in someone else's misfortune – here the inability of the Lord and his wife to have children).

'Exposure' – Wilfred Owen

Author and Context

Wilfred Owen (1893 – 1918) is widely regarded as the leading British poet of the First World War. He died in action on November 4th 1918 – just seven days before the war finally came to an end. Owen was an officer and was awarded the Military Cross for leadership and bravery in October 1918. The shock of what he saw in the front-line moved him to produce a great many poems in a very short time – most of which were not published until after his death. He seems to have been particularly keen to ensure that the British public was told the horrific truth about the war. He developed his own use of half-rhyme which was to influence other poets for the whole of the 20th century. Owen famously wrote that his subject was not war but the pity of war – a feeling that is especially apparent in this poem. *Above all I am not concerned with Poetry. My subject is War, and the pity of War. The Poetry is in the pity.*

It is over a hundred years since the First World War began, and, because of the many commemorations, many readers will have a visual sense of what that war was like. In fact, it was a world war with fighting taking place on almost every continent, but the abiding memory of the war – a memory based on photos, documentaries and even poems like this one, is of the trench warfare on the Western Front in Belgium and France. There are clear reasons for this. The war waged in the trenches resulted in battles with enormous loss of life with very little ground gained: on the first day of the Battle of the Somme the British army suffered 70,000 casualties, 20,000 of whom were killed. I think the other reason the Western Front holds such an important place in our image of the First World War is the trenches themselves and trench life: hundreds of thousands of soldiers living very close to each other in holes in the ground and suffering terrible, barbaric conditions, plagued by rats, lice and the cold. So the futility and loss of life in the battles, as well as the appalling conditions make the war in the trenches especially memorable.

Who? Owen uses the third person plural – we – to speak on behalf of British soldiers fighting in trenches on the Western Front during the First World War.

When? Not specified but in the depths of winter during the First World War.

Where? In the trenches of the Western Front. The First World War was a very static war: the trench systems of the Allies and of the Germans stretched from the coast of Belgium to the French border with Switzerland.

What? Owen describes a typical night and the following day in the trenches. The main enemy is not the Germans but the weather; the main feelings not fear or misgivings but boredom and pointlessness. Owen reflects on why he and his colleagues are there and what they are fighting for.

salient – a one-way trench dug out into No Man's Land to get closer to the enemy

melancholy – dejection, depression

glozed – decorated with

crickets – house crickets: insects which live near or behind old fireplaces and make a distinctive and rhythmic clicking sound

not loath – not unwilling

Throughout the poem, Owen speaks for all the soldiers on the Western Front by using *we* as they face an onslaught from – not the Germans – but the weather. The first stanza starts with a simple, straightforward statement: *Our brains ache in the merciless iced east winds that knive us* – the long vowels of the opening three words suggests tiredness followed by sibilance and assonance on shorter vowels describing the wind, and ending with *knive us* which turns the wind into a stabbing knife, cutting into them. In the next line, they cannot sleep; paradoxically it is because the night is silent and they anticipate an attack. They have confused memories of being in a salient and the only light comes from *low, drooping flares*; the sentries are *worried by silence... curious, nervous.* But, as Owen tells us in the last line *nothing happens* – words which are repeated four times in the poem.

Owen establishes in the first verse the structure he will use for all eight stanzas of the poem: a five line stanza with the first line half-rhyming with the fourth, and the second and third line rhyming with each other. Half-rhyme (because it sounds wrong - to put it simply) is an apt choice for a poem in which the poet describes a situation where many things are wrong. Very often the rhyme words are trochees as well as being half-rhyme (*nervous/knive us*) and this falling rhythm and the feminine endings to the lines intensify the sense of anti-climax and a poignant sort of futility. It also – along with the final shortened line produces a strange sense of apathy. The fifth and final line of each verse is much shorter than the others and acts as an anti-climax: again this is highly appropriate because, despite all the nervous anticipation, this is a poem in which nothing happens. The fact that the fourth line rhymes with the first is important too: by the time the reader reaches the fourth line we are directed back to the first line by the half-rhyme. The stanza looks inward so to speak and this is appropriate in a poem which describes a stalemate and which is concerned largely with the inner thoughts and feelings of the soldiers.

The first word of the second stanza – *Watching* – suggests the soldiers' passivity: they have nothing to do except wait, but their senses are keenly attuned to their surroundings and the possibility of attack. They hear the *mad gusts tugging on the [barbed] wire*, which only serves to remind them of the *twitching agonies* of men caught and dying on the wire. From the north, *the flickering gunnery rumbles*; a striking image which combines an image of light with onomatopoeia and is given aural cohesion by the assonance in *gunnery rumbles*, assonance is continued in the next line with *dull rumour*. The stanza ends with the poignant question: *What are we doing here?*

In the third stanza, dawn comes but it brings no respite, no hope. The soldiers give the impression of being reduced to survival of the elements: *We only know war lasts, rain soaks, and clouds sag stormy* Owen then introduces a metaphor related to the war to describe the heavy rain clouds that are heading their way:

Dawn massing in the east her melancholy army

Attacks once more in ranks on shivering ranks of grey.

The German army wore grey uniforms which makes the personification even more apposite, but only rain faces the soldiers. And once again *Nothing happens.*

The fourth stanza begins with a superbly written line, the sibilance of 's' giving an aural impression of the sound of gunfire. But it is not threatening and Owen remarks that the bullets are *less deadly than the air that shudders black with snow.* The next line alliterates on 'f' to describe the gentle snowflakes and the caesuras and verbs – *flock, pause and renew* attempt to suggest the swirling, random movement of the snowflakes. The soldiers are reduced to passivity again – watching the snowflakes. *But still nothing happens.*

The next stanza shows how exposed the British soldiers were to the elements: it's as if the snowflakes are deliberately seeking them out:

Pale flakes with lingering stealth come feeling for our faces.

And here the personification and the *stealth* make the snowflakes appear especially malevolent. The personification of the snowflakes and the phrase *come feeling for our faces* suggests a curiously evil intimacy. As the soldiers *cringe in holes* their minds reminisce about happier times – of *grassier ditches* and *blossoms trickling where the blackbird fusses.* But the stanza ends on an ominous note as Owen asks *Is it that we are dying?* The uncertainty engendered by the question is deliberately unnerving.

The sixth stanza is a respite from the weather. *Slowly our ghosts drag home* and the soldiers think about their homes, but the thought brings little joy as the house belongs to the crickets and the mice:

> *The house is theirs;*
>
> *Shutter and doors are closed: on us the doors are closed —*
>
> *We turn back to our dying.*

The seventh stanza appears to offer a justification for the war. If we follow the sense from the previous stanza:

> *We turn back to our dying.*
>
> *Since we believe not otherwise can kind fires burn;*
>
> *Nor ever suns smile true on child, or field, or fruit.*

These lines imply that the soldiers are there to ensure that *kind fires can burn* and that because of their participation in the war suns will smile true on *child, or field, or fruit.* Paradoxically, their love is made afraid of *God's invincible spring* which suggests that they believe that God is on their side. Winter will be displaced by Spring and – ironically – the better weather will allow real fighting to begin – which is why they are afraid. But, conscious that they are defending a just cause, *we lie out here; therefore were born,* which suggests that what they are doing is both their destiny and their duty; however, Owen's faith in the Christian God is given a tentative rebuke when he writes *but love of God seems dying* – how could God allow such horrendous suffering on such a colossal scale?

But despite this stanza of justification, Owen in the final stanza returns to the grim reality of winter in the trenches:

Tonight, His frost will fasten on this mud and us,

Shrivelling many hands and puckering foreheads crisp.

His frost is God's frost; there seems little evidence of God's love for suffering humanity in this poem: during the night some men will die of hypothermia and to be buried on the next day:

The burying party, picks and shovels in their shaking grasp,

Pause over half-known faces. All their eyes are ice.

But nothing happens.

Owen has succeeded in writing a poem which details in excruciating detail the desperate conditions endured in winter in the trenches, where the main enemy was not the German Army but the atrocious winter weather – men literally froze to death. He also conveys a sense of the sheer boredom of waiting for something, anything, to happen and questions repeatedly what the soldiers are doing there. He also includes two verses which allow the men to think about their homes and offers a justification for their being there – to allow kind fires to burn.

"Exposure" is not one of Owen's best-known poems, but perhaps it deserves to be: the use of half-rhyme, the stanza structure that turns in upon itself, and the truncated last line are wholly appropriate to the subject matter of the poem – the soldiers' doubts about why they are there and their doubt about God's role in their suffering. I find the last short line of each stanza especially effective since it leads nowhere – just as the men are going nowhere and seem to have lost all purpose.

Conflict

The central conflict in 'Exposure' is between the atrocious weather conditions and the British soldiers defenceless against the rain, the snow and the frost. In the final verse, some men have frozen to death overnight. The war is irrelevant in this poem. Another source of conflict is the sheer boredom the soldiers experience, waiting for something to happen and the doubts they have about why they are there as they do nothing except battling the atrocious weather conditions. Stanza six shows the conflict between the men's memories of home and their current experiences. While stanza seven introduces conflict with God and his part in all this: after all, in the following stanza it is *His frost* (the capitalization is all important) which kills the men in the night.

In terms of power, the weather seems all powerful, but, despite the toll taken by the winter, the soldiers show a hardy resilience and Owen's very act of writing the poem shows a certain triumph of art over horrendous living conditions.

Why?

This long poem:

- gives us a vivid picture of life in the trenches in winter.

- makes clear the boredom and the lack of action that the soldiers had to endure.

- shows the horrendous, life-threatening weather conditions in the trenches.

- expresses nostalgia for their homes.

- questions both God's part in the war and the very reason the men are fighting.

'The Charge of the Light Brigade' – Alfred, Lord Tennyson

Author and Context

Alfred Tennyson was born in 1809 and died in 1892. His early work received a mixed reaction, but his *Poems* published in 1842 established him as the leading poet of his day. In 1850 he was made Poet Laureate and was given a peerage in 1884. This poem is not especially typical of his work. It was published in 1855 in a collection called *Maud* and was written in response to a British military disaster during the Battle of Balaklava in October 1854. It is said that Tennyson read the report of the disaster in *The Times* and was moved to write the poem.

The Crimean War was fought largely in the Crimean Peninsula – then part of the Russian Empire and was until recently part of the Ukraine before the Crimean Peninsula was annexed by Russia in 2014. Britain and its allies – France and the Ottoman Empire – were fighting Russia over who would control the Dardenelles – the narrow strip of sea in Turkey that connects the Aegean Sea to the Black Sea. It was important for British sea-routes and trade that Russia did not control the Dardenelles, but it was important for Russia as it gave her access to the Mediterranean.

This is the report from *The Times* that Tennyson read:

At ten past eleven our Light Cavalry Brigade rushed to the front....The whole brigade scarcely made one effective regiment, according to the numbers of continental armies; and yet it was more than we could spare. As they passed towards the front, the Russians opened on them from the guns in the redoubts on the right, with volleys of musketry and rifles.

They swept proudly past, glittering in the morning sun in all the pride and splendour of war. We could hardly believe the evidence of our senses! Surely that handful of men were not going to charge an army in position? Alas! it was too true – their desperate valour knew no bounds, and far indeed was it removed from its so called better part – discretion. They advanced in two lines, quickening their pace as they closed towards the enemy. A more fearful spectacle was never witnessed than by those who, without the power to aid, beheld their heroic countrymen rushing to the arms of death. At the distance of 1200 yards the whole line of the enemy belched forth, from thirty iron mouths, a flood of smoke and flame, through which hissed the deadly balls. Their flight was marked by instant gaps in our ranks, by dead men and horses, by steeds flying wounded or riderless across the plain. The first line was broken – it was joined by the second, they never halted or checked their speed an instant. With diminished ranks, thinned by those thirty guns, which the Russians had laid with the most deadly accuracy, with a halo of flashing steel above their heads, and with a cheer which was many a noble fellow's death cry, they flew into the smoke of the batteries; but ere they were lost from view, the plain was strewed with their bodies and with the carcasses of horses. They were exposed to an oblique fire from the batteries on the hills on both sides, as well as to a direct fire of musketry.

Through the clouds of smoke we could see their sabres flashing as they rode up to the guns and dashed between them, cutting down the gunners as they stood. The blaze of their steel, as an officer standing near me said, was 'like the turn of a shoal of mackerel'. We saw them riding through the guns, as I have said; to our delight we saw them returning, after breaking through a column of Russian infantry, and scattering them like chaff, when the flank fire of the battery on the hill swept them down, scattered and broken as they were. Wounded men and dismounted troopers flying towards us told the sad tale – demigods could not have done what they had failed to do.

At the very moment when they were about to retreat, an enormous mass of lancers was hurled upon their flank…With courage too great almost for credence, they were breaking their way through the columns which enveloped them, when there took place an act of atrocity without parallel in the modern warfare of civilized nations. The Russian gunners, when the storm of cavalry passed, returned to their guns. They saw their own cavalry mingled with the troopers who had just ridden over them, and to the eternal disgrace of the Russian name the miscreants poured

186

a murderous volley of grape and canister on the mass of struggling men and horses, mingling friend and foe in one common ruin…At twenty five to twelve not a British soldier, except the dead and dying, was left in front of these bloody Muscovite guns.

And this is what *The Times* editorial said about the disaster:

Causeless and fruitless, it stands by itself as a grand heroic deed, surpassing even that spectacle of a shipwrecked regiment, setting down into the waves, each man still in his rank. The British soldier will do his duty, even to certain death, and is not paralyzed by feeling that he is the victim of **some hideous blunder.** [My emboldening.]

Why have I bothered to reprint this article? I think it is important for you to see the inspiration that Tennyson used. He had not been to the Crimea; he had never been on a battlefield; his only source was this article. *Some hideous blunder* is directly reflected in line 12 of the poem. Equally the reporter's assertion that the British soldier will *do his duty, even to certain death is* the main theme of the poem. The Light Brigade began the charge with 607 men and only 302 returned. I think *The Times* report is interesting – not simply because it is a first-hand account by a journalist who witnessed the event. The editorial admits there was *some hideous blunder* but the overwhelming tone of the report and the editorial is admiration for the courage of the men who obeyed such a senseless order. We can see in Tennyson's poem a similar balance: he does admit it was a terrible mistake but his emphasis is on the heroism of the men who simply obeyed their orders.

In reality, the incident was a complete failure and a pointless loss of life – it was a military disaster. However, it has become famous, partly through Tennyson's poem, but also because it moved other artists to produce work based on the incident. Perhaps it appealed to something that the public wanted to believe was part of being British – unflinching courage against the odds. Over the course of time, Tennyson's poem has lost some of its popularity perhaps because our attitudes to war have changed and we are more likely to question the justness of any war and the human cost of blindly following orders. In Tennyson's defence, one might say that as Poet Laureate it was his task to reflect the national mood at the time and it is certainly true that the men who charged on that day did display great courage.

league – three miles.

Valley of Death – an allusion to Psalm 23 in the Bible and to a novel called *Pilgrim's Progress* by John Bunyan. In both texts faith in God encourages people to be brave in dangerous places.

Light Brigade – at school I was confused about this title. It means that the brigade were on horseback but were lightly armed – they only carried swords. And, yes – there was a Heavy Brigade who moved more slowly because they carried more weaponry.

sabres – the specific type of sword carried by the soldiers.

Cossack – an ethnic group from south-eastern Russia, famed for their fighting skills and bravery.

sunder'd – broken apart.

Back from the mouth of Hell – anthropologists have noted that in cultures all over the world there are stories about brave men who visit hell or the underworld or the world of the dead and return alive. For example, in Greek mythology Hercules visits the underworld, but returns unscathed, adding to his heroic qualities. Tennyson is deliberately adding the members of the Light Brigade to this long and brave tradition.

Who? Tennyson writes about the cavalrymen of the Light Brigade; the enemy is present in the poem, as is the person who gave the order to charge the Russian guns. The reader is addressed directly in the final stanza.

When? October 25th, 1854, although Tennyson wrote the poem a few days later having read the report in *The Times*.

Where? Outside the Russian town of Balaklava in the Crimean Peninsula.

What? Tennyson describes the charge of the cavalry and what happened to them.

Commentary

This very famous poem relies a great deal on repetition throughout its length. Tennyson also uses alliteration in many lines and, if you read it aloud, the rhythm of the poem seems to imitate the motion of the horses galloping forward. It is these features, I would suggest, which make the poem so memorable.

The opening stanza highlights the order the brigade was given in lines 5 and 6. The opening phrase is repeated three times; *Valley of Death* is repeated twice as is *the six hundred* – giving these phrases prominence and emphasizing that they are going to die and their relatively small numbers. The phrase *Valley of Death* would have been very evocative to a Christian audience because it comes from such a well-known psalm.

The second stanza is directly related to the report in *The Times*. Line 9 repeats line 5. Line 12 picks up the word used by the journalist but makes the order anonymous – *Someone had blunder'd*. It is not part of Tennyson's aim to apportion blame for the order but to praise the men who followed it. And it is important, in the poem, that the soldiers knew it was a blunder yet still went ahead and charged: it shows their blind obedience to orders and their bravery. Lines 13 to 15 use repetition but also heap praise on their unquestioning obedience of the order, despite having a clear understanding that it would lead to death. The alliteration in line 15 – *do and die* – draws attention their clear courage and willingness to die.

In stanza three, Tennyson makes us aware of the enemy again through simple repetition which here gives us a real sense of the situation into which they rode, facing cannon fire from three sides. Note the onomatopoeia of *thunder'd* and the alliteration in line 22. In lines 24 and 25 Tennyson uses synonyms for the Valley of Death – *the jaws of Death* and *the mouth of Hell*. Although he concentrates on their bravery, line 23 also mentions their skill. They rode *well* and *boldly*, despite the terrible situation they were in.

Stanza four describes what happened when the cavalry reached the Russian positions. Tennyson uses vivid verbs – *flash'd, charging, plunged* – to give us an impression of close quarter fighting. *Charging an army* reminds us of the impossible odds they faced, while *All the world wonder'd* might mean that the world looks on amazed at their courage or astonished at the stupidity of the order – it probably means both! They have some limited success when in close contact with the enemy: the Russians *reel'd* and were *shatter'd and sunder'd*. Finally at the end of the stanza they turn to ride back to the British positions – those that are left. Note Tennyson's repeated use of the phrase *the six hundred*, except that it is now preceded by *not*.

The brigade ride back to their own positions in stanza five. Again Tennyson repeats several lines and phrases from earlier in the poem. The first three lines are identical to the start of stanza three with only one word being altered. He uses more alliteration in line 44 and pays tribute to the soldiers with the word *hero* and by pointing out that they had fought so well.

The sixth stanza is short and directly addressed to the reader. It begins with a question which stresses their glory (and not the idiocy of the order); the second line is an exclamation of admiration and is followed by a line we have seen before which suggests their charge will become famous all over the world. The final three lines are imperatives, orders to the readers – we are told to honour the Light Brigade because they were so noble.

How attitudes have changed since 1854! Today, if so many British soldiers died in one engagement that lasted only half an hour, there would be a public outcry and calls for an enquiry – particularly if it emerged that they died because of an incompetent order or an order that was misinterpreted. But Tennyson is not interested in that side of this story and in the past such an inquiry is much less likely to have occurred. He wants to praise their unthinking bravery and willingness to die following orders. You may find it hard to agree with the attitudes in the poem, but there is no doubt that Tennyson uses all his poetic skills to create something memorable.

Conflict

The questions of conflict and power are very ambivalent in this poem. Despite their appalling losses and the fact that this attack was a terrible failure, Tennyson manages to suggest the power of the Light Brigade's charge through his use of anapaests, coupled with the occasional trochee at the start of some lines. It is this which helps to make the charge sound heroic and brave. Of course, the Russian artillery are a major source of conflict and, throughout the charge, the Russians hold all the real power. More widely, the poem is about a wider conflict – the Crimean War. There is further conflict on the British side which Tennyson acknowledges: the ill-judged order for the Light Brigade to charge (*someone had blundered*), yet it is a tribute to the self-discipline of the Brigade that they obey the order. The power of discipline in the British Army is a quality which Tennyson's poem recognises and celebrates, despite the disastrous result. Yet the real power in the poem is that of the Russian cannon which caused such heavy losses on the Light Brigade. The ultimate conflict in the poem is the unwavering courage of the members of the Light Brigade who obeyed without question an order which sent many of them to certain death and whether it was right for them to do so. I think the modern reader might feel some conflict when reading Tennyson's poem, because he does glamourise war and its participants and our modern attitudes to war and its victims is very different because of the enormous suffering in two world wars and countless minor conflicts.

Why?

This very well-known and famous poem:

- gives a vivid impression of the speed of the charge and the atmosphere of battle.

- glorifies the courage and heroism of the men who followed orders and made the charge.

- tells us to remember the dead and their noble deeds.

- is unashamedly patriotic and celebratory of the courage shown by the soldiers.

'Half-caste' – John Agard

Author and Context

John Agard was born in the former British colony of Guyana in 1949 and he has written many books for children and adults. He moved to Britain in 1977 and lives in Sussex with his partner Grace Nichols, who is also a poet. Agard is well-known as a skilled and adept performer of his own poems and you may get the chance to see him perform his poems during your course. You should check out his performance of the poem 'Half-Caste' on YouTube because his performance helps to bring the poem alive. In many of his poems he uses Caribbean accent and dialect to bring a Guyanese identity to his work, but he also uses Standard English in some poems.

'Half-caste' is a term for a category of people of mixed race or ethnicity. It is derived from the term *caste*, which comes from the Latin *castus*, meaning pure, and the derivative Portuguese and Spanish *casta*, meaning race, and is generally considered offensive. Because of its derivation from the Latin, 'half-caste' implies someone who is half-pure or impure: it is for this reason that the term 'mixed race' is considered more accurate and acceptable.

yuself – yourself

yu - you

Picasso – a very famous 20th century painter

dat – that

some of dem cloud – some of those clouds

de – the

ah rass – oh shit

Tchaikovsky – a famous 19th century Russian composer

dah - the

an – and

wha - what

ah – I

wud – would

mih - my

Who? Although Agard addresses 'yu', the poem's message is directed at all those who use the term half-caste.

When? In modern Britain.

Where? In the United Kingdom.

What? In a deeply serious poem, Agard uses humour to mock and ridicule the term half-caste.

This poem deals with a very serious issue and one that the poet cares deeply about but does so at times in a funny way in order to mock those the poem is protesting about and attacking. Agard is angry at the use of the term 'half-caste' and uses mockery and ridicule to challenge the term, but the poem can be seen as hostile to any form of racial prejudice or judging anyone on the colour of their skin. This poem is also written to be performed so that the opening short verse:

Excuse me

standing on one leg

I'm half-caste.

would be visually funny as the poet mimics the words and starts the performance of the poem on one leg. Throughout the poem, Agard chooses his words very carefully, so that he writes words which are a mixture of standard 'correct' English and words which come from Black British patois or are phonetically spelt (spelt to mimic the way they are said). Therefore, even in his language Agard mirrors the theme of the poem – which is all about mixing – by deliberately mixing patois with standard English. For most of the poem, Agard rejects traditional punctuation to show that he does not need to conform to convention or to show his rebellion at convention.

After the first verse, the poem's speaker asks for an explanation of half-caste and asks a series of ridiculous rhetorical questions which serve to highlight the stupidity of the term. He asks whether Picasso, when he mixed *red and green,* produced a *half-caste canvas* and whether on a day of sunshine and clouds, light and dark, we speak of *half-caste weather.* It is white English people who use the term and Agard jokily points out that most English weather is:

nearly always half-caste

in fact some of dem cloud

half-caste til dem overcast

so spiteful dem don't want de sun to pass

Spiteful here is clearly referring to the clouds but it is easy, by extension, to see it as referring to the sort of people who unthinkingly and insensitively use the term *half-caste* to describe people. He goes on to ask whether Tchaikovsky's symphonies should be called *a half-caste symphony* because he used both the black and the white keys of the piano to compose them. The poet demonstrates his own cultured background by mentioning Picasso and Tchaikovsky – two giants of European culture.

The third verse paragraph changes direction. Agard still demands that the user of the term *half-caste'* should explain himself. These lines explore the effect of the term *half-caste* on the speaker. He says he is only listening to him with half of his ear and looking with only half of his eye; and he only offers half of his hand by way of greeting. These are silly, ridiculous notions but Agard uses them to attack the use of the term half-caste to show that he cannot engage fully with those who use that term and who show racial prejudice. The whole rhythm of his life is upset – when he sleeps he *close half-a-eye* and is only able to *dream half-a-dream*. The use of the term, he claims, stops him from being a full human being – *I half-caste human being* – in a society which calls him half-caste and which exhibits prejudice based on the colour of people's skin, he is not fully human. Indeed, one might argue that racists are what they are because they refuse to see the common humanity they share with people of all races.

The tone changes in the final few lines. Agard has moved from humour through anger at being rejected to a quiet determination and he asks the other person to come back tomorrow with his complete humanity

Wid de whole of your eye

an de whole of your ear

and de whole of your mind.

an I will tell yu

ae other half

of my story.

If people approach him with their full human consciousness and the right mind-set, they will accept him for what he is and understand that the term 'half-caste' reflects essentially racist attitudes – which is why 'mixed race' is less offensive and more accurate.

The poem is written in free verse – again like the lack of punctuation showing the poet's disregard for traditional convention. But the rhetorical questions and the anaphora – especially the number of times 'half-caste' is used – give the poem cohesion. Structure is also provided by the development of the thoughts of the poet and the final challenge to 'come back tomorrow'.

Conflict

The conflict in this poem is fairly straightforward. Put at its simplest, it is between people who are mixed race and those who use the insensitive term 'half-caste' to describe them. More widely, it is a poem about racial prejudice, between those who judge others by the colour of their skin and those who don't.

Why?

'Half-caste' by John Agard:

- uses humour and ridicule to mock the term 'half-caste'.

- ridicules racial prejudice in general.

- is a poem of protest about the way mixed race people are treated.

- highlights a serious social problem – racism.

'Catrin' – Gillian Clarke

Author and Context

Gillian Clarke who was born in 1937 in Cardiff is one of the leading poets of our time and is very much associated with Wales, where she has lived for most of her life. She and her husband live on a smallholding and keep sheep. Many of her poems are rooted in nature and she is highly aware of environmental issues. You can find a lot of very useful material for students on her website, including comments on most of her poems. Her writing is deeply rooted in everyday experience – sometimes as in this poem personal experience – but also touches on wider, deeper themes. Her poetry is widely studied in schools and she gives regular poetry readings and lectures about poetry.

the tight/ Red rope of love – the umbilical cord joining mother to baby

that old red rope – Gillian Clarke has said of this 'The invisible umbilical cord that ties parents and children even when children are grown up. I was also thinking of a boat tied to a harbour wall. The rope is hidden. The boat looks as if it is free, but it isn't.'

Who? The poet addresses her daughter, Catrin, directly.

When? Although the poem starts with Catrin's birth, the final stanza is written when she has grown older and, crucially, more independent.

Where? The first two stanzas are set in the delivery room and the hospital where Catrin was born, but the rest of the poem is set, if anywhere, in the family home.

What? As Gillian Clarke herself once said in an interview 'Catrin' answers the question: 'Why did my beautiful baby have to become a teenager?' The first stanza shows Catrin's complete dependence on her mother as a baby being born; the second stanza shows the desire for independence and freedom that many teenagers feel. It is an intensely personal poem that confronts the physical strain of childbirth and later the tensions that can arise in any parent/child relationship.

Commentary

The first stanza is written looking back at the memory of giving birth. The poet says *I can remember you* – a statement repeated in line 6 as if to emphasise the clarity and strength of the memory. In the opening sentence the poet is simply waiting for the process of child-birth to begin and has time to watch 'The people and cars taking/Turn at the traffic light'. Childbirth can be a very painful and traumatic experience for the mother and the poet describes the act of childbirth as 'our first/Fierce confrontation' fighting over 'the tight red rope of love' – alliteration helps give these lines aural cohesion but more importantly is the idea of childbirth as a fight and a fight that is fierce. The 'tight red rope of love' is a strikingly original phrase and seems as if it should be an oxymoron – we certainly do not associate 'love' with tight ropes or it may remind us of tug of war – one which the baby is bound to lose if it is to survive. The delivery room

> *... was square*
>
> *Environmental blank, disinfected*
>
> *Of paintings or toys*

The paintings and toys which will become such a feature of any child's life as it grows and develops, or which await the new-born baby in the family home. The pain of childbirth can cause women to shout and scream, and Clarke uses a metaphor of writing to describe the way she screamed:

> *I wrote*
>
> *All over the walls with my*
>
> *Words, coloured the clean squares*
>
> *With the wild, tender circles*

Of our struggle to become

Separate.

The circles are *wild* because of the pain but tender too because she is dealing with a new-born child. The scribbled *circles* may be a foretaste of Catrin in a few months' time and her first attempts with a crayon or they may be a hint that the mother's language became colourful (i.e. taboo) during the pain of childbirth. Notice how the poet positions the word *separate* on its own at the beginning of a line – separate from the rest of the sentence. The *environmental blank* of the delivery room has been coloured in by the shouts and cries and yells of childbirth, and the overwhelming joy and elation that a new healthy baby can produce in its parents. Clarke must have felt such an extreme mixture of emotions – *wild* and *tender* in their intensity

The first stanza ends:

We want, we shouted,

To be separate.

As the baby is born *I* changes to *we* and the new-born baby's crying is added to the noises in the delivery room. Although bound by the *tight, red rope of love*, the baby must be born and the umbilical cord must be cut.

The second stanza begins by reflecting of the poet and her daughter that *neither won nor lost the struggle* of childbirth – they both simply survived it. But the poet claims she is still *fighting [you] off*. Catrin is presented as strong and this is shown in the slowing down of the language and the three adjectives used to describe her hair – *your straight, long/ Brown hair* and her *glare* which is *defiant*. It turns out that mother and daughter are arguing about whether the daughter should be allowed to skate outside in the dark for one more hour.

More importantly, they are still (in Clarke's consciousness at least) joined by *that old rope* – once the umbilical cord, now the indissoluble ties between mother and daughter. In the poem Catrin's *defiant glare* brings up, Clarke writes

From the heart's pool that old rope,

Tightening about my life.

Trailing love and conflict.

All this comes from Catrin's glare and, now she is older, Clarke's heart is torn between two extremes – *love and conflict* – just as in the delivery room the emotions were of pain and physical strain but also the deeply psychological.

Linguistically, the two verse paragraphs contrast with each other: the *dark* of the night contrasts with the brightly-lit delivery room; the *wild... circles* are contrasted with Catrin's *straight, strong, long/Brown hair*; the delivery room was *hot* in the first stanza, but we might infer that in the second stanza Catrin's face is *rosy* because she has come indoors after going skating outside – an activity she wants to continue. But both stanzas contain struggle: the first struggle to give birth or to be born which is then contrasted with the mother's struggle to control her child and the child's struggle to get her own way. The dark is, of course, the darkness outside which Catrin wants to go skating in, but it may also symbolise the future of the mother and daughter relationship or Catrin's own individual future, both of which are unknowable.

The poem does not rhyme and has no regular pattern, although most lines have three stressed syllables. There is some internal rhyme. Clarke uses enjambment throughout and very simple language to give the impression of a natural speaking voice, which is appropriate in a poem addressed to your daughter.

The poem's tone shifts remarkably too, beginning with the calm and relaxed description of the poet simply watching people and cars waiting for the traffic lights to change, but, as the process of childbirth arrives, the poem, while still descriptive, becomes fraught with tension and pain.

The second verse paragraph, although containing some description of Catrin, is also more reflective about their relationship, and the tone, although rueful in the face of her daughter's defiance of maternal authority, we should note the celebratory nature of the poem – Clarke is proud of her daughter and the very close relationship that they have. In the poem, Clarke is torn between love for her daughter and care for her well-being – which is what causes the conflict. The old rope that joins them will last a lifetime and bring more conflict underpinned by love.

'Catrin' is an easy poem to relate to: all children as they grow up come into conflict with their parents or carers; many of us will also be parents.

Conflict

The *struggle* of the first stanza becomes the *fighting* of the second stanza and the conflict between mother and daughter is described vividly and intensely. There is also conflict within the poet herself: when faced with Catrin's *defiant glare* at being told she cannot skate outdoors in the dark for another hour, we are told that the glare brings up:

From the heart's pool that old rope,

Tightening about my life,

Trailing love and conflict.

Clarke's memory of giving birth to Catrin is still so intense and so paradoxical (the pain of childbirth versus the joy at new life) that she is torn between what she calls *love and conflict.*

Why?

In this poem which uses very simple vocabulary to describe a situation which must face every mother and her children, Clarke:

- vividly suggests the pain and suffering of the mother during childbirth, but also celebrates the strength and personality of her daughter.

- shows that the connection between mother and daughter, which started in the heat and trauma of the delivery room, will never fade.

- suggests that just as childbirth brings joy and feelings of tenderness, there will come a time when mother and daughter (despite their love for each other) will have confrontations as the child strives for independence.

'War Photographer' – Carole Satyamurti

Author & Context

Carole Satyamurti (born 1939) is a British poet, sociologist, and translator. She grew up in Kent, and lived in North America, Singapore and Uganda and she was a poet. She taught at the University of East London, and at the Tavistock Clinic where her main interest was relating psycholanalytic ideas to the stories people tell about themselves whether in formal autobiography or everyday encounters. She teaches for the Arvon Foundation and for the Poetry School. She is vice-president of Ver Poets. She runs poetry programs in Venice, Corfu and the National Gallery (London), with Gregory Warren Wilson. She has been writer in residence at the University of Sussex, and the College of Charleston. She lives and works in London.

Who? This is a dramatic monologue with Satyamurti adopting the voice of a press photographer.

When? The poem is contemporary.

Where? Mainly in a war-torn foreign country, but the second stanza is set at Ascot – a race meeting in Surrey attended by the rich and famous.

What? Satyamurti writes of taking different photographs and draws a contrast between our easy lives in the developed world compared to the sufferings of those in areas of war and conflict.

Commentary

Satyamurti begins the poem by writing

The reassurance of the frame is flexible

by which she means that in a photographic frame you can ignore what is outside the frame and imagine

people eat, sleep, love normally,

while she (as a war photographer seeks out *the tragic, the absurd.* Alternatively, if the photograph displays a happy scene you can convince yourself that all is right with the world:

Or if the picture's such that lifts the heart

the firmness of the edges can convince you

this is how things are.

As an example of a photo that lifts the heart she writes in the second verse of a photo she took at Ascot

... a pair of peach, sun-gilded girls

rolling, silk-crumpled, on the grass

in champagne giggles

The third stanza is set in a war zone and the photographer speaks of following a small girl – staggering down some devastated street – and carrying a baby on her hip.

She saw me seeing her, my finger pressed

and the photographer took a picture of her with the baby.

At the start of the fourth stanza comes *the first bomb of the morning* and the girl, *instinct prevailing* – dropped the baby and ran.

What gets printed is the photograph of the girl holding the baby with the caption

'Even in hell the human spirit

triumphs over all.'

Which is not a true representation of what happened after the shelling started.

Satyamurti ends the poem with a chilling message:

But hell, like heaven, is untidy,

its boundaries

arbitrary as a blood stain on a wall.

The word *boundaries* is crucial here: the frame of a photograph excludes things which are unpleasant or bad – you can't see the whole picture. But hell is *arbitrary* – it has no boundaries. The poem ends with the chilling image of a blood stain on a wall.

Conflict

The poem is set in an unidentified foreign war zone and focuses on a young girl – which increases our feelings of pathos. Satyamurti succinctly describes war as *hell* towards the end of the poem. However, there is another conflict at work in the poem to do with the truth that photographs reveal and the truths they conceal. A photograph shows what is in the frame not what is happening just outside the frame; photographs are also limited by time – they do not show what happened immediately before or immediately after the event captured in the frame. This creates a conflict between different versions of the truth and which photographs are selected to show the 'truth'. In the poem the photo chosen shows the young girl carrying the baby with the caption: '*Even in hell the human spirit / triumphs over all*'. However, we know from the poem that the next thing to happen is that the shelling starts, the girl drops the baby and, screaming, runs for her life. Therefore, the photograph is not completely accurate. As Satyamurti says hell is untidy – we might add that war and truth are also untidy.

Why?

In 'War Photographer' Satyamurti:

- contrasts our comfortable world (Ascot) with the suffering of war-torn regions.

- shows that photographs can never tell the whole truth – just give a partial version of it.

- implies that we are sheltered from the harsh reality of war.

- in the second half of the poem gives a frightening glimpse into a war-ravaged area – the stones of the buildings being shattered.

- ends the poem with a memorable image of blood smeared on the wall.

'Belfast Confetti' – Ciaran Carson

Author and Context

Carson was born in Belfast in 1948 and has lived there all his life. Violence and its effects are central to much of his writing. He has lived throughout the 'Troubles', which is the name given to the last forty years of the history of Northern Ireland. During the Troubles, terrorist groups representing both sides of the conflict attacked each other and the British Army and planted bombs which deliberately targeted civilians too. This poem was written in 1990, but the term 'Belfast confetti' was already in use in speech and means the shrapnel (pieces of metal) placed around explosives that would fly out and injure people when the explosive was detonated or it can mean random objects made of heavy metal, which rioters hurled at the soldiers or the police during riots.

There has been violence in Ireland ever since the English tried to conquer it and make it a colony in the 16th century. The most recent era of violence is known as the Troubles and flared up in the late 1960s. Tension between Catholic and Protestant communities erupted into violence and British troops were sent to Northern Ireland to keep the peace and to keep the opposing sides apart; however, because of various factors, the violence escalated and terrorist groups on both sides of the sectarian divide became involved and increasingly powerful. There were many deaths and many bombings, and the violence continued into the late 1990s. Carson was brought up in the Falls Road area – one of the most dangerous areas of Belfast.

It is dangerous to generalise about Ireland, but essentially the Catholic community favoured unification with the Republic of Ireland, while the Protestant community wanted to remain as part of the United Kingdom. More immediately, in the 1960s the Catholic community did not have equal rights because the Protestant majority dominated politics. The British government claimed the British soldiers were in Northern Ireland to keep the peace, but Irish Republicans felt they were an army of occupation

fount – this word means two things in this poem. It is a spring of water like a fountain, but it is also a fount of broken type: before computers, books and newspapers were printed using metal blocks to represent each letter and piece of punctuation which were laboriously put in position by hand. These metal blocks are not unlike the pieces of metal used as shrapnel.

Balaklava, Raglan, Inkerman, Odessa, Crimea – street names in the Falls Road area which ironically recall the Crimean War – another British imperial war, you might argue. You can read more about the Crimean War in the section devoted to *The Charge of the Light Brigade* by Alfred Tennyson.

Saracen – a British army armoured personnel carrier.

Kremlin-2 mesh – a type of mesh used over the windows of Saracens and designed to protect the windows from bombs and rockets.

Makrolon face-shields – Makrolon is a tough man-made substance which protects the face but is transparent.

fusillade – a continuous discharge of guns.

Who? The poet speaks as himself.

When? During the Troubles.

Where? In the Falls Road area of Belfast.

What? The poet is caught on the streets of Belfast when a bomb is detonated. He seems to get lost in the confusion and chaos after the explosion and describes the British Army's own confused reaction to the incident.

Commentary

This is a confused and confusing poem which you may struggle to make sense of; it is deliberately written in this way to suggest that this sort of incident is frightening and confusing and it also demonstrates the inability of language to describe adequately what is going on. The title of the poem 'Belfast Confetti' is an everyday, darkly-comic term for shrapnel or for odd pieces of metal thrown at the British soldiers during riots: it is a euphemistic slang term and derives its comic edge from our usual association of confetti with weddings which are happy, joyous occasions – unlike the riot described in this poem. It becomes darkly comic because we normally associate confetti with weddings not bombings. The *confetti* - the shrapnel - rains down on the streets of Belfast once the bomb has exploded and continues as the rioters use odd scraps of metal to bombard the British soldiers.

In the first stanza, the poet struggles to make sense of what is going on. He is caught up in a riot and then a bomb explodes, adding to the confusion. The very first word – *suddenly* – plunges us into the midst of the action. In the wake of the explosion, the air is *raining exclamation marks*: this metaphor suggests the pieces of shrapnel flying through the air; the shouts and cries of people near the bomb's blast; and also the sheer sense of shock and fear that courses through the poet. Carson continues this metaphor of the shrapnel as pieces of punctuation to suggest that language and its tools – punctuation – cannot make sense of, or convey the reality of, the riot and the bomb. *This hyphenated line* becomes *a burst of rapid fire*. The poet tries to formulate a sentence in his head, but he cannot complete it – his sense of fear and panic and shock is so strong that he has lost the ability to communicate. To make matters worse, at the end of the stanza he cannot escape – everywhere is *blocked with stops and colons*.

In the second stanza, the poet is lost in his home area. The tense switches to the present to give extra immediacy. He knows *this labyrinth so well* but cannot escape. The list of street names adds to his sense of confusion. As I have already mentioned, the names are highly ironic since they are named after places in the Crimea where the British Army fought except Raglan Street which is named after Lord Raglan, the British army commander-in-chief during the Crimean War. Everywhere he finds a dead-end. The short sentences echo his confusion and also give us the sense that he is trying to move quickly in order to get off the streets to the safety of his home. Line 15 is full of references to British soldiers, but they are described in terms of their equipment – in a list like the street names – which makes them seem dehumanised and threatening. The soldiers are not presented as human and in line 16 they fire a series of questions at him – a *fusillade of question marks*. *Fusillade* is a brilliantly chosen metaphor which is appropriate since the soldiers are asking the questions but also suggests how potentially dangerous these questions seem to the poet in his state of panic:

My name? Where am I coming from? Where am I going?

Clearly the soldiers are trying to catch the bombers and these are genuine questions which they might have asked someone running in the streets in the aftermath of a riot and a bombing, but they are more important than that. In fact, the whole poem (composed of two stanzas of equal length) is an extended metaphor which suggests that conflict destroys language and our ability to communicate normally: *raining exclamation marks* suggests rapid shouts of fear and alarm; *an asterisk on the map* would look like there had been an explosion on the paper; *stuttering* obviously shows the poet cannot get his words out because of his fear, but also suggests the sound of *the rapid burst of fire*; the alleyways are *blocked with stops* just as full stops block the reader at the end of the sentence.; a fusillade refers to several questions being fired at the narrator but also means rapid gunfire.

Carson's sense of total disorientation, his fear and total confusion, mean that he is unsure of who he is and where he's going, so great has been his sense of shock.

Conflict

The poem enacts the conflict of the riot situation very effectively through language, the disrupted rhythm and the extended metaphor. The British soldiers are dehumanised and it is easy to see them as an army of occupation – certainly their brief interrogation of the poet causes conflict. This conflict is internalised as the poet panics and is desperate to get to the safety of his home.

Why?

This poem:

- uses lists, questions and short, unfinished sentences to convey an atmosphere of fear and chaos.

- shows no overt interest in the political situation, but is wholly concerned with the reactions of one frightened and confused man.

- suggests, it could be argued, through its presentation of the soldiers and the careful selection of street names which recall foreign wars, that the British Army is an army of occupation.

- uses language to suggest the inability of language to adequately convey the reality of a riot and a subsequent bomb blast.

- enacts through its language and imagery the extreme sense of shock and disorientation that the poet feels.

'The Class Game' - Mary Casey

Author and Context

Not much is known about Mary Casey, except that she was a housewife from Liverpool. Casey was a contributor to a poetry magazine called 'Voices', which existed from 1972-1984. 'The Class Game', published in 1979, was one of four poems of Casey's that appeared in the magazine. 'Voices' published poems by working class writers. These authors were not professional poets and had no literary reputation; they were ordinary people who wrote largely about their everyday experiences. Some critics were rather snobby about 'Voices' and even the academic who had started the magazine, Ben Ainsley, wrote in the introduction that *I can make no great claims for these pieces, except that they are, it seems to me, varied, interesting, freshly written, and in most cases the work of men and women taking up a pen late in life; with some qualms, though with real curiosity as to how it will turn out.* This implies that he had some doubts about the 'literary value' of the work.

Ironically, to call into question the value or 'literary value' of a piece of poetry is playing a different version of the class game, because it assumes that untutored, working class poets will have little of value to communicate. This commentary aims to prove otherwise.

1979 was a turning point in British politics and society. Margaret Thatcher became Prime Minister and proceeded to implement monetarist economic policies. This led to a terrible recession with very high unemployment – especially in the northern cities like Liverpool. She went on to privatise previously nationalised industries and deliberately sought industrial confrontation with the unions – firstly, the National Union of Coalminers and the teaching unions. Britain moved from a system heavily dependent on income tax (direct taxation) to a system of indirect taxation - VAT, fuel tax – taxes whish are paid by everyone no matter what their income. The rich received tax cuts, while the poor were often unemployed or saw their wages drop in real terms. From one point of view, it is not hard to see the Tory policies of the 1980s as a form of class war – aimed at the working class.

In the 21st century, you often hear some people claim that we live in a classless society but I'm not sure that is true. If anyone has ever commented on the way you speak or the words you use or where you live or the occupations your parents have or the school you go to, then they are, in effect, making a class-based comment. I am writing this in the summer of 2015 and, with another Tory government in power, the gap between the rich and the poor is widening daily and food bank use is continuing to rise therefore it is hard to see the UK as a classless society.

wince – cringe, look embarrassed

Tara to me Ma – Goodbye to my mother

corpy – a Liverpool slang term for a council house

Wirral – part of Merseyside that is regarded as posh

Toil – work

gullet – throat

docker – someone who works in the docks or in a shipyard

Who? The poem is a dramatic monologue in which the author directly addresses a member or members of the middle or upper classes.

When? 1979 – although it could be argued that the issues the poem raises are still relevant today.

Where? No specific place, but clearly centred on Liverpool.

What? Casey asks the rhetorical question *How can you tell what class I'm from?* and proceeds to answer it mainly in terms of vocabulary – the words we use – although she also defines it in terms of where people live and their occupations. At the end of the poem Casey asserts that she is proud to be working class.

Commentary

The poem opens with a confident and challenging rhetorical question; *How can you tell what class I'm from?* The narrator of the poem asserts *I can talk posh like some* which shows that when she uses working class words she chooses to do so, though she knows how to talk 'posh'.

This is a first-person dramatic monologue reflecting on the speaker's feelings on being judged on her accent, her vocabulary, her father's job and her general social background. The speaker is clearly from the working class (*we live in a corp*) but she is addressing people from the middle classes who live in a 'pretty little semi' and in the Wirral, not Liverpool itself.

The poem is not divided into stanzas but it is presented as one long stanza, which suggests a sustained outpouring or outburst of anger and annoyance at being judged by her speech and her class. Separate stanzas would have impeded the flow of her emotions and thoughts as expressed in the poem. The use of the word 'game' in the title suggests very strongly that judging people on their class backgrounds is trivial and no more than a game as far as the speaker is concerned. Alternatively, it might refer to a game you play when you are people-watching – deciding what class they come from.

The poem itself might suggest the humour and fun of a game. However, the poet introduces internal rhyme – *nose/clothes* and *Tata/Ma* and rhyming couplets towards the end of the poem suggests that the focus of her anger and the target of her anger – the class system - is becoming more coherent and is starting to coalesce.

The short line lengths towards the end of the poem, along with the anaphora of *and* and the enjambment between the last two lines emphasise the passion and commitment the poet feels about this subject: anger, annoyance, irritation but also an exuberant pride in her background. The rhythm of the poem also contributes to the air of essential light-heartedness, but the lines get shorter towards the end of the poem which may indicate the speaker's growing anger and frustration at being judged and being labelled working class. The speaker's tone certainly becomes more confrontational as the poem progresses.

Throughout the poem, Casey uses rhetorical questions to put the reader under pressure. She also juxtaposes slang or colloquial words with standard English words; sometimes the slang words are used alone without their standard English equivalent; and sometimes the class differences are presented in physical form – for example, Casey asks *did I drop my unemployment card/ Sitting on your patio (we have a yard)?* Or later and much more bitterly:

Or is it because my hands are stained with toil,

Instead of soft lily-white with perfume and oil?

Casey is fully aware of the adverse effect that her words will have on a certain type of middle class reader when she asks *does it stick in your gullet like a sour plum.* Some middle class are very sensitive to class differences and would, as Casey suggests, *wince* at the use of words like *bog* for toilet and *pee* for urinate.

Conflict

Conflict in this poem revolves completely around class conflict and the judgments people make based on fear of the working class or disapproval of the way they speak or where they live or what job they do. Casey herself adds to this conflict by her accusatory tone and her proud defiance – she is proud to be working class.

Why?

In 'The Class Game' Mary Casey writes a poem which:

- sets out to confront and shock middle class readers with its use of slang and colloquial language.

- juxtaposes assumptions about working class speech with standard English.

- demonstrates and celebrates her pride in being working class.

- is essentially light-hearted in tone but contains a bitter, accusatory edge.

- implies that class differences still exist in modern England.

'Poppies' – Jane Weir

Author and Context

Weir grew up on the outskirts of Manchester and works as a poet, writer and textile designer. Her poetry has been highly praised. This poem was commissioned by Carol Ann Duffy along with nine other contemporary war poems in 2009, in response to the growing violence in Afghanistan and the inquiry into the invasion of Iraq. In an interview Weir commented:

I wrote this piece from a woman's perspective, which is quite rare, as most poets who write about war have been men. As the mother of two teenage boys, I tried to put across how I might feel if they were fighting in a war zone. I was subliminally thinking of Susan Owen [mother of Wilfred Owen] *and families of soldiers killed in any war when I wrote this poem.*

Armistice Sunday – the Sunday closest to November 11th, Remembrance Day, chosen because the First World War ended on November 11th, 1918.

tucks, darts, pleats – words associated with clothes and textiles.

Who? The poet speaks directly to a son who is taking leave of his mother, the narrator.

When? We are told it is three days before Armistice Sunday but apart from that no specific time is mentioned and no specific war is mentioned which gives the poem a universal quality. It could be any war at any time and any mother bidding farewell to her son, unsure of what will happen to him. Having said that, Armistice Sunday has only been commemorated since the First World War, and the habit of wearing poppies to remember the sacrifice of dead soldiers is also a modern phenomenon, so this is a modern poem. We know it was published in 2009.

Where? The action begins at the narrator's home and ends in the local churchyard in front of the war memorial.

What? She pins a poppy on his lapel and says goodbye at the front door. Filled with memories of his childhood, she goes to her son's bedroom and then is led to the local churchyard and the poem ends with the mother gazing at the war memorial, thinking about her son.

Commentary

The opening sentence fixes the day: it is three days before Armistice Sunday. Before her son leaves the narrator pins a poppy on the lapel of the person the poem is addressed to: it is her son, but this is only confirmed by later details. Even the gender of the speaker is not made explicit, but there are strong suggestions that it is his mother, which we will explore later. Armistice Sunday commemorates all those who have died in wars, but we might note that poppies have been placed on individual war graves to remind us that every serviceman who died was an individual. The final three lines of the first stanza use language which is rich in texture and sound qualities:

I pinned one onto your lapel, crimped petals,

spasms of paper red, disrupting a blockade

of yellow bias binding around your blazer.

Alliteration on *p* gives way to alliteration on *b*, and Weir also uses assonance to give further euphony to these lines: *pinned/crimped* and *spasms/paper/blazer* and *bias/binding*. A sense of war is introduced by the word *blockade* to describe the blazer's binding.

The second stanza gives us lots of recognisable domestic details: the mother (we assume that it is the mother because stereotypically it is mothers who would fuss over a son's appearance in this way) uses sellotape to remove the cat's hairs from her son's clothes and smooths his collar down. The sellotape is *bandaged around* her hand – a hint perhaps that she is finding this leave-taking painful. The narrator says *I wanted to* rub noses with her son as they did when her son was younger, but she doesn't; she also had to resist the *impulse* to run her fingers through his hair. These details suggest that now her son is older she feels she cannot do these things that a parent might naturally do to their child when they are younger. So as our children grow up, it seems, we lose some of the intimacy we enjoyed when they were small children. Another detail which confirms that the son is older is probably the gelled blackthorns of his hair; he is old enough to make decisions about his appearance. The speaker clearly feels sad that her son is growing up: in lines 10 and 11 we are told she *steeled the softening of my face* and in line 18 she tells us *I was brave* — it is as if her face will soften with tears at her son's departure, but she manages to control her feelings in order not to embarrass her son — just as she has not rubbed noses with him or run her fingers through his hair.

The words she wants to say to him won't come; they are slowly *melting* in line 18. When she opens the front door the world is overflowing *like a treasure chest* and her son is *intoxicated*: leaving home may be sad for the parent but it can be a time of excitement and opportunity for the child as these words suggest.

As soon as he has gone she goes to his bedroom and releases a song bird from its cage; I don't think we are meant to see this as literal, but it probably symbolises the speaker's son being released into the intoxicating, *treasure chest* world — a good thing despite his mother's obvious sadness at saying goodbye.

Weir then introduces a dove which leads the mother to the churchyard. The mother is still distracted: her stomach is busy and her nervousness about her son is conveyed to us in imagery drawn from textiles and the manufacture of clothes — *tucks, darts, pleats*; she is obviously distracted too because, although it is November, she has no coat and wears no gloves. Weir is a textile designer and often uses such vocabulary in her poems. However, the fact that she goes out improperly dressed is also a sign of her deep need to follow the dove and get to the war memorial.

Once in the churchyard the speaker traces the inscriptions on the war memorial while leaning against it *like a wishbone* – a simile that displays her fragility and which also raises the idea of wishes: presumably she would wish her son to be safe and happy. The dove flies above her and is described metaphorically as *an ornamental stitch*......... and then the poem ends:

I listened, hoping to hear

Your playground voice catching on the wind.

And that phrase - *playground voice* – suggests the speaker's nostalgia for her son's childhood and her regret that he has to grow up. *Playground* is a word we associate with primary schools and it is clear from earlier details in the poem that he is older and has left childish things behind.

This is a beautiful and powerful poem. The very writing of the poem can be seen to be a political act because Weir is writing about a topic (war) which is dominated by male poets, so to give a mother a voice is an important decision.

Some readers feel that the son is going off to war and that is why Weir is saying goodbye to him. I don't see the poem quite like that. Soldiers don't wear blazers; it is not a word used to describe what soldiers wear. I think Weir's son is going off to school – secondary school, perhaps even boarding school – and this poem is about a rite of passage for mother and for her son. A rite of passage is a ritual that marks a deep change in one's life: here it is all about sending your son off into the world, about not being able to rub noses with him because he is too old for that; it might contain the fear that later in the future he might join the army and his name might one day join the names on the war memorial.

And this fear of the future leads the mother to the war memorial, because on this day when she bids goodbye to her growing son, she feels real empathy for the mothers of the men listed on the war memorial. In their cases, they said goodbye to their sons and never saw them again because they died in war. So the poppy on the lapel and the fact that this poem takes place three days before Armistice Sunday are crucial to the poem's impact. It is as if our commemoration of Armistice Sunday makes the speaker acutely aware of the much worse sacrifices that mothers make in times of war and this alerts her to what might happen in the future if her on ever becomes a soldier. Becoming a soldier (or whatever your child's first job might be) would also be a rite of passage and death is the ultimate rite of passage.

What are we to make of the dove? It is a symbol of peace, but in the final stanza the metaphor used to describe it is an ornamental stitch, a stitch which is ornamental, not practical, not serving a purpose. Does this suggest that our hopes for peace will always be ornamental and never real, never realised, never practical? Does it suggest that war will always be with us because the dove will remain ornamental? This may seem a little fanciful to you, but the First World War, which led to so many monuments in British towns and churchyards was once thought of as the 'war to end all wars', but Weir is writing in 2009 when British soldiers were dying regularly in Afghanistan. War has continued to blight human history.

Conflict

The narrator has some power over her son's appearance: she pins the poppy on his blazer, but there is a conflict between her desire to keep her son safe and his possible participation in a war in the future. However, once he has left she realises that she has no power over war – these matters are decided by governments (although the poem does not mention this). Both the poppy and the dove are powerful symbols – one of remembrance for the dead and the other for peace – and together they draw her to the local churchyard where she traces the *inscriptions on the war memorial*. She leans against the memorial *like a wishbone*, showing her weakness compared with the power of the memorial and the implied power of governments in the future to send young men like her son to fight in foreign countries. There is clear conflict between her maternal instinct to keep her son safe, and the danger that in the future his name might appear on a similar war memorial. In war time, the mother would lose all control over what happens to her son – and, in fact, her position in the poem is one of powerlessness.

Why?

This interesting, modern poem:

- allows a woman's voice to speak on the subject of war.

- uses symbols very effectively and evocatively.

- presents an inevitable rite of passage for any mother and her child.

- links this rite of passage with the commemoration of the war dead through poppies and on Armistice Day.

- uses the language of textiles to suggest the gender of the parent.

- movingly presents the way parent/child relationships change over time.

- is more powerful because the mother in the poem represses her emotions in front of her son.

- sees the growing up of children and their loss of innocence as inevitable, but sad.

'No Problem' – Benjamin Zephaniah

Author and Context

Poet, novelist and playwright Benjamin Zephaniah was born on 15 April 1958.

He grew up in Jamaica and the Handsworth District of Birmingham, England, leaving school at 14. He moved to London in 1979 and published his first poetry collection, *Pen Rhythm*, in 1980.

He was Writer in Residence at the Africa Arts Collective in Liverpool, and was a candidate for the post of Professor of Poetry at Oxford University. He holds an honorary doctorate in Arts and Humanities from the University of North London (1998), was made a Doctor of Letters by the University of Central England (1999), and a Doctor of the University by the University of Staffordshire (2002). In 1998, he was appointed to the National Advisory Committee on Creative and Cultural Education to advise on the place of music and art in the National Curriculum, and in 1988, Ealing Hospital in London named a ward after him.

His second collection of poetry, *The Dread Affair: Collected Poems* (1985) contained a number of poems attacking the British legal system. *Rasta Time in Palestine* (1990), an account of a visit to the Palestinian occupied territories, contained poetry and travelogue.

His other poetry collections include two books written for children: *Talking Turkeys* (1994) and *Funky Chickens* (1996). He has also written novels for teenagers: *Face* (1999), described by the author as a story of 'facial discrimination'; *Refugee Boy* (2001), the story of a young boy, Alem, fleeing the conflict between Ethiopia and Eritrea; *Gangsta Rap* (2004); and *Teacher's Dead* (2007) .

In addition to his published writing, Benjamin Zephaniah has produced numerous music recordings, including *Us and Dem* (1990) and *Belly of de Beast* (1996), and has also appeared as an actor in several television and film productions, including appearing as Moses in the film *Farendg* (1990). His first television play, *Dread Poets Society*, was first screened by the BBC in 1991. His play *Hurricane Dub* was one of the winners of the BBC Young Playwrights Festival Award in 1998, and his stage plays have been performed at the Riverside Studios in London, at the Hay-on-Wye Literature Festival and on television. His radio play *Listen to Your Parents*, first broadcast on BBC Radio 4 in 2000, won the Commission for Racial Equality Race in the Media Radio Drama Award and has been adapted for the stage, first performed by Roundabout, Nottingham Playhouse's Theatre in Education Company, in September 2002.

Many of the poems in *Too Black, Too Strong* (2001) were inspired by his tenure as Poet in Residence at the chambers of London barrister Michael Mansfield QC and by his attendance at both the inquiry into the 'Bloody Sunday' shootings and the inquiry into the death of Ricky Reel, an Asian student found dead in the Thames. *We Are Britain!* (2002), is a collection of poems celebrating cultural diversity in Britain.

He has recently been awarded further honorary doctorates by London South Bank University, the University of Exeter and the University of Westminster. Recent books, both for children, are an autobiography: *Benjamin Zephaniah: My Story* (2011) and *When I Grow Up* (2011).

de – the

brunt - force

an – and

yu – you

dan – than

to have a chip on your shoulders – to bear a grudge about something

me – my

Mother country – Great Britain

Who? The poet speaks directly to the reader.

When? The poem has a contemporary setting.

Where? No specific location.

What? Despite having been the victim of *playground taunts/An racist stunts*, Zephaniah holds no grudges, but uses the poem to attack racism in general and racial stereotyping in particular.

'No problem' is a phrase you might hear several times in a single day; as the title of this poem it is clearly ironic, since racism and racial stereotyping clearly are social problems which have no place in civilised society. The title also shows Zephaniah's immunity to racist taunts and stunts – he is clearly proud of who and what he is and repeats, *I am not de problem' four times in the first verse paragraph, also giving it prominence as the opening line of the poem. This is repeated almost exactly in the second verse paragraph when Zephaniah writes 'Black is not the problem.* Black people in the United Kingdom are not the problem – the problem is the racist attitudes of white British people and their habit of stereotyping black people.

The first verse paragraph deals mainly with the stereotypes that white people have of black people. Zephaniah asserts *I am branded athletic* and *I can do more than dance* because the stereotypical and generalised view of black people is that they are all good at athletics and dancing, whereas it is probably the case that they have excelled at those activities because they have had opportunities to do so, while other professions remain closed to them in our society. *Branded* is a very emotive word: in the days of slavery slaves were branded with red-hot iron with a symbol to show who they belonged to. Zephaniah seems to be suggesting that casual racial stereotyping is almost a continuation of slavery. By contrast to athletics and dancing, he asserts 'I am a born academic' and *I a versatile*, although white people insist on pigeon-holing him because of his race.

But as the title asserts – 'no problem' – he can cope with racial stereotyping although he clearly does not think it is right or fair. He is still able to *greet yu wid a smile* and the racist taunts and stunts he has been the victim of have left him with no grudge – *I have no chip on me shoulders*. The poem ends with a joke. It is not uncommon to hear white people speak in racist terms or say things based on racist stereotypes and finish by asserting that *Some of my best friends are black*. Zephaniah, having asserted that he is *versatile*, cannot be pigeon-holed and that *Black is not the problem*, jokes by saying *Sum of me best friends are white*.

This is essentially quite a light-hearted poem but with very serious issues at its core. The language Zephaniah uses is a mixture of Black British words and standard English. The Black British words assert his pride in his identity, while the standard English words show his education – he is, after all, *versatile*. The poem uses rhyme throughout but rejects traditional punctuation, probably because it is too conventional. The title of the poem is double-edged: 'No problem' is often used in everyday speech and Zephaniah's use of it is appropriate given the jocular tone of the poem. However, racism is a real and serious problem.

Conflict

There is a clear conflict in this poem between real black people and the stereotypes we have of black people, and the poem mocks or ridicules our stereotyping of black people and argues that they cannot be pigeon-holed – they are as varied in their accomplishments as white people.

Why?

This poem by Benjamin Zephaniah:

- rejects the casual, unthinking racial stereotyping of black people by white people.

- celebrates the poet's black identity.

- is light-hearted in tone but deals with serious issues by ridiculing them.

'What Were They Like?' – Denise Levertov

Author and Context

Denise Levertov (24 October 1923 – 20 December 1997) was a British-born American poet. During the course of a prolific career, Denise Levertov created a highly-regarded body of poetry that reflects her beliefs as an artist and a humanist. Her work embraces a wide variety of genres and themes, including nature lyrics, love poems, protest poetry, and poetry inspired by her faith in God. Levertov was born and grew up in Ilford, Essex. Her mother, Beatrice Adelaide (née Spooner-Jones) Levertoff, came from a small mining village in North Wales. Her father, Paul Levertoff, had been a teacher at Leipzig University and as a Russian Hassidic Jew was held under house arrest during the First World War as an 'enemy alien' by virtue of his ethnicity. He emigrated to the UK and became an Anglican priest after converting to Christianity. In the mistaken belief that he would want to preach in a Jewish neighbourhood, he was housed in Ilford, within reach of a parish in Shoreditch, in East London. His daughter wrote, "My father's Hasidic ancestry, his being steeped in Jewish and Christian scholarship and mysticism, his fervour and eloquence as a preacher, were factors built into my cells". Levertov, who was educated at home, showed an enthusiasm for writing from an early age and studied ballet, art, piano and French as well as standard subjects. She wrote about the strangeness she felt growing up part Jewish, German, Welsh and English, but not fully belonging to any of these identities. She notes that it leant her a sense of being special rather than excluded: "[I knew] before I was ten that I was an artist-person and I had a destiny". She noted: "Humanitarian politics came early into my life: seeing my father on a soapbox protesting Mussolini's invasion of Abyssinia; my father and sister both on soap-boxes protesting Britain's lack of support for Spain; my mother canvasing long before those events for the League of Nations Union; and all three of them working on behalf of the German and Austrian refugees from 1933 onwards... I used to sell the *Daily Worker* house-to-house in the working class streets of Ilford Lane". The

Daily Worker was a Communist newspaper and in the Spanish Civil War a socialist government fought a war against fascist rebels - who won and who imposed a brutal fascist dictatorship on Spain.

When she was five years old, she declared she would be a writer. At the age of 12, she sent some of her poems to T. S. Eliot, who replied with a two-page letter of encouragement. In 1940, when she was 17, Levertov published her first poem. During the Blitz, Levertov served in London as a civilian nurse. Her first book, *The Double Image*, was published six years later. In 1947, she met and married American writer Mitchell Goodman and moved with him to the United States the following year. Although Levertov and Goodman would eventually divorce in 1975, they did have one son, Nikolai, together and lived mainly in New York City, summering in Maine. In 1955, she became a naturalised American citizen and is considered an American poet. She achieved fame through a series of books which dealt with the Vietnam War.

Vietnam had been a French colony until 1954. When the French withdrew a civil war broke out between Communist North Vietnam and capitalist South Vietnam. North Vietnam's aim was to unite the country, South Vietnam's to preserve its independence. However, this took place during the Cold War and America intervened (initially with military advisers) in order to help South Vietnam and to stop the spread of Communism. However, the South Vietnamese were clearly losing the war. So in 1964 the USA began to bomb North Vietnam and in 1965 it sent 200, 000 combat troops to Vietnam. The heavy bombing of North Vietnam continued: in May 1964 the American general, Curtis Le May, said in a quotation that became notorious: *Tell the Vietnamese they've got to draw in their horns or we're going to bomb them back to the Stone Age.*

As the 1960s wore on, the Americans committed more and more troops to Vietnam until there were half a million there by 1968. However, although the USA was the world's military superpower and possessed military technology that was far superior to the North Vietnamese army, it was clear that North Vietnam were winning the war by using hit-and-run guerrilla tactics and avoiding large-scale open battles with the American army.

Back home in the USA, the war became increasingly unpopular and a growing anti-war movement quickly grew and huge public protests were held. Marshall McLuhan, a cultural commentator, said in 1975:

TV brought the brutality of war into the comfort of the living room. Vietnam was lost in the living rooms of America – not on the battlefields of Vietnam.

From 1970, America began to withdraw its troops but continued to bomb North Vietnam with its aircraft. By 1973, all American ground troops has been withdrawn, leaving only advisers. By 1975, the North Vietnamese Army seized the capital of South Vietnam, Saigon, and the war was over and the country was unified. America's military might have been humiliated.

This poem (published in 1971) is part of domestic American protest against the Vietnam War.

jade – is a semi-precious rock, usually green in colour, which is used to make ornaments and jewellery.

paddies – flooded fields in Asia used to grow rice.

epic poem – a long narrative poem which tells of brave and heroic deeds.

Who? There are two speakers: the first asks questions which form the first stanza; the second answers each question in turn and in detail. We cannot tell who the speakers are but it is clear that the first speaker holds some sort of authority or importance because the second speaker address him as 'Sir'.

When? In an imagined future in which America has won the war and completely obliterated Vietnam, its people and culture.

Where? There is no specific location.

What? The questions are asked to ascertain the truth about the Vietnamese way of life and culture.

The first question is:

Did the people of Vietnam

use lanterns of stone?

To which the answer is;

Sir, their light hearts turned to stone.

it is not remembered whether in gardens

stone gardens illumined pleasant ways.

Their light hearts turning to stone is an effect of the war. The passive voice of 'it is not remembered' is chilling here as is the implication the pleasant ways no longer exist because they have been destroyed.

The second question is:

Did they hold ceremonies

to reverence the opening of buds?

The answer is:

Perhaps they gathered once to delight in blossoms,

but after their children were killed

there were no more buds.

A response that is full of anguished empathy for the child victims of the war.

The questioner asks: *Were they inclined to quiet laughter?* which elicits the response *Sir, laughter is bitter to the burned mouth* – a line which manages to suggest both the physical suffering of the Vietnamese (burned mouth) and their psychological suffering – they have forgotten how to laugh.

The next question – *Did they use bone and ivory/jade and silver for ornament?* – elicits a longer answer:

Ornament is for joy.

All the bones were charred,

it is not remembered. Remember,

Most were peasants; their life

was in rice and bamboo.

When peaceful clouds were reflected in the paddies

and the water buffalo stepped surely along terraces,

maybe fathers told their sons old tales.

I have quoted this answer at length because it gives us a more complete picture of how Levertov presents the Vietnamese people in the poem: they are presented by the poet as simple, innocent, gentle people living a humble and simple existence; however close that may be to the truth is irrelevant: in the poem and in the poem's context Levertov's presentation of their way of life like this is a direct and peaceful contrast to the destructive military might of the American Army with its ability to bomb the Vietnamese into surrender. They have no epic poem, although Levertov speculates that *fathers told their sons tales* – the past tense is significant since they no longer tell their sons tales because they no longer exist as a people.

The final question is: *Did they distinguish between speech and singing?* The respondent says that their speech was *like a song* and their singing *resembled moths in moonlight* – a gentle, peaceful image. But the truth is that no one knows because *it is silent now.* In Levertov's imagined future, Vietnamese culture and its people have been wiped out.

The poem is written in free verse which is appropriate as the respondent struggles to give coherent answers to the questions asked.

This poem became rapidly famous when it was published in 1971. Some readers felt she was being slightly patronising to the Vietnamese – who had a fully developed cultural life and were not all simple peasants; however, that is to miss the point of the poem, I think. The poem is for an American audience and it serves as a piece of anti-war propaganda and, in contrast to the brutality of American mass bombing of North Vietnamese cities, Levertov is quite consciously trying to create sympathy and empathy for the Vietnamese.

Conflict

This poem deals with the aftermath of a conflict and, within the poem itself, there is little conflict – but it only came to be written because of the Vietnam War. We might sense a minor conflict in the poem between the dryly academic and dispassionate questions of the opening stanza, and the answering voice which is keen to provoke sympathy and empathy for the Vietnamese people. There are also oblique references to the effects of the conflict between the USA and North Vietnam: *their children were killed*; *the burned mouth*; *All the bones were charred* and *When bombs smashed those/Mirrors there was only time to scream*. And thus the second voice gives us details of the conflict designed to shock the reader.

Why?

This poem by Denise Levertov:

- is set in an imaginary future (North Vietnam actually won the war and ejected the Americans).
- is a poem which protests about American tactics and involvement in Vietnam.
- arouses sympathy for the Vietnamese people.
- warns against the possible genocide of the Vietnamese people and uses chilling images to suggest that eventual fate.

TIME & PLACE

Introduction

Before we look at any of the poems from the anthology, I want to briefly examine some poems in which time and place are important to give you a taste of the approach that will be followed throughout the rest of the book. So we will start by looking at two completely different poems. I am not going to subject either to a full analysis, but I will demonstrate with both poems some crucial ways of reading poetry and give you some general guidance which will stand you in good stead when we deal with the poems in the anthology itself. This is not meant to confuse you, but to help. I cannot stress enough that these poems are not ones that you will be assessed on. They are my choice – and I would use the same method in the classroom – introducing a class very slowly to poetry and 'warming up' for the anthology by practising the sorts of reading skills which will help with any poem. Besides, you may find the method valuable in your preparation for answering on the unseen poem in the exam.

Here is a poem in which Place is important:

'Spellbound' – Emily Jane Brontë

The night is darkening round me,
The wild winds coldly blow;
But a tyrant spell has bound me
And I cannot, cannot go.

The giant trees are bending
Their bare boughs weighed with snow.
And the storm is fast descending,
And yet I cannot go.

Clouds beyond clouds above me,
Wastes beyond wastes below;
But nothing drear can move me;

I will not, cannot go.

Context

Emily Brontë (1818 – 1848) was one of the three famous Brontë sisters who lived in the village of Haworth in Yorkshire. They are famous for their writing, but also because they all had tragically short lives, as did their brother Branwell. Emily's poems were first published in 1846 in a volume of poetry along with others by her sisters – Charlotte and Anne. They published under the assumed names of Ellis, Currer and Acton Bell – so readers would not know they were women and not judge their work harshly as a result of knowing their sex. All three sisters went on to publish novels which you may come across in your other reading in English. Emily published *Wuthering Heights* which is an astonishing book. It has been televised and made into several different film versions. Emily adored the wildness and rugged beauty of the Yorkshire moors and this can be seen in *Wuthering Heights* and this poem.

This poem was written in November 1837 when Emily was nineteen. This poem is usually thought of as belonging to Emily's 'Gondal' period; 'Gondal' was an imaginary world created by the Brontë children in which heroes and heroines battled against terrible and desperate situations. The Brontës (including their brother) wrote poems and short stories set in Gondal which are all linked and interwoven with each other. Fannie Ratchford in *Complete Poems of Emily Jane Brontë*, suggests that this poem refers to an earlier incident in the Gondal chronicles when one of the heroines exposes her child to die on the moors in winter. She cannot bear to watch the child die but she cannot tear herself away from the scene.

tyrant – an absolute ruler, an oppressor.

drear – dreary, gloomy, cheerless.

Who? An unidentified narrator – although the context above suggests it is a mother who has abandoned her baby.

When? At the start of the night. The poem is written in the present tense.

Where? Outdoors. The narrator is vulnerable to the storm which is coming. We might also say, given what we know, that the setting is the Yorkshire moors near Haworth.

What? The narrator, despite the awful weather conditions, cannot leave the moors.

Commentary

This poem is written in the first person and the present tense and this gives it an immediacy and vibrancy. The poem begins as night is falling; in the second stanza there is snow on the trees and the storm is coming; in the final stanza the narrator is surrounded by clouds and wastes. The narrator is held by *a tyrant spell*, but there is a progression in her attitude: in the first two stanzas she says she cannot go, but in the final line she expresses defiance – *I will not go* – the act of braving the storm has become a conscious act.

The fact that it is written in the ballad form is important too: it gives it the feel of something old and ancient as well as creating an insistent rhythm. This rhythm is re-enforced by heavy alliteration – *wild winds, bending... bare boughs* – simple repetition – *clouds* and *wastes* and *cannot* – and the consonance on the letter *l* especially in the first stanza, but throughout the poem. The speaker is encompassed by the storm – it is round her, above her and below her: there is no escape. The poem is given an added air of mystery by the *spell* – which like the trees – is personified.

If we accept the context of this poem suggested above – a mother who has abandoned her child on the moors – then this is a poem about the strength of maternal bonds and the fierceness and passion of a mother's love. Even this terrible storm cannot force her away from her baby. In this interpretation the storm may be seen as a pathetic fallacy for her own mental state at the abandonment of her baby.

However, it was published on its own, without any reference to the original setting of Gondal and the poem means something different, we might argue, on its own. In Victorian times women really were second class citizens. Once they married all their property automatically transferred to their husbands; they did not have the vote and would not get it until the 20th century. The Brontë sisters growing up in a genteel, middle class vicar's family would have been protected from the harsh realities of life and would have been expected to excel at needlework, drawing, playing musical instruments, water-colouring, painting. We know that Emily liked to wander around the moors near the family home, even in appalling weather conditions – and this was probably seen as slightly odd behaviour at the time.

So what? You are probably thinking. But if this is true, then 'Spellbound' becomes a poem of great courage and the wilful pursuit of risk and danger. It can be seen as an assertion of Brontë's determination to experience the full energy and force of the storm, to give herself up to elemental forces, to rebel against the protected, insulated life that was expected of middle-class Victorian ladies. Remember the last line which expresses her wilful determination – *I will not go*. This can be seen as a determined cry for independence and freedom – despite the risks that exist from being exposed to the storm.

Why?

This simple ballad powerfully communicates:

- a sense of the power of nature which inspires awe not fear.

- a woman's determined struggle for freedom from the stifling conditions of Victorian middle class existence.

- a sense of courage and resilience even when faced with the most hostile conditions.

- the narrator's sense of isolation.

- the narrator's desire for danger, risk and excitement.

The poems by Wordsworth and Emily Brontë share important features: they both stress the power of nature, and they both connect their own feelings with the place in which the poem is set. Indeed, the two locations – the mountains surrounding Wordsworth's lake and the storm on the moors that Brontë's speaker endures - are both integral to the overall meaning of both poems, however they are interpreted.

The Wild Swans at Coole – W B Yeats

The trees are in their autumn beauty,
The woodland paths are dry,
Under the October twilight the water
Mirrors a still sky;
Upon the brimming water among the stones
Are nine-and-fifty swans.

The nineteenth autumn has come upon me
Since I first made my count;
I saw, before I had well finished,
All suddenly mount
And scatter wheeling in great broken rings
Upon their clamorous wings.

I have looked upon those brilliant creatures,
And now my heart is sore.
All's changed since I, hearing at twilight,
The first time on this shore,
The bell-beat of their wings above my head,
Trod with a lighter tread.

Unwearied still, lover by lover,
They paddle in the cold
Companionable streams or climb the air;

Their hearts have not grown old;
Passion or conquest, wander where they will,
Attend upon them still.

But now they drift on the still water,
Mysterious, beautiful;
Among what rushes will they build,
By what lake's edge or pool
Delight men's eyes when I awake some day
To find they have flown away?

Context

William Butler Yeats (1865 – 1939) lived through a momentous period of Irish history as there were growing calls for independence from Britain, much violence and finally, in 1922, the establishment of the Irish Free State. Yeats was very interested in the pagan roots of Irish culture and ancient Irish myths, as well as the occult and mysticism. In 1898 he met the Irish playwright Lady Augusta Gregory and from then on spent his summers at her home at Coole Park, County Galway – which is the setting for this poem. Yeats once described Coole Park as the most beautiful place on earth. This poem was the title poem in the collection *The Wild Swans at Coole*, published in 1917.

Who? Yeats, his younger self and the swans on the lake. Yeats writes in the first person and the present tense, although he uses the past tense to look backwards and switches to the future tense in the final stanza.

When? October 1916. The poem was dated when it was first published. Yeats was 51 and still unmarried and childless.

Where? At the lake at Coole Park in Ireland.

What? Yeats watches the swans and thinks about the first time he saw them and reflects on his life.

Commentary

The opening stanza is peaceful and describes the present. It is autumn and evening – there is a sense that things are coming to an end – the year and the day, but it is beautiful to look at. In the second stanza Yeats tells us that he first came to this lake 19 years ago and counted the swans, who rose up and flew away before he had finished. The third stanza starts to reveal the central idea of the poem: when Yeats first saw these swans he was younger and *trod with a lighter tread*; he was full of youthful optimism, but now his heart is *sore*. The swans, by way of contrast, are unchanged – *Their hearts have not grown old*, which implies that Yeats' heart has. He no longer has the energy for *passion* and *conquest* which still come naturally to the swans. The final stanza looks into the future and wonders where the swans will go next. There is certainty that they will delight men's eyes, but there will come a day when Yeats wakes up and the swans have gone.

The poem centres around two contrasts: Yeats as he is now compared with his younger self; and Yeats in contrast with the swans. The beauty and unchanging nature of the swans is emphasised throughout this poem. Compared to humans they have a beauty, power and grace which never changes. They almost become a symbol of the love that Yeats feels he has no energy for at his age and with a series of unsuccessful romances behind him. By contrast the swans are paired, *lover by lover*, but Yeats is alone and lonely. The swans are *brilliant creatures*: their wings are *clamorous*, like a bell-beat. They are *unwearied still; their hearts have not grown old*; they still have the energy for passion or conquest; they are beautiful and mysterious. They are also, as the title points out, *wild* – a word Yeats associated with passion and energy. Note the repetition of the word *still* throughout the poem: this suggests the unchanging nature of the swans and through the idea of stillness, the fact that we cannot tell what lies beneath the beautiful appearance of the lake and the scene: Yeats is deeply troubled and unhappy. The fact that the final stanza ends with a question shows Yeats' uncertainty about the future and his essential pessimism about love and growing old. Yeats has lost his youthful energy and passion. The second stanza expresses well the energy and passion of the swans:

All suddenly mount

And scatter wheeling in great broken rings

Upon their clamorous wings

Here the verbs of motion - *mount, scatter, wheeling* – all suggest an energy which Yeats no longer has. If the swans are a symbol for love then the final sentence imagines a time when there will no love at all in Yeats' life. It is also interesting to note that Yeats was going through a period during which he was producing hardly any poetry, so that his creative block might also influence his mood in this poem.

Why?

This very famous poem has certain key themes:

- it identifies the unchanging energy and beauty of nature.

- it reflects rather sadly on growing old and the lack of power and energy that older people may feel.

- it is a poem that seems to be bidding farewell to love and relationships.

- it uses the swans as a symbol, a symbolic contrast to everything that Yeats is.

- it meditates on human memory and the passing of time: the swans seem not to have changed, but everything about Yeats has changed.

Just like Wordsworth and Rossetti, Yeats uses Place to reflect on his own feelings, but there is a difference: in Wordsworth Nature takes on a moral force which educates the young Wordsworth; in Brontë, as we have seen, the storm takes on symbolic meanings and helps to define the poet's resistance and rebelliousness; Yeats is more interested in the contrast between him and the swans.

Now one last poem on Place before we start to look at the Anthology itself.

Storm in The Black Forest
By D H Lawrence

Now it is almost night, from the bronzey soft sky

jugfull after jugfull of pure white liquid fire, bright white

tipples over and spills down,

and is gone

and gold-bronze flutters beat through the thick upper air.

And as the electric liquid pours out, sometimes

a still brighter white snake wriggles among it, spilled

and tumbling wriggling down the sky :

and then the heavens cackle with uncouth sounds.

And the rain won't come, the rain refuses to come!

This is the electricity that man is supposed to have mastered

chained, subjugated to his own use!

supposed to!

Context

David Herbert Lawrence (1885 – 1930) is better known as novelist. He was born in the coal-mining town of Eastwood near Nottingham and came from a working class background. He travelled widely and also wrote over 800 poems, most of them in free verse. He also wrote some well-known short stories and three plays. Lawrence believed in spontaneity and naturalness, and many of his poems are about love and relationships or, as this one is, the power of nature. He felt that modern man was insulated by technology and civilization from his true self and from nature. This attitude can be seen in the final stanza of this poem.

We think this poem was written late in his life. In a notebook entry for July 20th 1929, Lawrence wrote: *Last night a long and lurid thunderstorm poured out endless white electricity.* He was staying at a hotel in Lichtenthal on the edge of the Black Forest in Germany.

cackle – to laugh.

uncouth – awkward, ungraceful.

subjugated – to be conquered or overpowered.

Who? The poet speaks as himself in the present tense.

When? It is almost night on July 19th 1929.

Where? On the edge of the Black Forest in Germany.

What? Lawrence describes the coming of a thunder storm.

Commentary

This poem is written in a very fluid free verse form with four stanzas of varying lengths. Lawrence liked to experiment and there is some truth in the observation that he was the first British-born poet in the twentieth century to embrace fully the lack of restrictions that free verse allows.

The first two stanzas describe the approach of the storm; the third single line stanza describes the rain which still has not started to fall; and the final stanza is Lawrence's comment on what he has seen.

The choice of free verse does seem especially suited to the subject matter here. The lines are very unequal in length; some are end-stopped; some use enjambment – it is all very unpredictable like the storm itself, like the natural world. The opening stanza describes the lightning in a series of beautiful and awe-filled phrases. Look at the combination of assonance and consonance in the opening line:

Now it is almost night, from the bronzey soft sky.

There is a tendency amongst some readers to think that free verse requires less skill and craft to write, but it can involve a very high level of patterning to do with sounds or repetition. Lawrence uses assonance again in lines two and three: the long *i* sounds of *white/fire/bright/white* and the shorter *i* sounds of *liquid/tipples/spills*. There is more assonance in *gold-bronze* and the unusual collocation *flutters bent*. The storm is alive.

The second stanza continues the metaphor of the lightning as *liquid fire* and introduces a new metaphor – the *white snake*. Here Lawrence continues to use assonance on short and long *i* sounds, and he combines it with verbs of great energy and movement – *pours, wriggles, spilled, tumbling, wriggling*. In the final line we hear the thunder:

And then the heavens cackle with uncouth sounds

and the alliteration on *c* and the longer vowel sounds in *cackle, uncouth* and *sounds* act as a contrast to the shorter sounds associated with the lightning – *electric liquid*. The heavens are personified here too and we cannot say that the lightning has been personified but it has been animated and brought alive.

Ironically the rain refuses to come. The final stanza represents a complete change of tone. Lawrence sounds amused - not at the storm and its lightning and thunder, but at the human assumption that we have somehow tamed electricity, that we can make nature do what we want. Lawrence seems delighted that nature cannot be mastered, cannot be chained by human beings. Lawrence uses the language of slavery to show the human desire to control nature, but laughs at our inability to do so.

Why?

Lawrence uses the extreme liberty of free verse to

- celebrate the power and majesty of nature.

- to mock human boasts that we can tame nature.

- to suggest that we should show a greater sense of awe and respect towards nature.

- gives a vivid impression and shows admiration for the dangerous strength of nature.

TIME & PLACE

'To Autumn' – John Keats

Author and Context

John Keats (31 October 1795 – 23 February 1821) was an English Romantic poet. He was one of the main figures of the second generation of Romantic poets along with Lord Byron and Percy Bysshe Shelley, despite his work having been in publication for only four years before his death. Although his poems were not generally well received by critics during his life, his reputation grew after his death, so that by the end of the 19th century, he had become one of the most beloved of all English poets. He had a significant influence on a diverse range of poets and writers, and the Pre-Raphaelite painters.

The poetry of Keats is characterised by sensual imagery, most notably in the series of odes. Today his poems and letters are some of the most popular and most analysed in English literature. Keats suffered from tuberculosis, for which, at the time, there was no cure and as a result, perhaps, many of his poems are tinged with sadness and thoughts of mortality, as well as having a keen eye for the beauties of nature and the pains of unrequited love.

gourd – a large hard-rinded fleshy fruit of the cucumber family – often hollowed out and used as a container.

kernel – the edible part of a nut.

granary – a store house for grain.

winnowing – to separate the edible part of grain from the inedible part (the chaff) – which used to be done by the wind as the chaff is lighter.

hook – a scythe, a cutting implement to harvest the corn.

gleaner – someone who gathers any ears of corn left by the main reaper.

barrèd clouds – clouds arranged to looks like bars in the sky.

sallows – shallows.

Who? The poet writes an Ode to celebrate all the good things autumn and harvest time brings us.

When? In autumn. Keats wrote the poem on September 19th, 1819, after a long walk in the countryside. He wrote to a friend; ' How beautiful the season is now – How fine the air. A temperate sharpness about it. Really, without joking, chaste weather – Dian skies – I never liked stubble fields as much as now – Aye better than the chilly green of the spring. Somehow a stubble plain looks warm – in the same way that some pictures look warm – this struck me much in my Sunday's walk that I composed upon it.'

Where? Locations shift throughout the poem, but the whole poem is set in the countryside.

What? Some poets in some poems see autumn as a precursor of winter, but Keats is concerned to emphasize autumn's richness and the beauty of the harvest.

Commentary

'To Autumn' is an ode split into three stanzas of eleven lines and with a complex rhyme scheme. The first four lines rhyme ABAB and the next seven CDECDDE. An ode is a serious and dignified lyric poem which eulogizes its subject matter: it is a poem of praise and celebration. The rhyme scheme (which is grand and difficult)Keats uses could be said to befit the beauty and seriousness of his subject matter: it is aesthetically pleasing.In the ode Keats personifies Autumn: the first stanza personifies Autumn (and the sun) in a generalized way and this personification is given added force in the second and third verses by use of apostrophe – Keats addresses Autumn directly. Furthermore, Autumn is personified as a woman who, along with the sun, brings the fruits to ripeness.

The opening line of the poem is justly famous and memorable:

Season of mists and mellow fruitfulness

The preponderance of the soft letters – s, f, l and m – give a warm and tender tone to the line. The first stanza presents the early stages of Autumn – the weather is still hot, so much so that the bees 'think warm days will never cease' and the stanza celebrates the growth and sheer plenitude of autumn with all the fruits and nuts swelling as they approach ripeness. In another famous phrase Autumn is described as the

Close bosom-friend of the maturing sun,

Conspiring with him

how to swell and ripen all the fruits in time for the harvest. Everything in the stanza comes to ripeness – the sun, the vines, the apples, the gourds, the nuts – even the hives are 'o'erbrimmed' with honey. The opening stanza is full of words which suggest repleteness and fullness: 'fill all fruit', 'swell', 'plump', 'o'erbrimmed' – as well as the apples bending with the weight of their ripeness.

The second stanza starts by apostrophizing the season (addressing Autumn):

Who have not seen thee oft amid thy store?

In this stanza the ripening process is complete and Keats describes the outcome. The personified Autumn is to be found in a granary surrounded by the harvested grain or asleep in a 'half-reaped furrow'. Autumn also appears as 'a gleaner' and at the end of the stanza is to be found

... by a cider-press, with patient look,

Thou [Autumn] watchest the last oozings, hours by hours.

The second stanza has a sleepy, lazy tone and mood because the harvest has been gathered in and all the hard work has been done. Keats celebrates the sheer bounty of nature with a tone of wonder and intense satisfaction.

The third stanza looks forward to winter and the scene is evening: the poem progresses through time in two ways: the development of autumn and, broadly, the progression through the day. However, Keats starts the stanza in an original way by asking a question:

Where are the songs of Spring? Aye, where are they?

Think not of them – thou hast thy music too.

There are many poems in English which praise the Spring: Keats is arguing that Autumn too deserves praise for its songs and its attractions. Keats paints the beauty of Autumn:

... while barrèd clouds bloom the soft dying day,

And touch the stubble-plains with rosy hue.

But winter is approaching:

... in a wailful choir the small gnats mourn

and the 'light wind lives or dies'. The gnats are mourning because winter will come and they will die. Just as the first verse was full of images of ripeness and fullness, the third verse is full of images of dying – because the end of Autumn is the start of winter – but it is not as simple as that.

On line 30 Keats mentions the 'full grown lambs' but this implies the new-born lambs that the following spring will bring. In the final line Keats writes of the 'gathering swallows' that 'twitter in the skies': they are gathering to make their annual migration, but they will return the following year in late spring. Therefore, while the final stanza contains images of death and precursors of winter, it also contains hints of spring and the seasons' annual cycle of renewal. The poems progress through Autumn and through a single day is complete as the day is 'soft-dying' as the sun sets. This stanza is given added piquancy because Keats suffered from tuberculosis and knew that he would probably die at a relatively young age.

This leads neatly on to the poem's other themes. Keats' poem is at heart a celebration of Autumn and the harvest – the sheer fullness of the harvest and the combined companionship of the sun and the season. Keats presents the harvest in all its glorious plenitude, but the final stanza mentions that winter is on its way. The other great themes of 'Ode to Autumn' are mutability and stability. In the final stanza the swallows are gathering to migrate – winter with its harsh weather is on its way – so the seasons are mutable – they change. But they also represent stability too: the swallows will return next summer and the process of growth to the autumnal harvest will begin again. Reassuringly in one sense the seasons will continue in their natural cycle even after Keats' death.

Keats does not write about one specific named place (unlike many of the poets in the Anthology), but summons up a sense of a generic English landscape at harvest time: specific places are mentioned – the granary, the room with the cider press, the bank on which the tired gleaner dozes – but these have a generic quality and this is surely appropriate because Keats wants to suggest a whole country's harvest coming to fruition at the same time. If there is a single place in Keats' poem, it is the English countryside.

In 'Ode to Autumn' Keats:

- eulogizes the fecundity and plenitude of the English harvest;
- captures the lazy, hazy days of late summer through his word choice;
- brings the harvest and the sun alive through personification;
- introduces more serious themes such as mutability, stability and death and time.

'Composed upon Westminster Bridge, September 3rd, 1802' – William Wordsworth

Author and Context

You can read about Wordsworth on page 24. Here I want to stress how important a city London was in 1802. Although the British Empire was not at its height, London was the capital city of an enormous empire and much of the trade connected with Empire passed through the port of London. It was the biggest city in the world and must have been a truly impressive sight. However, as a poem, it presents a major contrast to William Blake's 'London', the next poem in the Anthology.

garment – article of clothing.

temples – mainly churches and cathedrals, but some synagogues.

Who? The poet as himself writes a sonnet of praise to the city he sees in front of him. (In reality he was accompanied by his sister but she is not mentioned in the poem.)

When? Dawn on September 3rd, 1802.

Where? Halfway across Westminster Bridge.

What? Wordsworth writes a eulogy about the city's magnificence and splendour.

Commentary

'Composed upon Westminster Bridge, September 3rd, 1802' is a Petrarchan sonnet and one of Wordsworth's most famous. Its subject matter is slightly surprising because the vast bulk of Wordsworth's poetry is about nature and the poems are frequently set in the English Lake District, and so the fact that he chose to write a sonnet about London is itself somewhat surprising. He generally sticks to the iambic pentameter, but the first two lines begin with a trochaic foot – an abrupt and arresting start to the poem.

The sonnet is a eulogy to London and its *majesty*:

Earth has not anything to show more fair.

Anyone who can pass by without being impressed is *dull... of soul*. In a simple simile the city is said to wear *the beauty of the morning like a garment* – showing how suited it is to its grandeur and appropriate and natural its majesty is to it. In line 6 the asyndetic list draws attention to the 'official' buildings of London – the buildings which are part of the architectural wonders of the city. The ships remind us that the port of Lonon was the hub of a fast-growing and prosperous empire. The whole scene is arresting and memorable (and a complete contrast to William Blake's 'London'). It is

All bright and glittering in the smokeless air.

In line 9 there is a turn or volta as Wordsworth turns to nature to heap more hyperbolic praise on London. He asserts that

Never did sun more beautifully steep

In his first splendour valley, rock or hill;

Ne'er saw I, never felt, a calm so deep!

The river glideth of his own sweet will!

It is interesting that Wordsworth turns to his habitual subject (nature) in order to better express the marvel and wonder that London presented to Wordsworth on the morning of September 3rd, 1802.

The penultimate line begins with an exclamatory spondee and a wonderful sense of the city about to burst into life:

Dear God! the very houses seem asleep;

And all that mighty heart is lying still.

In this sonnet Wordsworth:

- eulogizes London as the most magnificent sight on earth;
- compares it favourably to natural phenomena;
- is impressed by the power it wields through its institutions;
- likes and enjoys the quietness of the city;
- uses the volta to introduce natural imagery;
- time and place are integral to this poem – even the fact that it is dawn and there is no-one about.

'London' – William Blake

Context and Author

William Blake (1757 – 1827) is now seen as the foremost artist and poet of his time, but his work was largely unknown during his lifetime. He was a painter as well as a poet and you can see some of his paintings in art galleries like Tate Britain in London or the Fitzwilliam Museum in Cambridge. 'London' comes from a collection *Songs of Innocence and of Experience* which appeared together for the first time in 1794. *The Songs of Innocence* (which originally appeared on their own in 1789) are positive in tone and celebrate unspoilt nature, childhood and love. *The Songs of Experience* (from which 'London' comes) depicts a corrupt society in which the prevailing mood is one of despair and in which children are exploited and love is corrupted.

This poem is often read as a profound criticism of the society Blake lived in. Everything in London is owned (*chartered*) - even the River Thames which is a natural force which one might expect to be free. Blake was writing at a time when Britain was the wealthiest country in the world because of its global empire and because of the Industrial Revolution which produced goods which were exported all over the world. But not everyone shared in this enormous wealth; the gap between rich and poor was huge, with the poor suffering really terrible living and working conditions. This poem first 'appeared' (this term will be explained below) in 1794. The date of publication is crucial: Blake is partly seeing London in this way because of events in France. In 1789 the French Revolution began, changing French society forever and ushering in a new age of freedom, equality and brotherhood. Many English people saw what was happening in France and thought it was good to have a society based on greater equality; they looked critically at British society and saw appalling inequalities and injustices. For example, you may be aware that this was the period in British history that some people campaigned against slavery in the British Empire: what is less well-known is that forms of slavery existed in London. There are recorded cases of parents selling their sons to master chimneysweeps in London. The life of a chimney sweep was likely to be short: they were sent up the chimneys of large houses to clean them. Some suffocated; others were trapped in the confined space and died; sometimes their masters would light fires below them to encourage them to work faster – they sometimes were burnt alive. For those who survived, their health was affected: they suffered from terrible lung complaints as a result of breathing in coal dust and, because of poor hygiene, might also succumb to testicular cancer brought on by the accumulated layers of biting coal dust.

Blake had produced *Songs of Innocence* on its own in 1789, although we can tell from his surviving notebooks that he always intended to write *Songs of Experience*. I have used the term 'appeared' because they were not published in a conventional sense. Blake produced each copy of *Songs of Innocence and of Experience* at home by hand and copies were then given to friends and acquaintances. Part of this was Blake's own choice, but we can easily see that his views about Britain and its government would have been highly controversial, so open publication of them may have led to charges of sedition or treason. The British government at the time were terrified of a revolution here, like the one in France, and were doing everything they could to silence people like Blake who were critical of the society in which they lived.

Blake earned his living as an engraver. Before photographs and modern ways of reproducing images, engravings were the cheapest and easiest way of illustrating a book. Blake produced illustrations for other people's books throughout his life – that was how he earned a living. To create an engraving, the engraver has to carve, with a specialist knife, lines on a metal plate; when the plate is then covered in ink and pressed on paper the lines appear on the paper.

Blake used the same technique for reproducing his own poems. After coating the metal plate with ink and producing the outline, Blake coloured each page of each copy of *Songs of Innocence and of Experience* by hand with water colour paint. It is estimated that only 25 copies were produced in his lifetime. If you go to the British Museum you can see one copy: it is tiny and exquisitely detailed and, of course, very personal, because Blake coloured it by hand himself. In addition, to produce his poems in this way was time-consuming and arduous, since in order for the words to appear the right way round when the page was printed, they had to be written in mirror hand-writing on the plate – a painstaking process that must have taken hours and shows not only Blake's artistry, but also his devotion to hard work.

chartered – owned. The charter was a legal document proving possession.

mark – to notice.

marks – signs.

ban – a government edict banning people from doing something.

manacles – handcuffs or leg-irons.

hapless – unlucky.

harlot – prostitute.

marriage hearse – an oxymoron; Blake juxtaposes the idea of death (hearses carry the dead body to the graveyard) with life – marriage often produces children.

Who? The narrator recounts what he sees in the first stanza and in the next three stanzas what he hears as he wanders around London. The poem is written in the present tense which gives it an immediacy and greater impact.

When? 1794.

Where? London.

What? The narrator sees and hears a population suffering and full of pain and despair.

Commentary

The poem's narrator wanders through the streets of London looking at the suffering of his fellow citizens which is apparent on their faces. The first stanza concentrates on what he sees; the second stanza changes to the sounds he can hear and this continues until the end of the poem. Everywhere he goes he sees people who are repressed and downtrodden; in the third stanza he hears the cry of a chimney sweep and the sigh of a soldier; in the final stanza, at night, at midnight, he hears the curse of *the youthful harlot* (very young prostitute) whose *curse* rings out in the night and *blasts* the *marriage-hearse*. We might note that there is no interaction between Blake and the sights and sounds he sees; the only interaction that there is evidence of is the *new-born infant* in the final stanza – the product of a sexual act – but the baby cries and is born into a world of misery and degradation. Nowhere in the poem do we meet a complete human being: we see their marks and hear them, but there is no encounter with any complete human being, suggesting at once their isolation, but also their lack of completeness and community in this horrifying city.

In the first stanza Blake uses simple repetition of the word *chartered* and *marks* (although with a slightly different meaning). The oppression he sees is all-consuming – he sees it in every face he meets. Note the last line which uses parallelism of sound:

Marks of weakness, marks of woe.

The word *mark* is repeated and is then followed by two words which alliterate. This combination of the letter *m* and *w* is very soft and gentle and creates a sense of overwhelming sadness. Note how *mark* starts as a verb in a very innocuous sense and then becomes a repeated noun, suggesting that there is an indelible mark on all the citizens of London.

The second stanza picks up the word *every* and repeats it five times to suggest the situation he is describing is all–encompassing. Again the final line is significant. The manacles that imprison people are *mind-forged* – they are forged, made in the mind. Is Blake suggesting that the people of London are not even aware of their own oppression? Is it something in their mentality, their minds, which prevents them from protesting? Do they have too much faith in their own rulers? Do they not question the system? Note too how Blake delays the verb of the second stanza – *I hear* – until the very last two words of the stanza. Blake's use of repetition in the first two stanzas has another purpose: his language becomes as restricted and limited as the lives of the people he describes. The word *ban* often stirs some debate: you may read elsewhere that it is a reference to the marriage banns – the announcements of a couple's intention to marry. This ties in with the final stanza, but, according to the Oxford English Dictionary, marriage banns have never been spelt with a single *n*. Isn't it more likely that Blake means prohibitions, banning something? Such as public meetings to protest about the condition of the country?

The third stanza continues with the sounds of London: the cry of the chimney sweep and the sigh of the soldier. Why is the church *black'ning*? Some readers suggest that it is a result of pollution caused by industry, but it could be a comment on the moral corruption of the church – it is evil. Why? I think Blake would suggest it is hypocritical: it is appalled by the cry of the chimney sweep, but does nothing to stop slavery. The sibilance in lines 11 and 12 suggest the agony of the soldier. It is an astonishing image – sighs do not run in blood. But the soldier is badly wounded or dying – and he seems to be defending the palace or at least in the pay of the place where the royal family live. Blake uses synecdoche to great effect in this stanza with his use of the words *church* and *palace*: its use here is partly to protect Blake in the repressive society he lived in, but it also serves to distance the establishment and the royal family even further from their subjects.

The worst horrors are saved until the fourth stanza and Blake signals this by stating – *but most* – and what he hears most of all is the curse of the youthful harlot. You can sometimes read that this is a curse in the sense of a bad spell, but it might just as well be a shouted swear word (*curse* had that meaning too). Who she is cursing is unclear, but the curse *blasts the new-born infant's tear*. Perhaps this is an unwanted baby, another mouth to feed, its father one of her clients? The baby is crying and in the final cryptic, oxymoronic line, her curse

blights with plagues the marriage hearse.

The phrase *marriage hearse* is an oxymoron because we normally associate marriage with new life and happiness, whereas we associate hearses with funerals and sadness, so to put the two ideas together is striking and original. Does Blake mean that some marriages are like death? Or that marriage is the death of love? Is marriage something that the youthful harlot will never know? Or is it the marriage of one of her clients? Why do married men visit prostitutes? Some readers even suggest that the curse of the harlot is some sort of sexually transmitted sexual disease which the harlot has given to her client who has then passed it on to his wife – this reading might be supported by the word *plagues*. But *plagues* can be a metaphor too – whatever interpretation you choose, it is wise not to be too dogmatic – the beauty and brilliance of Blake is that he is able to suggest all the above possibilities – and even more.

What is certain is that there is something very wrong with marriage in this final stanza and that the curse of the harlot is frightening and chilling: note Blake's use of harsh plosive consonants in *blasts, blights and plagues* – this is almost onomatopoeic in its presentation of a diseased, corrupt society and Blake's angry reaction to it. We have already mentioned the oxymoron with which the poem ends, but Blake in the third stanza had already juxtaposed things which are not normally associated with each other: the cry of the chimney sweep with the church, and the sigh of the soldier with the palace walls – both these images in a way are oxymoronic. Think back to our comments on 'The Sick Rose' in the introduction – this is a profound and moving criticism of Blake's society.

Finally, Blake's use of the ballad form is important. The ballad form is associated with the oral tradition and with anonymity – it is a more democratic form than the sonnet. However, traditional ballads have a strong narrative drive which this poem lacks. So we can say that Blake takes a form that is popular and egalitarian, and then turns its narrative conventions upside down by writing a poem that is descriptive.

The Final Unpublished Stanza

This is the stanza that was found in Blake's notebooks when he died and which some editions of his complete works publish. As you read it, think about why Blake did not publish this stanza during his lifetime:

Remove away that blackening church;

Remove away that marriage hearse;

Remove away that man of blood –

You'll quite remove the ancient curse!

This makes explicit what is implied in the poem: Blake is calling for a revolution which will *remove* the church and the monarchy: *man of blood* is a phrase famously used by Oliver Cromwell to describe Charles I, the English king who was executed after losing the English Civil War. One can only guess why Blake did not include this stanza, but we can speculate that in 1794 it was too dangerous and that Blake might have got in trouble with the authorities for publishing such a call. Artistically the stanza has its limitations: *remove away* is tautological and, because it makes completely clear Blake's attitude to the things described in the poem as we read it today, one can argue that takes away the cryptic, mysterious quality of Blake's poem as it first appeared. This cryptic nature of the poem encourages us to think and analyze what Blake is saying and thus we are encouraged by the poem to break out of our own *mind-forged manacles*, to expand our minds in order to realize the full impact, the complete implications of what Blake's view of London is. London needs to be changed urgently and by a revolution.

Why?

This very famous poem is remarkable.

- It is a political poem of protest against the authorities.

- This sense of protest makes it an angry and bitter poem.

- Blake speaks up for the marginalized in his society.

- It uses the ballad form in a revolutionary way.

- It is remarkable for its compression of language. Blake manages to pack so much meaning into so few words.

- Its use of simple repetition, sound effects and oxymoronic imagery make it memorable and striking.

'I started Early – Took my Dog' – Emily Dickinson

Author and Context

 Emily Elizabeth Dickinson (December 10, 1830 – May 15, 1886) was an American poet. Dickinson was born in Amherst, Massachusetts. Although part of a prominent family with strong ties to its community, Dickinson lived much of her life highly introverted. After studying at the Amherst Academy for seven years in her youth, she briefly attended the Mount Holyoke Female Seminary before returning to her family's house in Amherst. Considered an eccentric by locals, she developed a noted penchant for white clothing and became known for her reluctance to greet guests or, later in life, to even leave her bedroom. Dickinson never married, and most friendships between her and others depended entirely upon correspondence.

While Dickinson was a prolific private poet, fewer than a dozen of her nearly 1,800 poems were published during her lifetime. The work that was published during her lifetime was usually altered significantly by the publishers to fit the conventional poetic rules of the time. Dickinson's poems are unique for the era in which she wrote; they contain short lines, typically lack titles, and often use slant rhyme as well as unconventional capitalization and punctuation. Many of her poems deal with themes of death and immortality, two recurring topics in letters to her friends.

Frigates – sailing ships of medium size.

Hempem Hands – ropes made of hemp.

Bodice – a woman's outer garment covering the waist and bust.

Who? A young woman narrates the poem which is about a visit to the sea.

When? No specific time of day.

Where? By the sea shore and in the local town.

What? A young woman walks to the sea with her dog. She enjoys herself until being intimidated by the force of the waves. She retreats and seeks sanctuary in the town

Commentary

The opening line – *I started Early – Took my Dog* – begins the poem with a sense of light-hearted energy and the fanciful element continues as on her visit to the sea

The Mermaids in the Basement

Came out to look at me.

The metaphor of a house is solid, ordinary and domestic, and is extended with the *Frigates - in the Upper Floor* extend helping hands and ropes. The air of whimsicality is continued by the frigates, the poet writes, *Presuming Me to be a Mouse.*

The third stanza represents a change of tone. It begins with the blunt statement – *But no Man moved Me* – and the Tide rapidly overtakes her, the suddenness of which is reflected in Dickinson's staccato delivery of the lines

...the Tide

Went past my simple Shoe –

And past my Apron – and my Belt

And past my Bodice – too –

Dickinson's use of dashes here is effective in showing the speed with which the tide caught her.

In the next stanza the sea (resolutely masculine) *made as He would eat me up* – but the sense of danger is defused to a large extent by the simile Dickinson uses to present herself:

As wholly as a Dew

Upon a Dandelion's Sleeve –

Dickinson starts and the sea follows:

And then – I started – too –

And He – He followed – close behind –

I felt his Silver Heel

Upon my Ankle – Then my Shoes

Would overflow with Pearl –

In the final stanza Dickinson reaches the safety of the *Solid Town* where the sea seems to know no one and then

…bowing – with a Mighty look –

At me – The Sea withdrew –

The poem is straightforward at a literal level. A young woman walks to the sea with her dog; she enjoys herself until the sea catches her; she becomes frightened and runs to the town for safety. The metaphors of *his Silver Heel* and *Pearl* can be taken to describe a wave breaking and the foam produced.

Most readers would agree that the poem also has a symbolic meaning. Clearly the speaker is initially welcomed by the sea and then attacked and frightened by it. Your reading of the poem will depend on what you feel the sea represents. Readers of the poem generally agree that the sea represents either - sex, the unconscious, death or nature. We will explore the sexual symbolism of the poem.

The speaker is female, timid and innocent, while the sea is male, assertive and aggressive. At the start she is attracted to the sea which is welcoming:

mermaids come and look at her and ships offer help, although they see her as a mouse – a tiny, easily-scared creature.

In stanza three the Sea is personified as a man. The speaker is sexually innocent (*But no Man moved Me*) and felt secure and safe up until this point. But she actually writes that *no Man moved Me – till the Tide* caught up with her and made her wet. The sea engulfs almost her whole body – as high as her bodice and chest. She *started* – is this a frisson of sexual feeling? If we read the poem as sexually symbolic, then his *Silver Heel* and the *Pearl* which overflows her shoes can be seen as the sea's sperm.

On the one hand, the speaker seems to fear the loss of selfhood that sex would entail – she fears that *He would eat me up* – but on the other hand, the rhythm of the verse and the whimsicality of some of the imagery suggest the speaker also finds the whole experience exciting. Her fear may be real, but the safety of the town is easily attainable and at the end of the poem the personified sea bows to her *with a Mighty look* – in a sort of parody of a lover's farewell. Is his look *Mighty* because the speaker acknowledges the power of sexual feeling, despite the fact that she has escaped this time? Or is *Mighty* ironic because the speaker has escaped relatively easily and is now back in the safety of the town? Is her fear, in fact, only light-hearted mock fear?

Emily Dickinson once wrote in a letter: "The shore is safer... but I love to buffet the sea" – a good quotation to summarize the mixture of fear and attraction that is apparent in this poem.

In this short, cryptic poem, Emily Dickinson:

- clearly shows her attraction to a particular place which lies outside the safety of the town;
- describes a potentially frightening experience in a light-hearted and whimsical way;
- uses the sea as a symbol of sex to explore her fears and attractions to sexuality;
- uses language and punctuation in an original and refreshing way.

'Where the Picnic Was' – Thomas Hardy

Author and Context

Author

Thomas Hardy (1840 – 1928) is best known as a novelist. He wrote 15 novels, most of which are set largely in Dorset and the surrounding counties, and which deal with the ordinary lives of ordinary people in stories in which they struggle to find happiness and love – often battling against fate or their own circumstances. His final two novels *Tess of the D'Urbervilles* (1891) and *Jude the Obscure* (1895) both portray sex outside marriage in a sympathetic way and there was such a hysterical public outcry about the novels that Hardy stopped writing fiction and devoted the rest of his life to poetry. Although some of his poetry is intensely personal, this poem is also typical of his work in that it gives a voice to an ordinary man. Although Hardy trained as an architect, he came from a fairly poor family and, in both his novels and his fiction, he never forgets his roots.

An important note. On various internet sources I have read that this poem is about Hardy's dead wife, Emma. There are two reasons why I think this is not the case. The facts of the matter are these: In 1870, while on an architectural mission to restore the parish church of St Juliot in Cornwall, Hardy met and fell in love with Emma Lavinia Gifford, whom he married in 1874.[1] In 1885 Thomas and his wife moved into Max Gate, a house Hardy had designed himself and his brother had built. Although they later became estranged, her subsequent death in 1912 had a traumatic effect on him and after her death, Hardy made a trip to Cornwall to revisit places linked with their courtship; his *Poems 1912–13* reflect upon her death. In 1914, Hardy married his secretary Florence Emily Dugdale, who was 39 years his junior. However, he remained preoccupied with his first wife's death and tried to overcome his remorse by writing poetry. 'Where the Picnic Was' is NOT included in *Poems 1912 – 13*, suggesting it is not about Emma Hardy. Furthermore, 'Where the Picnic Was' has a time-frame of a single year, yet we know that Hardy's estrangement from Emma lasted many years – again strongly suggesting the poem is not about his dead wife.

sward – green turf, an area of grass.

Who? Hardy – and the three other people who attended the picnic.

When? A year or so after the picnic. In the autumn after the previous year's summer.

Where? On a hill overlooking the sea.

What? Hardy pokes around the remnants of the bonfire they lit at the picnic and reflects on the fate of those who attended the picnic.

Commentary

The first verse contrasts the summer time when *we made the fire, on the hill to the sea* with winter: now Hardy climbs through *winter mire* and the site of the picnic is a *forsaken place*. The identity of *we* is not revealed – this is important for the overall effect of the poem.

The second stanza begins by stressing the wintry weather: *a cold wind blows/ And the grass is gray*, but the evidence of the fire they made – the *burnt circle*, *stick-ends*, *charred* – are still clearly visible. The end of the second stanza impels us to read on as Hardy admits he is

Last relic of the band

Who came that day!

What has happened to the rest of the band?

The final stanza asserts that Hardy is still there – *Just as last year* – and the sea is the same:

And the sea breathes brine

From its strange, straight line

Up hither, the same

As we four came.

Here the alliteration draws attention to the sea and makes the lines memorable.

The last five lines reveal what has become of the band that had the picnic: two have moved to the city (to the *urban roar/ Where no picnics are*). Most poignantly the fourth has died:

… one has shut her eyes

For evermore.

The image of her shutting her eyes forever is a delicate and beautifully tender way of making clear she has died.

Looking back on the poem it can now be seen that the wintry atmosphere (apart from being literal) also acts as a pathetic fallacy representing Hardy's feelings of loss and sadness at the dispersal of the band that had the picnic together. The first two stanzas are both nine lines long and they follow a similar rhyme scheme: ABACBADDC in the first stanza and ABABCCDDB in the second stanza. It could be argued that this lack of regularity reflects Hardy's unease and unhappiness. The final stanza breaks the pattern still further: it is twelve lines long and has the following rhyme scheme: AABBCCDEFDEF. It seems appropriate that the opening of the final stanza should rhyme so simply given Hardy's assertion that he and the sea are unchanged and immutable – the verse reflects this.

And so we have a poem about four friends who went for a picnic one summer day and by autumn of the following year, only one is left: the poet. Two have moved away to try city life and the fourth has died. Place is important in this poem because the place where they had the picnic still shows traces of it, and the sea remains the same, but this is also a poem about the passing of time, the breaking of friendships (through distance) and human mortality. It is a lament about change and the passing of time.

Why?

In this short lyric poem, Hardy:

- expresses his desolate sadness at the death of a friend and the removal of two others associated with a specific place;
- uses pathetic fallacy to represent his feelings of loss;
- expresses mild amazement that he should still be there unchanged;
- venerates the place where the picnic was as the place where all four friends were last together.

'Adlestrop' – Edward Thomas

Author and Context

 Philip Edward Thomas (3 March 1878 – 9 April 1917) was a British poet, essayist, and novelist. He is commonly considered a war poet, although few of his poems deal directly with his war experiences, and his career in poetry only came after he had already been a successful writer and literary critic. Thomas agonized about whether to enlist in the Army, but after months of indecision finally decided to enlist in the army – against the advice of many friends. In 1915, he enlisted in the British Army to fight in the First World War and was killed in action during the Battle of Arras in 1917, soon after he arrived in France. 'Adlestrop' was one of the last poems Thomas ever wrote and he wrote it in the trenches of the Western Front.

Unwontedly – not accustomed to.

No whit less – in the same way, just as.

Who? The poet is on a train which makes an unscheduled stop.

When? We assume that it is set during the First World War.

Where? At a small local railway station at a village called Adlestrop in Gloucestershire. Thomas took the railway trip in June 1914 – before the war – but only wrote about it later as an act of memory.

What? The railway train makes a short, unscheduled stop at a tiny station: no one leaves the train or boards it; Thomas is emotionally overwhelmed by the trees and bushes, and by the sound of bird-song.

Commentary

The poem begins with an affirming *Yes* as if Thomas is speaking to another person or even directly addressing the reader. The poet remembers the tiny village of Adlestrop because one hot afternoon in late June the express train stopped there unexpectedly. He is aware of sounds - the train's *steam hissed* and *someone cleared his throat* – partly because there are no passengers are waiting on the platform and no one leaves the train, so sounds are more easily heard. Through repetition Thomas stresses the fact that the station was completely deserted:

No one left and no one came

On the bare platform.

Perhaps the railway station is so devoid of people because Thomas is writing during the First World War when millions of British men were fighting overseas.

Thomas in the third stanza describes what he remembers of the station at Adlestrop: he saw the name of the station

And willows, willow-herb, and grass,

And meadowsweet, and haycocks dry,

No whit less still and lonely fair

Than the high cloudlets in the sky.

The first two verses had several full stop caesuras which broke up the rhythm and slowed them down. It is significant that here in the third stanza, Thomas avoids such heavy caesuras and uses enjambment too as he writes with enthusiasm about the natural world. His knowledge of the plants he sees proves his enthusiasm for them and for rural England.

The silence on the station is important again in the final stanza:

And for that minute a blackbird sang

Close by, and round him, mistier,

Farther and farther, all the birds

Of Oxfordshire and Gloucestershire.

The silence allows him to hear the blackbird, and to make the imaginative leap to imagine all the birds of two entire counties singing their hearts out in celebration of the weather and the English countryside. In many cultures blackbirds are seen as birds of ill omen – so perhaps the huge chorus of birds is warning of the huge loss of life that will occur (and had already started to occur) when Thomas wrote the poem.

We know that Thomas wrote this poem in the trenches of the Western Front, after he had enlisted as a soldier. I think that must make a difference to the way we read the poem. It is important that the poem is an act of memory as the first line clearly signals – a memory of a beautiful, tranquil day which brings consolation and comfort to a man suffering in the trenches. The natural beauty Thomas describes in the poem might be said to represent the best of the English countryside and acts, therefore, as a beautiful reminder of home and what the soldiers are fighting for. It is typical of Thomas that when he writes a poem about home he chooses to write about a tiny and obscure railway station and the ordinary plants and birds of the English countryside.

Thomas conveys a clear sense of place in this poem and sees the haunting beauty in this obscure Gloucestershire village. His lovingly detailed description of the wild plants and his ability to imagine all the birds of two whole counties joining in song, elevate Adlestrop to the very heights of English pastoral beauty.

In this short but famous poem, Edward Thomas:

- remembers a tiny incident from before the war;
- writes with genuine affection and love about the English countryside;
- perhaps uses the war as background and, therefore contrast to, this picture of a rural idyll;

- perhaps uses this idyllic memory as a consolation to him in the battlefields of France.

'Home Thoughts from Abroad' – Robert Browning

Author and Context

Robert Browning was born in 1812 and became one of the most famous English poets of the Victorian era. He was married to Elizabeth Barrett Browning who was a semi-invalid with an over-protective father. The couple were married in secret and then went to live in Italy. Browning's best work is often set in the past and he was a master of the dramatic monologue, in which the imagined speaker of the poem reveals their innermost thoughts and feelings, often going on to uncover uncomfortable truths about themselves. In this context 'Home Thoughts from Abroad' is not a typical Browning poem because it is largely natural and descriptive.

Who? The poet speaking as himself.

When? In springtime.

Where? Browning lived in Italy but is yearning for England.

What? Browning evokes the joys and pleasures of an English spring from far away in Italy.

Commentary

Browning wrote the poem in 1845 and it was first published in *Dramatic Romances and Lyrics*. On the surface it seems a straightforward poem: living with his family in Italy, Browning is home-sick and nostalgic for an English spring. Spring carries with it connotations of renewal and re-birth after the hiatus of winter – and the promise of new life. In this

Browning owes a lot to the tradition of English Romanticism and its veneration of nature.

The opening stanza has a rhyme scheme, but the line lengths are irregular - perhaps to suggest the joyful frenzy that the thought of England in April causes Browning. It has been suggested by some readers that the rise and fall of lines of different lengths may also suggest his longing for home, along with an acceptance that he cannot return. The poem begins with an exclamation which also suggests his excitement simply at the thought of England in April. Browning is not really being nostalgic: in line three he writes of *whoever wakes in England* – in other words he is imaginatively creating what they will see. Also significant is the tiny detail that Browning writes about are typical of the English spring:

The lowest boughs and the brushwood sheaf

Round the elm-tree bole are in tiny leaf

While the chaffinch sings on the orchard bough.

The final word of the stanza – *now!* – emphasizes his longing to be back home in England.

The second stanza is more regular in its line length and Browning goes on to expatiate on the joys of May in England. The opening of the stanza celebrates the building of nests by birds – the whitethroat and the swallows. There is metrical variation in lines 11, 12 and 13 – each line starting with a trochaic foot which helps to convey enthusiasm and energy – the predominant rhythm in the second stanza being iambic. Browning then imagines his *blossomed pear-tree* scattering *blossoms and dew-drops*. His attention turns to the thrush who

… sings each song twice over

Lest you think he never could recapture

The first fine careless rapture.

With the mention of the fields *rough with hoary dew*, Browning admits that all is not ideal, but the dew will be dissipated when the noontime wakes anew. In short, as the final line admits, Browning yearns for an English spring in contrast to what surrounds him in Italy: the *gaudy melon flower*.

Browning wrote this poem in exile and for British men and women of the Victorian era, exile from Britain was becoming more normal. Of course, very few ended up in Italy like Browning: most were stretched out all over the world as the British Empire continued to grow and needed people to settle it or to run the colonial administration. In the minds of these exiles, Britain, or England as they often called it, came to have the idealized presentation that it does clearly have in Browning's poem.

This short but memorable poem:

- acts as a paean to the English spring;
- includes lovingly-recalled details of England in April and May;
- shows Browning's wider homesickness for his native land;
- presents an idealized picture of an English spring;
- Browning's patriotism extends to the tiny features of rural England – chaffinches, thrushes, swallows – and the blossom on his pear tree coming into bloom.

'First Flight' – U A Fanthorpe

Author and Context

Born in south-east London, the daughter of a barrister, Fanthorpe was educated at St Catherine's School, Bramley in Surrey and at St Anne's College, Oxford, where she received a first-class degree in English language and literature, and subsequently taught English at Cheltenham Ladies' College for sixteen years. She then abandoned teaching for jobs as a secretary, receptionist and hospital clerk in Bristol – in her poems, she later remembered some of the patients for whose records she had been responsible.

Fanthorpe's first volume of poetry, *Side Effects*, was published in 1978. She was "Writer-in-Residence" at St Martin's College, Lancaster (now University of Cumbria) (1983–85), as well as Northern Arts Fellow at Durham and Newcastle Universities. In 1987 Fanthorpe went freelance, giving readings around the country and occasionally abroad. In 1994 she was nominated for the post of Professor of Poetry at Oxford. Her nine collections of poems were published by Peterloo Poets. Her *Collected Poems* was published in 2005. Many of her poems are for two voices. In her readings the other voice is that of Bristol academic and teacher R. V. "Rosie" Bailey, Fanthorpe's life partner of 44 years. The couple co-wrote a collection of poems, *From Me To You: love poems*, that was published in 2007 by Enitharmon. Fanthorpe died, aged 79, on 28 April 2009, in a hospice near her home in Wotton-under-Edge, Gloucestershire.

cumulus – a kind of cloud consisting of rounded heaps with darker bases;

mackerel wigs – 'wigs' makes this a metaphor but the word 'mackerel' refers to a type of cloud cover – so called because it resembles the pattern on the skin of a mackerel.

Who? The poet as herself and (in italicized speech) a selection of her fellow travellers.

When? In daylight towards sunset.

Where? On an aeroplane – it is Fanthorpe's first flight. She describes the view of the clouds from 28,000 feet.

What? There is a consistent contrast between the banal and clichéd reactions of the other travellers (printed in italics) and the more nuanced and perceptive reactions of the main speaker. Meanwhile, Fanthorpe is entranced by the view from the aeroplane, particularly in its position above the clouds.

Commentary

This poem details Fanthorpe's first flight in an aeroplane – and she readily admits that she doesn't *like the feel of it*. The poem also consists of two voices: Fanthorpe's own voice, open to the beauty of the world above the clouds and also, in italics, the words said by seasoned travellers – almost all banal clichés and truisms. These interjections in italics serve as a contrast with Fanthorpe's more innocent, more open sense of wonder. The two voices always occur in different stanzas, so visually the poem is easy to follow.

Fanthorpe describes take off:

A sudden swiftness, earth slithers

Off at angle.

The more experienced travellers exchange small talk (*This is rather a short hop for me*, read newspapers and discuss secretaries), but Fanthorpe is excited now and cranes to see through a window to look at England below. She sees

Familiar England, motorways, reservoir,

Building sites.

All the time Fanthorpe is reminding us of the other passengers' reactions - rather mundane compared with Fanthorpe's enthusiasm: *I'm doing it just to say I've done it, Tell us when we get to water, The next lot of water'll be the Med.*

Once they are above the clouds Fanthorpe uses a striking metaphor to describe the cloud and the effect of the sun shining on it:

Under us the broad meringue kingdom

Of cumulus, bearing the crinkled tangerine stain

That light spreads on an evening sea at home.

Once again Fanthorpe's thoughts are interrupted by a fellow passenger's words:

You don't need an overcoat, but

It's the sort of place where you need

A pullover. Know what I mean?

Theses interjections contrast the banal reality of air travel with Fanthorpe's thoughts and impressions, but they also keep the poem grounded in a reality that the reader is likely to recognize.

Fanthorpe expresses great excitement at the freedom air travel brings, She writes:

We have come too high for history.

Where we are now deals only with tomorrow,

Confounds the forecasters, dismisses clocks.

They have come too high for history as no history has been made at such a height and their thoughts are on the future, on the trips they are making. The weather forecasters are confounded because the plane is above the cloud line and the forecasters deal with weather at ground level. Now they are in flight all that matters is their destination and clocks have been dismissed as they are travelling through different time zones – so there is no fixed time on the aeroplane.

Fanthorpe conveys a sense of awe and excitement at her first flight. The poem ends with an intriguing paradox:

Mackerel wigs dispense the justice of air.

At this height nothing lives. Too cold. Too near the sun.

The mackerel wigs are a common cloud pattern. The poem ends with a seeming paradox: nothing lives at this height, because it's too cold, yet ironically it is closer to the sun and should logically be hotter… if one did not take into account they are flying at 28,000 feet.

Altogether an engaging poem about the excitements of a first flight. Fanthorpe mixes well the comments of her fellow travellers with her own more excited and more interesting account of the flight.

In 'First Flight' U A Fanthorpe

- captures the thrill and excitement of one's first flight;
- finds beauty above the cloud line;
- accurately imitates the inane things that most people say.

'Stewart Island' – Fleur Adcock

Author and Context

Fleur Adcock was born in Auckland, but spent the years between 1939 and 1947 in the UK. Her father was Cyril John Adcock, her sister is the novelist Marilyn Duckworth. Fleur Adcock studied Classics at Victoria University of Wellington, graduating with an MA. She worked as an assistant lecturer and later an assistant librarian at the University of Otago in Dunedin until 1962. She was married to two famous New Zealand literary personalities. In 1952 she married Alistair Campbell (divorced 1958). Then in 1962 she married Barry Crump, divorcing in 1963.

In 1963, Adcock returned to England and took up a post as an assistant librarian at the Foreign and Commonwealth Office in London until 1979. Since then she has been a freelance writer, living in East Finchley, north London. She has held several literary fellowships, including the Northern Arts Literary Fellowship in Newcastle upon Tyne and Durham in 1979–81.

Adcock's poetry is typically concerned with themes of place, human relationships and everyday activities, but frequently with a dark twist given to the mundane events she writes about. Formerly, her early work was influenced by her training as a classicist but her more recent work is looser in structure and more concerned with the world of the unconscious mind.

Stewart Island - (officially named Stewart Island/Rakiura) is the third-largest island of New Zealand. It lies 30 kilometres (19 miles) south of the South Island, across the Foveaux Strait. Its permanent population is 381 people as of the 2013 census, most of whom live in the settlement of Oban on the eastern side of the island. It is inhospitable and very sparsely populated.

Who? The poet appears to speak as herself in this poem.

When? No specific time.

Where? Stewart Island, New Zealand.

What? The poet writes rather critically of Stewart Island which makes the final sentence a logical conclusion to the poem.

Commentary

Fleur Adcock does not like Stewart Island and makes it clear throughout this short but biting poem.

The first stanza begins with the local hotel manager's wife saying 'But look at all this beauty' but, significantly, she has been asked 'how she could bear to/live there' and in the third stanza Adcock sardonically notes that the hotel manager's wife 'ran off' with a Maori fisherman 'that autumn' – abandoning her husband and 'all this beauty'.

In the first stanza Adcock grudgingly admits

True; there was a fine bay,

all hills and atmosphere; white

sand and bush down to the sea's edge.

There is something dismissive about the phrase 'all hills and atmosphere' – Adcock cares so little for Stewart Island that she cannot be bothered to describe or give details of the atmosphere, but just dismisses it with that general word which tells us nothing of the sort of atmosphere it was.

However, the second half of the poem is more critical of Stewart Island: the poet 'walked on the beach', but only because it was too cold to swim; her seven-year-old collects shells 'but was bitten by sandflies'; and her 'four-year-old paddled' until

a mad seagull jetted down

to jab its claws and beak into

his head.

Overall, then, we get the impression of a place which is wild and beautiful, but lacks the trappings of civilization and which is positively antagonistic to human beings. The sandflies and the mad seagull present Adcock's view that this place is hostile to human beings and she is naturally, as any parent would be, protective of her children. The final sentence of the poem, therefore, comes as no surprise, although it is expressed in a weary tone of the inevitable:

…I had already

decided to leave the country.

Biographical context is important here: disliking the raw nature of Stewart Island, Adcock has chosen to live and work for most of her life in London - a bustling metropolis free of sandflies and mad seagulls. In many ways this is an unusual poem because poets often write poems in praise of unspoilt nature – unspoilt by human beings and the things they bring with them. We are especially aware of green or environmental concerns and how human activity can damage the natural environment, and so seek comfort in nature which is unharmed or untouched by human activity. Therefore, Adcock's poem is original in selecting the unpleasant parts of nature and pointing out the uncivilized parts of Stewart Island. Her final sentence too is dismissive in its brevity and simplicity – as if it is a foregone conclusion that she will leave New Zealand and its unspoilt nature. I find this poem quite comical given our current obsession with holidays in 'wild' nature – this is what wild nature is really like!

In this poem Fleur Adcock makes clear

- her detestation of wild nature and Stewart Island in particular;
- her dislike of the uncivilized parts of New Zealand;
- her disdain for the cultural emptiness of Stewart Island;
- her determination to leave New Zealand.

'Presents from my Aunts in Pakistan' – Moniza Alvi

Author and Context

Moniza Alvi was born in Lahore, Pakistan. She was born to a Pakistani father and a British mother. Her father moved to Hatfield, Hertfordshire in England when she was a few months old. She did not revisit Pakistan until after the publication of one of her first books of poems - *The Country at My Arm*. She worked for several years as a high school teacher, but is now a freelance writer and tutor, living in Norfolk. She and her husband, Robert, have one daughter. Alvi says: "Presents from My Aunts...was one of the first poems I wrote. When I wrote this poem I wasn't actually back in Pakistan. The girl in the poem would be me at about 13. The clothes seem to stick to her in an uncomfortable way, a bit like a kind of false skin, and she thinks things aren't straightforward for her. I found it was important to write the Pakistan poems because I was getting in touch with my background. And maybe there's a bit of a message behind the poems about something I went through, that I want to maybe open a few doors if possible."

salwar kameez – a long tunic worn over a pair of baggy trousers.

sari – a long cloth wrapped around the waist and covering the shoulder, neck and head.

filigree – ornamental metallic lacework of silver or gold.

prickly heat – a skin disease, inflammation of the sweat glands with intense irritation.

the Shalimar Gardens – a beautiful complex of gardens, fountains and trees in Lahore, Pakistan.

Who? The poet speaks as herself – a woman of Pakistani origin growing up in the UK.

When? The poem focuses on her childhood and teenage years at about the age of 13.

Where? The poem is set in the UK but there are frequent references to Pakistan.

What? Much of the poem discusses the clothes that the speaker was sent by relatives in Pakistan and the speaker's desire to wear Western clothes and, therefore, to fit in with British society.

Commentary

One of the first things one notices about this poem is the way it is set out with lines beginning half way across the page. The reason for this, as will become clear in the commentary, is that Alvi is torn between her ethnic heritage in Pakistan (shown in the illustration of the salwar kameez) and her upbringing in the UK. The seeming confusion on the page represents the two conflicting forces playing on the young Alvi and her own confusion about where she belongs. In this sense, the lay out of the poem is entirely appropriate and enhances the meaning of the words. The left and right hand side of the page represent her English growing up and her Pakistani heritage. She is torn between the two just as the words move from side to side.

Moniza Alvi contrasts the exotic and beautiful clothes sent to her by her aunts in Pakistan with what she sees around her in Britain. She has two problems with the gifts: firstly, they seem too beautiful, too exquisite for her to wear; secondly, they seem out of place in modern Britain. Many of the lines are centralized, showing how she is caught in the middle between two cultures. The salwar kameez are brightly coloured and exotic –

peacock-blue

and another

glistening like a split orange.

They send bangles and an apple-green sari bordered in silver for her teens.

Alvi tried the clothes on but felt *alien in the sitting room* -

I could never be as lovely

> *as those clothes.*

In fact, Alvi admits *I longed for denim and corduroy*. She describes her salwar kameez as her *costume* which suggests it is not ordinary clothing, but more a theatrical costume she wears when she is playing at being Pakistani – but the problem is she is half-English. She writes

My costume clung to me

> *and I was aflame,*

I couldn't rise up out of its fire,

> *half-English,*

> > *unlike Aunt Jamila.*

The image of her being *aflame* (because of the beautiful colours) is a striking metaphor because it shows how distraught she is about her cultural identity.

She turns on the camel-skin lamp in her bedroom

to consider the cruelty

> *and the transformation*

from camel to shade.

She is appalled by the cruelty involved, but is still able to

> *marvel at the colours*

like stained glass. –

once again showing her ambivalence to her mixed identity.

We are told in the fourth stanza hat her mother cherishes her jewellery, but that it was stolen from their car. The presents from her aunts were *radiant* in her wardrobe – suggesting that that is where they stayed and that she never wore them. In return, somewhat ironically, the aunts in Pakistan request to be sent cardigans from Marks and Spencer.

Alvi's eastern clothes did not impress the school friend she showed them to, but she herself used to admire the mirror work and it prompted memories of how her mother, her father and Alvi had first travelled to England. She sees herself in the miniature glass circles – and because the mirrors are tiny she sees multiple images of herself – again suggesting the fragmentary sense of self that Alvi has.

She never visited Pakistan but pictured it from 1950s photographs and, as she got older, became aware of it on the news – *conflict, a fractured land. Throbbing through newsprint.* Sometimes she imagined Lahore and her aunts

screened from male visitors,

> *sorting presents,*

>> *wrapping them in tissue.*

At the end of the poem she pictures other scenes from Lahore:

Or there were beggars, sweeper girls

> *and I was there – of no fixed nationality,*

staring through the fretwork

> *at the Shalimar Gardens.*

Alvi imagines other destinies for herself, had she not emigrated to England with her mother and father. Of course, she would be staring at the fretwork of the Shalimar Gardens because a beggar girl would not be allowed in. the poem ends on a note of poignant sadness: Alvi still feels of *no fixed nationality*.

This poem expresses well the problems that people with diverse cultural backgrounds have. It is good to compare this poem with 'Hurricane Hits England' – which has a very different ending.

In this poem Alvi

- demonstrates the pressures that those from dual cultural heritages have to suffer;
- gives a fascinating insight into British Pakistani home life;
- fails to resolve the problems of duality;
- reminds us of the richness of Pakistani culture and mores.

'Hurricane Hits England' – Grace Nichols

Author and Context

Grace Nichols was born on the Caribbean territory of Guyana in 1950. Since 1977 she has lived in Britain with her partner, John Agard. They are both poets. Although she lives in the UK, she is very aware of her past and the traditions of Guyana, and many of her poems explore the clash or conflict between British or European values and those of her West Indian and African ancestors or, as this one does, they celebrate her African heritage, contrasting it with life in the UK. Nichols herself has said:

I am a writer across two worlds; I just can't forget my Caribbean culture and past, so there's this constant interaction between the two worlds: Britain and the Caribbean.

These two worlds are contrasted and juxtaposed in this poem.

'Hurricane Hits England' - The Great Storm of 1987 was a violent extratropical cyclone that occurred on the night of 15–16 October, with hurricane-force winds causing casualties in England, France and the Channel Islands as a severe depression in the Bay of Biscay moved northeast. Among the most damaged areas were Greater London, the East Anglian coast, the Home Counties, the west of Brittany and the Cotentin Peninsula of Normandy which weathered gusts typically with a return period of 1 in 200 years.

Forests, parks, roads and railways were strewn with fallen trees, and the British National Grid suffered heavy damage, leaving thousands without power. At least 22 people were killed in England and France. The highest measured gust of 117 kn (217 km/h; 135 mph) was recorded at Pointe Du Roc, Granville, France and the highest gust in the U.K. of 100 kn (190 km/h; 120 mph) was recorded at Shoreham-by-Sea.

That day's weather reports had failed to indicate a storm of such severity, an earlier, correct forecast having been negated by later projections. The storm remains famous because of the damage it caused; because it was not forecast; and because hurricanes do not normally occur in the United Kingdom.

howling ship – perhaps an allusion to the original ships which brought African slaves to the Caribbean and the Americas.

Huracan – the Carib god of the hurricane.

Oya – goddess of the Niger river in Africa.

Shango – Caribbean god of thunder and lightning.

Hattie – name of a Caribbean hurricane.

Who? The poem is a third person narrative about an unnamed woman of Caribbean descent living in the UK, but switches to the first person.

When? 1987. The southern counties of England were hit by hurricane-force winds: many trees were uprooted and lots of buildings were damaged.

Where? Mainly along the South Coast of England and in the Home Counties.

What? Grace Nichols herself has said: 'Because I'd never associated hurricanes with England (a regular Caribbean phenomenon) the manifestation of one in England took on a deep significance for me. It was as if some invisible but potent connection has taken place between the two landscapes. As if the voice of the old gods from Africa and the Caribbean were in the winds of the hurricane as it raged around Sussex.' This is a key quotation and informs the first half of the poem.

Commentary

Nichols uses the occasion of the Great Storm to link two places that are close to her heart – England and Guyana. The opening litany of original Carib gods and ones brought by the slaves to the New World serves as a litany which melds the two cultures together and brings the Caribbean to England – just as the two cultures are blended in Nichols herself. The Great Storm has come to England but England is not prepared for the Great Storm. The Caribs were the original inhabitants of the region – all killed in war or died because of a lack of immunity to European diseases.

In the opening stanza (written in the third person) we are told

It took a hurricane, to bring her closer

To the landscape.

The hurricane keeps her awake half the night and it is frightening – we hear of its *gathering rage.* There is also an allusion to the slave trade – *the howling ship of the wind* – the original ships used to transport Africans to the Americas to act as slaves – a tragic episode in human history. The final line of the first stanza describes the storm as *Fearful and reassuring.* This oxymoron conveys the fear of the storm, but also that the hurricane reminds the young woman of home in the Caribbean – and is, therefore, reassuring.

In the second stanza the speaker appeals to the ancient Carib and African gods to talk to her and refers to Hattie as My sweeping, back-home cousin – which clearly shows her closeness to her Caribbean roots and an element of nostalgia.

The speaker in the third stanza is perplexed and confused:

Tell me why you visit,

An English coast?

What is the meaning

Of old tongues

Reaping havoc

In new places?

The lightening in the fourth stanza is a blinding illumination which disrupts the electricity supply and forces them into *further darkness*.

The speaker remains confused and perplexed in the fifth stanza and gives a vivid idea of the destructiveness of the storm with trees

Falling heavy as whales

Their crusted roots

Their cratered graves?

The speaker is still searching for meaning in the hurricane and its ferocity. 'Whales' is an interesting simile – chosen no just because of the comparison with size, but also because it is a huge ocean-going mammal and this fits in the other imagery to do with the sea. 'Roots' can also be linked with the speaker's roots which are crusted – suggesting they are in need of renewal.

The arrival of the hurricane which she associates with home in the Caribbean, the speaker says, has *unchained [her] heart*. Grace Nichols has written that it is "as if the hurricane has broken down all barriers between her and the English landscape." She is at last able to reconcile her two cultural tradition – the Caribbean and the English.

The speaker asserts that she is aligning herself to the goddess Oya:

Tropical Oya of the Weather,

I am aligning myself to you,

I am following the movement of your winds,

I am riding the mystery of your storm.

Oya, the speaker says, has come to break the frozen lake in me – to unite her Caribbean and English selves. Grace Nichols has remarked of the ending of the poem:

"In some mysterious way, it seems as if the old gods have not deserted her completely, connecting her both to the Caribbean and to England which is now her home. Indeed to the wider planet as she asserts

the earth is the earth is the earth."

In this poem, Grace Nichols:

- makes clear the devastating power of the Great Storm;
- uses it as a way of summoning old Caribbean and African gods;
- summons up the past historical wrong of slavery;
- uses the storm to allow the speaker to feel at home in England and reconciled to living in two cultural traditions;
- allows the speaker to be perplexed and confused, but to feel joyful and liberated at the end of the poem;
- *the earth is the earth is the earth* – expresses our common humanity and the unity of the world.

'Nothing's Changed' – Tatamkhulu Afrika

Author and Context

Tatamkhulu Afrika was born in 1920 and lived in Cape Town's District Six, which was then a flourishing mixed-race community. People of many different racial backgrounds lived there harmoniously and Afrika claimed that he felt at home there. In 1948 the South African government brought in the apartheid system, based on segregating the races rigidly and denying black South Africans and what the white government called 'coloureds' (people of mixed race and Asian backgrounds) citizenship and the vote. Inevitably non-whites had the least education, the worst jobs and the worst pay. It was a thoroughly iniquitous system, and caused international protests and sanctions, and riots and protests on the streets of South Africa.

During the 1960s, the government designated District Six a 'whites-only' area and evacuated the population. It bulldozed the entire area, much of which remains unbuilt on.

Tatamkhulu was brought up as a white South African, but discovered in his teens that he was the child of an Arabian father and a Turkish mother. He turned down the chance to be classified as white, converted to Islam and was classified by the government as 'coloured'.

The African National Congress (the ANC) was a political and terrorist organization fighting the injustice of apartheid. In 1984 Afrika joined the ANC but was arrested in 1987 on terrorism charges and was banned from writing or speaking in public for five years. He changed his name to Tatamkhulu – which had been his ANC code name. He was able to carry on writing despite the ban.

Afrika has said:

"I am completely African. I am a citizen of Africa – that is my culture. I know I write poems that sound European, because I was brought up in school to do that, but, if you look at my poems carefully, you will find that all of them, I think, have an African flavour".

In 1990 Nelson Mandela, the imprisoned leader of the ANC, was released from prison and the apartheid laws were repealed, but most count 1994 as the real end of apartheid when all South Africans – regardless of skin colour or ethnic background – were allowed to vote in national elections.

Afrika wrote this poem when it was clear that political change was coming to South Africa, and it expresses pessimism for the continuing economic and financial gulf between blacks and whites – something that may take decades to change.

linen fall – the linen table cloths that cover the tables in the new expensive restaurant.

Port Jackson trees – trees imported from Australia.

bunny chow – bread stuffed with sardines or pilchards. A cheap and unsophisticated dish.

Who? The poet returns to the scene of District Six and notes the disparity between an expensive restaurant and a cheap café.

When? In the post-apartheid era.

Where? In Cape Town, South Africa.

What? The poet reflects on the demolition of District Six and his feelings about it. He reflects on the new South Africa and concludes that *nothing's changed* – the blacks and any other non-whites are still mired in poverty and economically excluded from certain places.

Commentary

The poem is written in free verse – a frequent choice for poets writing outside the mainstream. To choose a traditional form would be submitting to the prevailing traditional white culture, so free verse signals their independence from that culture and their rebellion against it. Despite being in free verse, on the page the poem consists of six stanzas, all made up of six short lines, which gives it a visual coherence: Afrika is in control of his material and knows precisely what he wants to express, and this is reflected in its regular appearance on the page.

The entire poem is written in the present tense which gives it a vibrant immediacy and a sense of authenticity. Although the poem is based on Afrika's memory of District Six, the poem is set in the present. The opening stanza immediately immerses the reader in the poet's sensibility as he walks on the land which was once District Six – his home before it was bulldozed. The site is derelict and uncared for:

Small round hard stones click

under my heels

…cans

trodden on, crunch

in tall, purple-flowering,

amiable weeds.

The second stanza makes clear that although there is no sign that says the area was once District Six, Afrika lived there for so long that he recognizes it:

…my feet know,

and my hands,

and the skin about my bones,

and the soft labouring of my lungs,

and the hot, white, inwards turning

anger of my eyes.

The reader has to wait until the third stanza to know what has provoked his anger: a *new, up-market, haute cuisine* restaurant has opened, *brash with glass* and *a guard at the gatepost.* Afrika calls it a *whites-only inn,* but admits there is no sign while ruefully admitting *we know where we belong.* The poet presses his nose to the windows of the restaurant knowing he will see a luxurious interior with *crushed ice white glass,* immaculate table linen and a rose on each table.

The fifth stanza presents a contrast:

Down the road,

working man's café sells

bunny chows

The tables are made of plastic, there are no napkins (you wipe your fingers on your jeans) and people spit on the floor. Afrika explains – *It's in the bone* – it is what people are accustomed to. The mass of South Africans – the black and Asian and mixed race South Africans are excluded from the posh new restaurant by a lack of money and by social habit.

In the final stanza he backs away from the glass. What he has seen moves him to passionate, violent anger:

Hands burn

for a stone, a bomb

to shiver down the glass.

And he comes to the conclusion that forms the title of the poem: *Nothing's changed.* The political system has changed and true democracy has arrived in South Africa, but there is still a yawning economic gulf between whites and non-whites in the country.

Tatamkhulu wrote about the poem:

'Nothing's Changed' is entirely autobiographical. I can't quite remember when I wrote this, but I think it must have been about 1990. District Six was a complete waste by then, and I hadn't been passing through it for a long time. But nothing has changed. Not only District Six…. I mean, we may have a new constitution, we may have on the face of it a beautiful democracy, but the racism in this country is absolutely redolent. We try to pretend to the world that it does not exist, but it most certainly does, all day long, every day, shocking and saddening and terrible. Look, I don't want to sound like a prophet of doom, because I don't feel like that at all. I am full of hope. But I won't see it in my lifetime. It's going to take a long time. I mean, in America it's taken all this time and it's still not gone… so it will change. But not quickly, not quickly at all.

'Nothing's Changed' by Tatamkhulu Afrika

- evokes a clear sense of different, contrasting places;
- clearly conveys an angry bitterness about the new restaurant and wants to destroy it;
- adds a political dimension to his description of place;
- makes clear his political views regarding the new South Africa – both during the Apartheid era and the post-Apartheid era.

'Postcard from a Travel Snob' – Sophie Hannah

Author and Context

Sophie Hannah was born in Manchester, England; her father was the academic Norman Geras and her mother is the author Adèle Geras. She attended Beaver Road Primary School in Didsbury and the University of Manchester. She published her first book of poems, *The Hero and the Girl Next Door*, at the age of 24. Her style is often compared to the light verse of Wendy Cope and the surrealism of Lewis Carroll. Her poems' subjects tend toward the personal, utilizing classic rhyme schemes with understated wit, humour and warmth. She has published five previous collections of poetry with Carcanet Press. In 2004, she was named one of the Poetry Book Society's Next Generation poets.

Hannah is also the author of a book for children and several psychological crime novels. Her first novel, *Little Face*, was published in 2006 and has sold more than 100,000 copies. Her fifth crime novel, *Lasting Damage*, was published in the UK on 17 February 2011. *Kind of Cruel*, her seventh psychological thriller to feature the characters Simon Waterhouse and Charlie Zailer, was published in 2012.

Her 2008 novel *The Point of Rescue* was produced for TV as the two-part drama *Case Sensitive* and shown on 2 and 3 May 2011 on the UK's ITV network. It stars Olivia Williams in the lead role of DS Charlie Zailer and Darren Boyd as DC Simon Waterhouse. Its first showing had 5.4 million viewers. A second two-part story based on *The Other Half Lives* was shown on 12 and 13 July 2012.

In 2013, Sophie's novel, *The Carrier*, won the Crime Thriller of the Year Award at the Specsavers National Book Awards. Two of Sophie's crime novels, *The Point of Rescue* and *The Other Half Lives*, have been adapted for television and appeared on ITV1 under the series title Case Sensitive in 2011 and 2012. In 2004, Sophie won first prize in the Daphne Du Maurier Festival Short Story Competition for her suspense story *The Octopus Nest*, which is now published in her first collection of short stories, *The Fantastic Book of Everybody's Secrets*. Sophie has also published five collections of poetry. Her fifth, *Pessimism for Beginners*, was shortlisted for the 2007 T S Eliot Award. Her poetry is studied at GCSE, A-level and degree level across the UK. From 1997 to 1999 she was Fellow Commoner in Creative Arts at Trinity College, Cambridge, and between 1999 and 2001 she was a fellow of Wolfson College, Oxford. She lives with her husband, children and dog in Cambridge, where she is a Fellow Commoner at Lucy Cavendish College.

philistine – a person indifferent or hostile to culture.

connoisseur – a well-informed judge of, for example, wine or food.

Who? The speaker is a person who despises ordinary British tourists who go abroad for good weather and cheap alcohol.

When? No specific time of day but the poem is set in the present.

Where? Nowhere specific, but various general foreign locations are evoked. Two types of foreign holiday resort are evoked: one which caters for British people who just go abroad for good weather and cheap alcohol and who are not interested in the local culture; the other type of location is that preferred by the speaker, the travel snob – which offers a supposedly authentic holiday experience.

What? The 'travel snob' derides the behaviour and activities of the average British tourist, and, in so doing, comes across as arrogant and self-satisfied.

Commentary

In many ways this is a satiric poem, but as we shall see by the end of this commentary both ordinary holidaymakers and the speaker of the poem are being satirized.

Millions of Britons take overseas holidays each year. The vast majority go to hot, sunny places to escape the miserable and changeable English weather: they go to resorts packed with other foreign tourists where the food and the alcohol are cheap and plentiful. One gets the sense that such holiday makers do not care which country they go to as long as the sun shines and the alcohol is cheap: they appear to have no interest in the local culture and history.

In the last few years there has risen a trend where more discerning tourists seek out less well-known holiday destinations in order to avoid the typical British holidaymaker and attempt to enjoy – unadulterated – the local culture. This poem is about these different types of holiday maker. The speaker is a more discerning holiday maker who denigrates those who travel to recognized holiday resorts.

In the first stanza the speaker, the travel snob, glories in her isolation from ordinary holiday resorts and pours scorn on conventional holiday resorts

with karaoke nights and pints of beer

for drunken tourist types – perish the thought.

The speaker takes pride in their isolation

I do not wish that anyone were here

and

This place is not a holiday resort.

In the second stanza the speaker derides 'your seaside-town-consumer-hell' and glories in the authenticity of her holiday – she's sleeping in a 'local farmer's van' miles away from guest houses and hotels.

The speaker returns to the difference between her and the average British tourist in stanza three:

I'm not your sun-and-sangria-two weeks-

Small-minded-package-philistine-abroad.

The speaker is highly critical of ordinary tourists who go abroad and get drunk and behave appallingly, while soaking up the sun and having no interest in the local culture. But this raises important questions: can the travel snob experience the real culture and life of a place? After all, she is a tourist too – albeit a richer, more discerning one.

However, the final stanza turns the tables on the travel snob. The travel snob declares themselves to be 'multicultural' and claims that their friends are 'wine connoisseurs, not drunks' – although the words are very different, it is still possible for a wine connoisseur to get drunk. The final two lines of the poem clinch the double satire that is going on in this poem:

I'm not a British tourist in the sea;

I am an anthropologist in trunks.

That final phrase – 'an anthropologist in trunks' – is so pretentious and pompous that the speaker becomes part of the satire.

This is a very interesting poem: the speaker mounts a sustained attack on the average British tourist's obsession with sun, booze and karaoke – but it is all presented with no warmth, no compassion, no understanding. The speaker himself (I think it is male because of the trunks in the last line) is a pretentious snob – precious, opinionated and derogatory to his fellow human beings. Overall the poem is amusing because it manages to satirise two very different groups of tourists – one through his own words!

Why?

This highly amusing poem:

- satirizes the conventional British tourist interested in cheap booze and sunshine;
- also satirizes the speaker of the poem for his/her pretentiousness and his/her derogatory attitude to the other type of tourist;
- achieves its object succinctly and with humour.

'In Romney Marsh' – John Davidson

Author and Context

John Davidson (11 April 1857 – 23 March 1909) was a Scottish poet, playwright and novelist, best known for his ballads. He also did translations from French and German. In 1909, financial difficulties, as well as physical and mental health problems, led to his suicide.

Romney Marsh is an inhospitable and sparsely populated unspoilt wetland area situated in the counties of Kent and East Sussex in the south-east of England. It covers about 100 square miles (260 km²) and it is very flat.

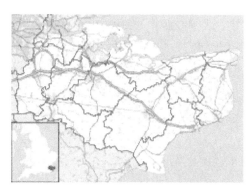

Dymchurch has had a sea wall since Roman times, with the original development being constructed to protect the harbour at Port Lympne., and then continuing throughout the centuries to help protect the Marsh itself.

knolls – a small round hill.

the wire – the telephone wire carrying messages from Romney to Hythe.

The Straits – the Straits of Dover. The English Channel.

the offing – the area between the shore and the horizon.

brands – lit pieces of wood used as torches.

Who? The poet describes the beauty of Romney Marsh, but does not let his personality intrude at all.

When? The late nineteenth century.

Where? Romney Marsh.

What? In this largely descriptive poem, Davidson concentrates on the sights and sounds of the marsh.

Commentary

The title of the poem '**In** Romney Marsh' suggests Davidson's complete immersion in the marsh. This is not just a poem about Romney Marsh: the word 'in' suggests that from within the marsh Davidson is able fully to appreciate the natural world of the marsh: he is absorbed in it and part of it. Davidson writes in four line stanzas - quatrains – in which the first and the third lines rhyme and the second and the fourth. This highly traditional and controlled form suggests that Davidson is fully in control of his material; it also strongly suggests the perfect beauty of the scene. – nothing spoils the beauty of the scene, just as nothing spoils the perfection and controlled order of the poem.

Much of the poem details what Davidson can see and hear and he is alive to the natural phenomena on the marsh as well as the human. In the first stanza Davidson says he 'went down to Dymchurch Wall' and he writes that he

…heard the South sing o'er the land

I saw the yellow sunlight fall

On knolls where Norman churches stand.

The south wind is personified as it sings over the flat land and the yellow sunlight suggests warmth and brightness. The Norman churches suggest the history and antiquity of the area. Already in the first stanza Davidson's senses are heightened and much of the poem consists of what he hears and what he sees – his senses are highly attuned to his surroundings.

In the second stanza Davidson can hear the telephone wire carrying messages from Romney to Hythe – and he can hear it 'ringing shrilly, taut and lithe/Within the wind a core of sound'. Perhaps the wire is reverberating in the wind. Ringing shrilly is a sharp and penetrating sound. The 'airy journey' perfectly describes the journey that the words on the telephone make.

The third stanza switches to the sense of sight and Davidson notices 'A veil of purple vapour' out at sea, while the upper air

... like sapphire glowed.

And roses filled Heaven's gates.

This is an especially beautiful stanza, helped by the poetic techniques that Davidson uses: the metaphor of the 'veil of purple vapour' is augmented by the simile – 'The upper air like sapphire glowed' – and the whole stanza is rounded off by the unusual and original image of the roses filling Heaven's gates. Davidson is overwhelmed by the natural beauty of the sky above the Marsh.

In the fourth stanza Davidson turns to the shoreline and begins by personifying the masts who 'wagged their tops' in the wind, which makes them sound playful. The rest of the stanza concentrates on the sound and visual qualities of the waves hitting the shore. 'Pealed', 'surge' and 'roar' are all onomatopoeic, while 'saffron' and 'diamond' suggest how beautiful and precious the beach and the waves are, while 'beads' is a metaphor related to jewellery which describes the drops of water being flung up the shore.

The fifth stanza marks a break and a reversal of the first line of the poem. Now Davidson writes

As I came up from Dymchurch Wall

and evening is approaching. In a metaphor Davidson describes the fiery and beautiful sunset:

The crimson brands of sunset fall,

Flicker and fade from out the West.

The personified 'crimson brands' suggest that the sky is streaked with red, while the alliteration that follows on the letter 'f' emphasizes the movement of the colours in the sky.

The first line of the sixth stanza begins with a strong caesura after 'Night sank' which emphasizes its speed. Davidson follows this with a simile – 'like flakes of silver fire' which once again evokes precious metals and accentuates the beauty of the stars which 'in one great shower came down' – and the enjambment between lines one and two of the stanza stresses the speed at which the stars descended. Davidson is still attuned to the noises around him. The wind is shrill and the wire is shrill and the wire 'Rang out'. 'Shrill' and 'rang' are both onomatopoeic.

The final stanza returns to the shore line to describe vividly the waves crashing on the beach:

The darkly shining salt sea drops

Streamed as the waves clashed on the shore

In these two lines the sibilance on the letter 's' and the onomatopoeic 'clashed' give an accurate sense of the sound of the sea. And in the final two lines the beach is compared in a metaphor to an organ with 'pealing' and 'roar' both being onomatopoeic.

The tone of this intensely vivid poem is admiring and full of a love and fascination with this place.

In 'In Romney Marsh' John Davidson

- makes clear his love and closeness to the landscape;
- makes extensive use of metaphor, simile and onomatopoeia to bring the landscape alive;

- has all his senses attuned to the sights and sounds of Romney Marsh;
- gives a vivid and evocative sense of Romney Marsh.

'Absence' – Elizabeth Jennings

Author and Context

Jennings was born in Boston, Lincolnshire. When she was six, her family moved to Oxford, where she remained for the rest of her life.[2] There she later attended St Anne's College. After graduation, she became a writer. Jennings' early poetry was published in journals such as *Oxford Poetry*, *New English Weekly*, *The Spectator*, *Outposts* and *Poetry Review*, but her first book was not published until she was 27. The lyrical poets whom she usually cited as having greatly influenced her work were Hopkins, Auden, Graves and Muir. Her second book, *A Way of Looking*, won the Somerset Maugham award and marked a turning point, as the prize money allowed her to spend nearly three months in Rome, which was a revelation. It brought a new dimension to her religious belief and inspired her imagination.

Regarded as traditionalist rather than an innovator, Jennings is known for her lyric poetry and mastery of form. Her work displays a simplicity of metre and rhyme shared with Philip Larkin, Kingsley Amis and Thom Gunn, all members of the group of English poets known as The Movement. She always made it clear that, whilst her life, which included a spell of severe mental illness, contributed to the themes contained within her work, she did not write explicitly autobiographical poetry. Her deeply held Roman Catholicism coloured much of her work.

She died in a care home in Bampton, Oxfordshire and is buried in Wolvercote Cemetery, Oxford.

Who? The poet writes as herself and addresses her former lover or companion.

When? In summer perhaps – there are lots of birds singing.

Where? The place is not specified except as the place where she and a former lover last met and ended their relationship.

What? The poet reflects on the beauty and serenity of her surroundings contrasted with the emotional turmoil she feels inside.

Commentary

This is a sad and melancholy poem. It is based on a place – which is as attractive and as beautiful as it ever was – but the speaker of the poem is there alone – without her companion or lover – and so her perceptions and feelings have changed completely.

In the first stanza the speaker visits *the place where we last met* alone, we assume the relationship has ended. Ironically nothing has changed which must sharpen the memory of their last visit there:

Nothing was changed, the gardens were well-tended,

The fountains sprayed their usual steady jet;

The poet writes that *there was no sign that anything had ended/ And nothing to instruct me to forget.* It's almost as if had the place fallen to rack and ruin that would have been an appropriate metaphor for the breakdown in their relationship. It's also galling in the breakup of a relationship that a special place with particular connotations continues to thrive. As it is the place the poet revisits is as nice as it ever was. The relationship and its ending has had a profound effect on the poet and she wants something to instruct her to forget.

In the second stanza the *thoughtless birds* are *singing an ecstasy I could not share.* They are thoughtless because they do not, cannot, take into account her feelings of misery. In the second half of the second stanza Jennings admits that faced with the beauty of the birdsong she should feel no *pain* or *discord.*

However, in the third stanza Jennings allows the depths of her sorrow to become apparent. She starts by saying:

It was because the place was just the same

That made your absence seem a savage force.

The place has not changed but their relationship has. She then imagines that underneath the essential gentleness of the scene – the fountains, the trees, the birds, the well-tended gardens – there comes an *earthquake tremor* when she thinks of her former lover's name.

The overall tone of this poem is relatively calm until we reach the cataclysmic events of the last stanza. This is, in part, because Jennings uses a conventional rhyme scheme which gives the poem order and shape. However, it is important to note that as the poem becomes more emotional in stanzas two and three, Jennings uses more enjambment to increase the emotional momentum of her words. However, nothing prepares us for the *earthquake tremor* of the last verse. Because the place is unchanged it is almost as if Jennings wants to destroy it, so that she can at the same time destroy the once-happy memories she had of the place.

In this poem Elizabeth Jennings:

- revisits a place she had once visited with a former lover – this time she is alone;
- she seems cheated to find that the place has not changed, although time has changed her relationship;
- restrains her emotions (through a tight and regular rhyme scheme) until the last verse where she admits the intense sadness she feels.

Glossary

The Oxford Concise Dictionary of Literary Terms has been invaluable in writing this section of the book. I would again remind the reader that knowledge of these terms is only the start – do NOT define a word you find here in the examination. You can take it for granted that the examiner knows the term: it is up to you to try to use it confidently and with precision and to explain why the poet uses it or what effect it has on the reader.

ALLITERATION   the repetition of the same sounds – usually initial consonants or stressed syllables – in any sequence of closely adjacent words.

ALLUSION   an indirect or passing reference to some event, person, place or artistic work which is not explained by the writer, but which relies on the reader's familiarity with it.

AMBIGUITY   openness to different interpretations.

ANAPHORA   In writing or speech, the deliberate repetition of the first part of the sentence in order to achieve an artistic effect is known as Anaphora.

ASSONANCE   the repetition of similar vowel sounds in neighbouring words.

BALLAD   a folk song or orally transmitted poem telling in a simple and direct way a story with a tragic ending. Ballads are normally composed in quatrains with the second and fourth lines rhyming. Such quatrains are known as the ballad stanza because of its frequent use in what we call ballads.

BLANK VERSE   unrhymed lines of ten syllable length. This is a widely used form by Shakespeare in his plays, by Milton and by Wordsworth.

CAESURA   any pause in a line of verse caused by punctuation. This can draw attention to what precedes or follows the caesura and also, by breaking up the rhythm of the line, can slow the poem down and make it more like ordinary speech.

CANON   a body of writings recognized by authority. The canon of a national literature is a body of writings especially approved by critics or anthologists and deemed suitable for academic study. Towards the end of the 20th century there was a general feeling that the canon of English Literature was dominated by dead white men and since then there has been a deliberate and fruitful attempt made to give more prominence to writing by women and by writers from non-white backgrounds. Even your Anthology is a contribution to the canon, because someone sat down and decided that the poems included in it were worthy of study by students taking GCSE.

CARPE DIEM   a Latin phrase from the Roman poet Horace which means 'seize the day' – 'make the best of the present moment'. It is a very common theme of European lyric poetry, in which the speaker of a poem argues that since time is short and death is inevitable, pleasure should be enjoyed while there is still time.

COLLOCATION   the act of putting two words together. What this means in practice is that certain words have very common collocations – in other words they are usually found in written or spoken English in collocation with other words. For example, the word *Christmas* is often collocated with words such as *cards, presents, carols, holidays*, but you won't often find it collocated with *sadness*. This can be an important term because poets, who are seeking to use words in original ways, will often put two words together which are not often collocated.

COLLOQUIALISM   the use of informal expressions or vocabulary appropriate to everyday speech rather than the formality of writing. When used in poetry it can make the poem seem more down-to-earth and real, more honest and intimate.

CONCEIT   an unusually far-fetched metaphor presenting a surprising and witty parallel between two apparently dissimilar things or feelings.

CONSONANCE   the repetition of identical or similar consonants in neighbouring words whose vowel sounds are different.

CONTEXT   the biographical, social, cultural and historical circumstances in which a text is produced and read and understood – you might like to think of it as its background. However, it is important sometimes to consider the reader's own context – especially when we look back at poems from the Literary Heritage. To interpret a poem with full regard to its background is to contextualize it.

COUPLET   a pair of rhyming verse lines, usually of the same length.

CROSSED RHYME   the rhyming of one word in the middle of a long line of poetry with a word in a similar position in the next line.

DIALECT   a distinctive variety of language, spoken by members of an identifiable regional group, nation or social class. Dialects differ from one another in pronunciation, vocabulary and grammar. Traditionally they have been looked down on and viewed as variations from an educated 'standard' form of the language, but linguists point out that standard forms themselves are merely dialects which have come to dominate for social and political reasons. In English this notion of dialect is especially important because English is spoken all over the world and there are variations between the English spoken in, say, Yorkshire, Delhi and Australia. Dialects now are increasingly celebrated as a distinct way of speaking and writing which are integral to our identity.

DICTION   the choice of words used in any literary work.

DISSONANCE   harshness of sound.

DRAMATIC MONOLOGUE   a kind of poem in which a single fictional or historical character (not the poet) speaks to a silent audience and unwittingly reveals the truth about their character.

ELEGY   a lyric poem lamenting the death of a friend or public figure or reflecting seriously on a serious subject. The elegiac has come to refer to the mournful mood of such poems.

ELLIPSIS — the omission from a sentence of a word or words which would be required for complete clarity. It is used all the time in everyday speech, but is often used in poetry to promote compression and/or ambiguity. The adjective is elliptical.

END-RHYME — rhyme occurring at the end of a line of poetry. The most common form of rhyme.

END-STOPPED — a line of poetry brought to a pause by the use of punctuation. The opposite of enjambment.

ENJAMBMENT — caused by the lack of punctuation at the end of a line of poetry, this causes the sense (and the voice when the poem is read aloud) to 'run over' into the next line. In general, this can impart to poems the feel of ordinary speech, but there are examples in the Anthology of more precise reasons for the poet to use enjambment.

EPIPHANY — a sudden moment of insight or revelation, usually at the end of a poem.

EPIZEUXIS — the technique by which a word is repeated for emphasis with no other words intervening

EUPHONY — a pleasing smoothness of sound

FALLING RHYTHM the effect produced by several lines in succession which end with a feminine ending

FEMININE ENDING — the ending of a line of poetry on an unstressed syllable

FIGURATIVE — Not literal. Obviously 'figurative' language

covers metaphor and simile and personification

FIGURE OF SPEECH — any expression which departs from the ordinary literal sense or normal order of words. Figurative language (the opposite of literal language) includes metaphor, simile and personification. Some figures of speech – such as alliteration and assonance achieve their effects through the repetition of sounds.

FOREGROUNDING — giving unusual prominence to one part of a text. Poetry differs from everyday speech and prose by its use of regular rhythm, metaphors, alliteration and other devices by which its language draws attention to itself.

FREE VERSE — a kind of poetry that does not conform to any regular pattern of line length or rhyme. The length of its lines are irregular as is its use of rhyme – if any.

HALF-RHYME — an imperfect rhyme – also known as para-rhyme, near rhyme and slant rhyme – in which the final consonants or the vowel sounds do not match. Pioneered in the 19th century by Emily Dickinson and Gerard Manley Hopkins, and made even more popular by Wilfred Owen and T S Eliot in the early 20th century,

HOMONYM — a word that is identical to another word either in sound or in spelling

HOMOPHONE — a word that is pronounced in the same way as

another word but which differs in meaning and/or spelling.

HYPERBOLE exaggeration for the sake of emphasis.

IDIOM an everyday phrase that cannot be translated literally because its meaning does not correspond to the specific words in the phrase. There are thousands in English like – *you get up my nose, when pigs fly, she was all ears.*

IMAGERY a rather vague critical term covering literal and metaphorical language which evoke sense impressions with reference to concrete objects – the things the writer describes.

INTERNAL RHYME a poetic device in which two or more words in the same line rhyme.

INTERTEXTUALITY the relationship that a text may have with another preceding and usually well-known text.

INVERSION the reversal of the normally expected order of words. 'Normally expected' means how we might say the words in the order of normal speech; to invert the normal word order usually draws attention or foregrounds the words.

JUXTAPOSITION two things that are placed alongside each other.

LAMENT any poem expressing profound grief usually in the face of death.

LATINATE Latinate diction in English means the use of words derived from Latin rather than those derived from Old English.

LITOTES	understatement – the opposite of hyperbole.
LYRIC	any fairly short poem expressing the personal mood of the speaker.
METAPHOR	the most important figure of speech in which one thing is referred to by a word normally associated with another thing, so as to suggest some common quality shared by both things. In metaphor, this similarity is directly stated, unlike in a simile where the resemblance is indirect and introduced by the words *like* or *as*. Much of our everyday language is made up of metaphor too – to say someone is *as greedy as a pig* is a simile; to say *he is a pig* is a metaphor.
MNEMONIC	a form of words or letters that helps people remember things. It is common in everyday sayings and uses some of the features of language that we associate with poetry. For example, the weather saying Red sky at night, shepherd's delight uses rhyme.
MONOLOGUE`	an extended speech uttered by one speaker.
NARRATOR	the one who tells or is assumed to be the voice of the poem.
OCTAVE or OCTET	a group of eight lines forming the first part of a sonnet.
ONOMATOPOEIA	the use of words that seem to imitate the sounds they refer to (*bang, whizz, crackle, fizz*) or any combination or words in which the sound echoes or seems to echo the sense. The adjective is onomatopoeic, so you can say that *blast* is an onomatopoeic word.

ORAL TRADITION the passing on from one generation to another of songs, chants, poems, proverbs by word of mouth and memory.

OXYMORON a figure of speech that combines two seemingly contradictory terms as in the everyday terms bitter-sweet and living death.

PARALLELISM the arrangement of similarly constructed clause, sentences or lines of poetry.

PARADOX a statement which is self-contradictory.

PATHETIC FALLACY this is the convention that natural phenomena (usually the weather) are a reflection of the poet's or the narrator's mood. It may well involve the personification of things in nature, but does not have to. At its simplest, a writer might choose to associate very bad weather with a mood of depression and sadness.

PERSONA the assumed identity or fictional narrator assumed by a writer.

PERSONIFICATION a figure of speech in which animals, abstract ideas or lifeless things are referred to as if they were human. Sometimes known as personal metaphor.

PETRARCHAN characteristic of the Italian poet Petrarch (1304 – 1374). Mainly applied to the Petrarchan sonnet which is different in its form from the Shakespearean sonnet.

PHONETIC SPELLING a technique writers use which

involves misspelling a word in order to imitate the accent in which the word is said.

PLOSIVE — explosive. Used to describe sounds that we form by putting our lips together such as *b* and *p*.

POSTCOLONIAL LITERATURE — a term devised to describe what used to be called Commonwealth Literature (and before that Empire Writing!). The term covers a very wide range of writing from countries that were once colonies of European countries. It has come to include some writing by writers of non-white racial backgrounds whose roots or family originated in former colonies – no matter where they live now.

PUN — an expression that derives humour either through using a word that has two distinct meanings or two similar sounding words (homophones).

QUATRAIN — a verse stanza of four lines – usually rhymed.

REFRAIN — a line, or a group of lines, repeated at intervals throughout a poem – usually at regular intervals and at the end of a stanza.

RHYME — the identity of sound between syllables or paired groups of syllables usually at the end of a line of poetry.

RHYME SCHEME — the pattern in which the rhymed line endings are arranged in any poem or stanza. This is normally written as a sequence of letters where each line ending in the same rhyme is given the same alphabetical letter. So a Shakespearean sonnet's rhyme scheme is ababcdcdefefgg, but the rhyme scheme of a Petrarchan sonnet is abbaabbacdecde. In other poems the rhyme scheme might be arranged to suit the poet's convenience or intentions. For example, in Blake's 'London' the first stanza rhymes abab, the second cdcd and so on.

RHYTHM

a pattern of sounds which is repeated with the stress falling on the same syllables (more or less) in each line. However, variations to the pattern, especially towards the end of the poem, often stand out and are foregrounded because they break the pattern the poet has built up through the course of the poem.

ROMANTICISM

the name given to the artistic movement that emerged in England and Germany in the 1790a and in the rest of Europe in the 1820s and beyond. It was a movement that saw great changes in literature, painting, sculpture, architecture and music and found its catalyst in the new philosophical ideas of Jean Jacques Rousseau and Thomas Paine, and in response to the French and Industrial Revolutions. Its chief emphasis was on freedom of individual self-expression, sincerity, spontaneity and originality, but it also looked to the distant past of the Middle Ages for some of its inspiration.

SATIRE

any type of writing which exposes and mocks the

foolishness or evil of individuals, institutions or societies. A poem can be satiric (adjective) or you can say a poet satirizes something or somebody.

SESTET a group of six lines forming the second half of a sonnet, following the octet.

SIBILANCE the noticeable recurrence of *s* sounds.

SIMILE an explicit comparison between two different things, actions or feelings, usually introduced by *like* or *as*.

SONNET a lyric poem of 14 lines of equal length. The form originated in Italy and was made famous as a vehicle for love poetry by Petrarch and came to be adopted throughout Europe. The standard subject matter of early sonnets was romantic love, but in the 17th century John Donne used it to write religious poetry and John Milton wrote political sonnets, so it came to be used for any subject matter. The sonnet form enjoyed a revival in the Romantic period (Wordsworth, Keats and Shelley all wrote them) and continues to be widely used today. Some poets have written connected series of sonnets and these are known as sonnet cycles. Petrarchan sonnets differ slightly in their rhyme scheme from Shakespearean sonnets (see the entry above on rhyme scheme). A Petrarchan sonnet consists of two quatrains (the octet) followed by two tercets (the sestet). A Shakespearean sonnet consist of two quatrains (the octet) followed by another quatrain and a final couplet (the sestet).

STANZA a group of verse lines forming a section of a poem and sharing the same structure in terms of the

	length of the lines, the rhyme scheme and the rhythm.
STYLE	any specific way of using language, which is characteristic of an author, a period, a type of poetry or a group of writers.
SYLLOGISM	a form of logical argument that draws a conclusion from two propositions. It is very characteristic of Metaphysical poetry and is exemplified in the anthology by Marvell's 'To His Coy Mistress'.
SYMBOL	anything that represents something else. A national flag symbolizes the country that uses it; symbols are heavily used in road signs. In poetry symbols can represent almost anything. Blake's 'The Sick Rose' and Armitage's 'Harmonium' are two good examples of symbols dealt with in this book.
SYNECDOCHE	a figure of speech in which a thing or person is referred to indirectly, either by naming some part of it (*hands* for manual labourers) or by naming some big thing of which it is a part (the law for police officers). As you can see from these examples, it is a common practice in speech.
TONE	a critical term meaning the mood or atmosphere of a piece of writing. It may also include the sense of the writer's attitude to the reader of the subject matter.
TURN	the English term for a sudden change in mood or line of argument, especially in line 9 of a sonnet.
VERSE	another word for poetry as opposed to prose. The use of the word 'verse' sometimes implies writing that rhymes and has a rhythm, but perhaps lacks

the merit of real poetry.

VERISIMILITUDE truth-like; giving a strong sense of reality.

VERSE PARAGRAPH   a group of lines of poetry forming a section of a poem, the length of the unit being determined by the sense rather than a particular stanza pattern.

VOLTA   the Italian term for the 'turn' in the argument or mood of a sonnet which normally occurs in the ninth line at the start of the sestet, but sometimes in Shakespearean sonnets is delayed until the final couplet.

WIT   a general term which covers the idea of intelligence, but refers in poetry more specifically to verbal ingenuity and cleverness.

Printed in Great Britain
by Amazon

22315836R00185